THE STOIC SAGE

After Plato and Aristotle, the Stoics, from the third century BCE onwards, developed the third great classical conception of wisdom. This book offers a reconstruction of this pivotal notion in Stoicism, starting out from the two extant Stoic definitions, 'knowledge of human and divine matters' and 'fitting expertise'. It focuses not only on the question of what they understood by wisdom, but also on how wisdom can be achieved, how difficult it is to become a sage, and how this difficulty can be explained. The answers to these questions are based on a fresh investigation of the evidence, with all central texts offered in the original Greek or Latin, as well as in translation. *The Stoic Sage* can thus also serve as a source book on Stoic wisdom, which should be invaluable to specialists and to anyone interested in one of the cornerstones of the Graeco-Roman classical tradition.

RENÉ BROUWER is a lecturer at the University of Utrecht, where he teaches on law and philosophy in the Faculty of Law. He works on theory of law and topics in ancient philosophy, with a special focus on Stoicism, its origins and reception, and the tradition of natural law.

CAMBRIDGE CLASSICAL STUDIES

Aelbert Cuyp, *Herdsmen with Cows*
Source: Dulwich Picture Gallery, by permission of the Trustees of Dulwich Picture Gallery

THE STOIC SAGE

The Early Stoics on Wisdom, Sagehood and Socrates

RENÉ BROUWER

CAMBRIDGE
UNIVERSITY PRESS

University Printing House, Cambridge CB2 8BS, United Kingdom

One Liberty Plaza, 20th Floor, New York, NY 10006, USA

477 Williamstown Road, Port Melbourne, VIC 3207, Australia

314-321, 3rd Floor, Plot 3, Splendor Forum, Jasola District Centre, New Delhi - 110025, India

79 Anson Road, #06-04/06, Singapore 079906

Cambridge University Press is part of the University of Cambridge.

It furthers the University's mission by disseminating knowledge in the pursuit of education, learning and research at the highest international levels of excellence.

www.cambridge.org
Information on this title: www.cambridge.org/9781107641778

First published 2014
First paperback edition 2018

A catalogue record for this publication is available from the British Library

Library of Congress Cataloging in Publication data
Brouwer, René.
The Stoic Sage: The Early Stoics on Wisdom, Sagehood and Socrates / René Brouwer.
pages cm – (Cambridge Classical Studies)
Includes bibliographical references and indexes.
ISBN 978-1-107-02421-2 (Hardback : alk. paper) 1. Stoics. 2. Wisdom.
3. Socrates. I. Title.
B528.B735 2013
188–dc23
2013028613

ISBN 978-1-107-02421-2 Hardback
ISBN 978-1-107-64177-8 Paperback

CONTENTS

PREFACE

My interest in the topic of wisdom dates back to the time when I first read Plato's *Apology*. I became particularly interested in how the Stoics seemed to have picked up on this Socratic theme, and it is to their treatment of wisdom that I devoted my Cambridge dissertation. After I had published one article, 'Stoic Sagehood', directly out of it, and developed sections of the dissertation into longer articles, I became convinced that I needed to present them as part of a more integrated account, which has now resulted in this book on the Stoic sage. Chapter 2 goes back to 'The Early Stoic Doctrine of the Change to Wisdom', *Oxford Studies in Ancient Philosophy* 33 (2007), Chapter 3 is a reworked version of 'Stoic Sagehood', *Oxford Studies in Ancient Philosophy* 23 (2002), and an earlier version of sections in Chapter 4 appeared in 'Hellenistic Philosophers on *Phaedrus* 229B–230A', *Cambridge Classical Journal* 55 (2008). I am grateful to the publishers for their permission to re-use this material.

In the long period of gestation that led to this book I have benefited from the help of many people. Here I wish to thank those who have been particularly important in the writing of the present book: Alice van Harten for discussing its set-up; the editors of Cambridge Classical Studies for taking the book for the series; the readers for the Press for their generous and constructive comments at various stages; David Sedley for annotating – in his inimitably careful manner – the penultimate version, and thus for making me rethink a number of passages; Jörn Mixdorf, for his proof-reading, and help throughout. Finally, I would like to express my gratitude towards Malcolm Schofield, who already as the supervisor of my PhD thesis formulated these pertinent, fundamental questions that always turned out to advance my work. He has remained supportive of it ever since, giving me valuable advice even at the very last stages of writing.

For the cover image I have chosen a painting by the seventeenth-century Dutch painter Aelbert Cuyp, *Herdsmen with Cows*, now in the Dulwich Picture Gallery, which I take to show some of the characteristics of the Stoics' 'ordinary' ideal of living in harmony with nature, in its idyllic version. Even more than the low viewpoint, the evening light is the most striking feature of the painting. It can be seen as a reminder of the elusiveness of the ideal: if it can be attained at all, it will be only late in life, or as Cleanthes put it, 'at the setting of the sun'.

INTRODUCTION

The present study is an attempt to bring the early Stoic notions of the sage and wisdom to the fore again. To judge by von Arnim's standard collection of the ancient evidence on early Stoicism, *SVF*,[1] the sage as the embodiment of wisdom must have been an important subject for the Stoics. Despite this importance, in modern scholarship the sage has not yet been given comparable attention.[2] Perhaps von Arnim himself is, at least partly, to blame here. He separated much of the evidence on the stark contrast the Stoics drew between sage and non-sage, in distinct sections devoted to the sage and non-sages, respectively.[3] He also omitted quite a few passages that show the Stoics' enthusiasm for their ideal.[4]

A further reason for this study is that interest in the notion of wisdom is on the rise again.[5] In the Western philosophical tradition this interest has varied considerably. The history of the reception of the Stoic interpretation of wisdom offers an illustration of these changes in popularity. In Antiquity one of the Stoic definitions was so well liked that at some point it was even regarded as commonplace. In the Renaissance this Stoic definition became fashionable again. According to a modern Renaissance scholar, it 'can be found in Salutati and Bruni, in Reuchlin's *Breviloquus vocabularius* and in Elyot's *Governour*,

[1] For the explanation of *sigla* and references see the bibliography (p. 180).

[2] This is not to say that modern scholarship has completely neglected the Stoic sage. Valuable earlier work was done by Lipsius (1604), Hirzel (1877–83), Deißner (1930), Kerferd (1978), Bénatouïl (2005), Vogt (2008), Liu (2009), Togni (2010), Vimercati (2011).

[3] See Pohlenz (1904) 933–4.

[4] See Pohlenz (1904) 936: 'Gern hätte ich es auch gesehen, wenn eine von den Stellen abgedruckt wäre, wo die Stoiker bei der Schilderung ihres Weisen einmal wirklich warm werden, wo man etwas von der Begeisterung merkt, die sie für dieses Ideal empfanden.'

[5] See e.g. Tiberius and Swartwood (2011).

in Erasmus, Cardanus, Pontus de Tyard, and Bodin, in every country of Europe and in virtually any year between the end of the fourteenth century and 1600'.[6] In the early modern period the interest in the Stoic notion of wisdom remained, examples being Descartes' *Principles of Philosophy* (1644),[7] Spinoza's *Ethics* (1677)[8] and Leibniz's *On the Happy Life* (1676).[9] In the eighteenth century, however, its popularity started to wane. In this process Kant's rejection of what he called 'worldly wisdom' (*Weltweisheit*), which followed from his influential repositioning of philosophy as the critical investigation of the conditions under which knowledge of nature or moral acts are possible, will surely have played its role.[10]

With the renewed contemporary interest in the notion of wisdom, the classical interpretations provide a rich source. Next to the unreflected use of 'wisdom' (*sophia*) as a mastered expertise, as in Homer, who gives the example of a carpenter who has mastered his craft,[11] or as attributed to the traditional 'Seven Sages',[12] Plato and Aristotle are among the thinkers who in the fourth century BCE start to develop their own conceptions of wisdom. Plato (*c.* 429–347) gives a new meaning to the term *philo-sophia*: next to the traditional meaning of philosophy as the 'love of or exercise of wisdom', philosophy gets the meaning of 'desire for wisdom'. In the slipstream of this new meaning, Plato in his *Republic* appears to offer a new meaning of wisdom, too, consisting in the

[6] Rice (1958) 93.

[7] *illae [virtutes] purae et sincerae, qui ex sola recti cognitione profluunt, unam et eandem omnes habent naturam, et sub uno sapientiae nomine continentur. quisquis enim firmam et efficacem habet voluntatem recte semper utendi sua ratione, quantum in se est, idque omne quod optimum esse cognoscit exsequendi, revera sapiens est, quantum ex natura sua esse potest* (2–3).

[8] *laetitia afficimur, eo ad maiorem perfectionem transimus, hic eo est, eo nos magis de natura divina participare necesse est. rebus itaque uti . . . viri est sapientis* (IVP45s). See further Wolfson (1934) 2.255–60, Nadler (2007) 230–8.

[9] *sapientia est perfecta earum rerum quas homo novisse potest scientia, quae et vitae ipsius regula sit, et valetudini conservandae, artibusque omnibus inveniendis inserviat* (636).

[10] See Marquard (1989) 715.

[11] Homer, *Iliad* 15.410–13. See further Section 2.4.

[12] On the lists of Seven Sages see Busine (2002), Engels (2010); on their traditional wisdom see Snell (1971) and Althoff and Zeller (2006).

all-encompassing knowledge of a higher reality, which the philosopher-king ought to possess in order to rule well.[13] Aristotle (384–322) distinguishes between practical and theoretical wisdom, re-using the traditional term for wisdom but giving it a rather different meaning by defining it explicitly as the theoretical knowledge of first principles and causes.[14] After Plato and Aristotle, from the third century BCE onwards, the Stoics developed the third of the great classical conceptions of wisdom. Like Aristotle, they re-used the traditional term for wisdom but, unlike him, they appear to have built on the unreflected traditional meaning of wisdom as mastered expertise, while putting it to work in their own systematic framework.

In order to show the importance of the notion of wisdom within Stoic thought, as well as the richness of their conception for modern discussions, one of the main topics in this study will be to provide an answer to the obvious question of what the Stoics understood by wisdom. Furthermore, I will discuss how, according to the Stoics, this wisdom can be achieved, how difficult it is to become a sage, and how this difficulty can be explained.

Before introducing these questions in somewhat more detail, it may be useful to set out the assumptions under which this study has been carried out. For a start, one of the main aims has been to offer a reconstruction of the Stoic notion of wisdom and to discern what the Stoics may have been after, rather than to stress any possible inconsistencies. This study is therefore an attempt 'to understand rather than to undermine' Stoicism.[15]

A related assumption is that Stoicism should principally be investigated as a unified system of thought, rather than as the

[13] In the ps.-Platonic *Definitions*, a philosophical dictionary containing definitions formulated by members of the Academy in the fourth century BCE, the Platonic definition of wisdom is formulated at 414B as ἐπιστήμη ἀνυπόθετος· ἐπιστήμη τῶν ἀεὶ ὄντων· ἐπιστήμη θεωρητικὴ τῆς τῶν ὄντων αἰτίας ('non-hypothetical knowledge, knowledge of what always exists, knowledge which contemplates the cause of beings').

[14] See further Section 1.2.1.

[15] The expression is by Craig (1987) 213, who used it in his splendid account of the 'activist' philosophical tradition that emerged on the European continent from the early sixteenth century onwards.

overarching name given to a movement of thinkers who all held their own sets of doctrines. Under the influence of two late nineteenth-century studies in particular, Hirzel (1882) and Schmekel (1892), much attention has been given to the development of Stoic thought, to the possible neglect of the idea of a set of core doctrines shared by individual Stoics, irrespective of the difference of opinions that certainly existed among them. The developmental aspect was highlighted especially in relation to the Cynic origins of Stoicism, the role of which may well have been exaggerated, as well as in relation to the classification of Stoicism into early, middle and late periods. For reasons of feasibility I will, however, restrict myself in this study to a reconstruction of doctrines of the founders of the Stoic school. Later Stoics can and will be taken into account, in as far as they provide reliable information on the doctrines of the founders of the school.

That brings me to my last assumption. As so little ancient evidence on Stoicism has survived (let alone the writings of the Stoics themselves), we will have to rely on a variety of sources. A simple reference to von Arnim's collection cannot suffice, first because most of the texts as printed by von Arnim have since been re-edited (his collection is after all now more than a hundred years old), and secondly because this collection does not include quite a few of the passages that will be discussed here. For this reason I decided to add most of the Greek (and sometimes Latin) in the footnotes, to give the reader direct access to the texts on which my interpretations are based. Nevertheless, I have still added references to *SVF* (and to other collections of fragments, where I thought it appropriate) for those readers who want to check the immediate contexts of the Greek or the combination of texts as printed in these collections.

As for the structure of this study, in Chapter 1 I will set out the Stoic interpretation of wisdom. There are surely different ways in which our understanding of it can be enhanced. One method would be to offer a systematic overview of the extant passages in which either the sage or the notion of wisdom occurs. Although such an overview is certainly helpful, the main drawback is that it suffers from the fortunes of the surviving textual evidence, as with regard to some topics the sage figures prominently, and with regard to others the sage seems to get limited attention only. I therefore want to propose another approach, via a discussion of the two Stoic definitions of wisdom. The two definitions are 'knowledge of human and divine matters' and 'fitting expertise'. Although these definitions may at first sight appear to be formulated in a rather general manner, I submit that by concentrating on the terms in the definitions and the relation between the terms in each definition, a connection with core Stoic doctrines can be made, such that the definitions of wisdom lose their abstract character and a coherent conception of Stoic wisdom can emerge.

In Chapter 2, the central question will be how to become a sage. While most modern scholars tend to pay most of their attention to the long and difficult process of developing 'reason',[16] I will focus on the last step in this process, which is crucial for an understanding of the Stoic conception of wisdom. The characteristics of this last step are remarkable: the change to wisdom is not only instantaneous, it is also radical in the sense that it is a transition between two completely opposite states. Perhaps the most remarkable of all these features is that this change, however instantaneous and radical, at first remains unnoticed. As most of these characteristics can be found in the relatively comprehensive but hostile Plutarchean treatise, *Synopsis of the Treatise 'The Stoics talk More Paradoxically than the Poets'*, I will use this *Synopsis* as the main starting point of my discussion.

In Chapter 3, I will deal with the question of whether the Stoics believed that someone had ever achieved this state of perfection, and in particular whether they took themselves to be sages. I will give an answer to these questions on the basis of a long passage in Sextus Empiricus' *Against the Professors*. In that passage Sextus Empiricus, as a sceptic a hostile witness against the Stoics, maintains that the Stoics would not claim to

[16] E.g. Rabbow (1914), Hadot (2002) and Sellars (2009).

be sages. I will assess the reliability of this source against the other available evidence.

In the final Chapter 4, I will explain the sage's rarity by discussing the intellectual settings against which the Stoics developed their notion of wisdom. I will submit that they consciously fashioned themselves as followers of Socrates (469–399), who did not claim wisdom for himself, but nevertheless devoted his life to striving for it, and perhaps even – without him being aware thereof – found it. Against this Socratic background even the Stoic definition of wisdom can be understood as an attempt to make explicit what Socrates had left implicit in various 'dogmatic' assertions, in passages that can be found in Plato's and in Xenophon's texts alike. If this is indeed correct, then an underlying reason for the Stoics to develop their notion of wisdom must have been to give the best possible answer to the question of what Socrates, surely one of the most inspiring figures in the history of Greek or indeed Western philosophy, had been looking for, and what he – as we will see – had perhaps even found.

CHAPTER 1

TWO DEFINITIONS

1.1 Introduction

In this chapter I will offer an answer to the question of what the Stoics understood by wisdom. As already explained in the Introduction, I will do so by concentrating on two extant Stoic definitions: 'knowledge of human and divine matters' and 'fitting expertise'.

I will start with the best-known definition of wisdom as knowledge of human and divine matters. In fact, it became so well known that it has often been designated a commonplace, with its Stoic character thus played down. Moreover, in some of our sources the definition is actually attributed to Plato. Hence, before I deal with the meaning of the definition, the attribution of the definition to the Stoics will need to be discussed. In Section 1.2.1, then, I aim to show that the definition is firmly Stoic: the Stoics were the first who formulated this definition explicitly, and were thus really the first to whom the definition should be attributed. In Section 1.2.2 I will reconstruct the meaning of the definition by showing that the three elements in it – i.e. knowledge, human matters and divine matters – can be connected to the three parts of philosophical discourse as distinguished by the Stoics – i.e. logic, ethics and physics. I will first discuss the relation between ethics and physics. I will then move on to a discussion of 'logic', which the Stoics understood broadly, and which included epistemology as one of its main topics. The Stoics' two definitions of knowledge will provide a key to an understanding of the interrelatedness of the parts of philosophy or of the elements in the definition of 'wisdom' (*sophia*).

In Section 1.3 I will move on to the second definition, wisdom as fitting expertise. I will reconstruct its meaning by dealing first with the two Stoic definitions of expertise, and then offer an answer to the question of what it is that makes wisdom an expertise that is fitting.

1.2 The first definition

The first definition of wisdom, 'knowledge of matters human and divine', can be found in the so-called *Placita*, a treatise which survived in the works of Plutarch (*c.* 50–120), and which is now usually taken to be an abridgement of a work by Aëtius,[1] who probably wrote this work in the first century CE.[2] In the introduction of the treatise, at 874E in the standard pagination of Plutarch's works (*SVF* 2.35, LS 26A, *FDS* 15), the definition occurs in the following context (with my subdivisions added):

> The Stoics said that [i] wisdom is knowledge of human and divine matters, and [ii] philosophy exercise of fitting expertise; [iii] the single and supremely fitting expertise is excellence, [iv] and excellences at their most general are three: in nature, in behaviour, in reasoning. [v] For this reason philosophy is also divided into three parts: physical, ethical and logical. [vi] Physical is when we investigate the world and the matters in the world, ethical is that which is occupied with human life, logical is that concerned with reasoning – the last they also call dialectical.[3]

This condensed piece of writing constitutes our single most important piece of evidence on the Stoic notion of wisdom and the related notions of 'philosophy' (*philosophia*), 'expertise' (*technē*) and 'excellence' (*aretē*). In what follows I will discuss these notions. In Stoicism each of these notions was understood in a specific manner, often going back to the more traditional meaning of the respective terms, but also going beyond their ordinary meaning. We will see that, with regard to philosophy, for example, the Stoics went back to its

[1] This thesis was propounded by Diels (1879) and by and large accepted by Mansfeld and Runia (1997). For some sceptical remarks see e.g. Gourinat (2011). For ease of reference I will below refer to this *epitome* of the treatise as 'Aëtius'.

[2] For the dating see Mansfeld and Runia (1997) 319–23, cf. Runia (1996).

[3] οἱ μὲν οὖν Στωικοὶ ἔφασαν [i] τὴν μὲν σοφίαν εἶναι θείων τε καὶ ἀνθρωπίνων ἐπιστήμην, [ii] τὴν δὲ φιλοσοφίαν ἄσκησιν ἐπιτηδείου τέχνης, [iii] ἐπιτήδειον δ' εἶναι μίαν καὶ ἀνωτάτω τὴν ἀρετήν, [iv] ἀρετὰς δὲ τὰς γενικωτάτας τρεῖς, φυσικὴν ἠθικὴν λογικήν· [v] δι' ἣν αἰτίαν καὶ τριμερής ἐστιν ἡ φιλοσοφία, ἧς τὸ μὲν φυσικὸν τὸ δ' ἠθικὸν τὸ δὲ λογικόν· [vi] καὶ φυσικὸν μὲν ὅταν περὶ κόσμου ζητῶμεν καὶ τῶν ἐν κόσμῳ, ἠθικὸν δὲ τὸ κατησχολημένον περὶ τὸν ἀνθρώπινον βίον, λογικὸν δὲ τὸ περὶ τὸν λόγον, ὃ καὶ διαλεκτικὸν καλοῦσιν.

traditional meaning of 'love of wisdom', next to the 'new' Platonic meaning of 'striving for wisdom', and that they gave a broad application to both 'expertise' and 'excellence', such that the otherwise standard translations as 'craft' and '[moral] virtue' do not properly cover the scope of the Stoic use.

1.2.1 The attribution

First, however, a preliminary issue needs to be dealt with – the attribution of the definition to the Stoics. Although accepted by quite a few modern scholars,[4] it has been seriously questioned in recent times, for three reasons.[5] First, the definition would simply be a commonplace, a general formula to which most ancient philosophical schools would adhere, and which stands in no particular relationship to the Stoics. In the second place, Cicero, one of our main sources for the definition, often ascribes the definition to the 'ancients' (*veteres*), thereby suggesting that the definition had already been formulated before the Stoics. Finally, some later Platonists maintained that the definition went back to Plato, a position that has recently been defended again. As we shall see, none of these reasons can stand a critical examination of the extant evidence.

With regard to the first reason it can indeed be said that *at some point* the definition became so successful that it was simply regarded as a commonplace. For that Philo, Origen or Augustine, or even one of the apocryphal books in the *Septuagint*, the Greek translation of the Old Testament, have good examples on offer.[6] But, when we take a closer look at the sources, it turns out that the definition is not attributed to other

[4] See e.g. O'Meara (1951) 173 n. 40, Chadwick (1953) 176 n. 4, Kerferd (1978), Mansfeld (1979) 135 n. 22, Assmann (1991) 23, Dörrie and Baltes (1996) 245, Fiodora and Werner (2007) 17. Cf. Rice (1958) 2: 'For them [the Stoics] wisdom was not simply the knowledge of divine things only, as it was for Plato and Aristotle, but of both human and divine things.'

[5] See Männlein-Robert (2002).

[6] Philo of Alexandria (*c.* 15 BCE–50 CE), *Questions and Answers on Genesis* 1.6, 3.43, Origen (*c.* 184/5 – 254/5), *Against Celsus* 3.72, *Homily on Jeremiah* 8.2, 57.11–12 (on *Jeremiah* 10.12), Augustine (354–430), *On the Trinity* 14.1.3, *4 Maccabees* 1.16. Cf. e.g. Renehan (1972) 228, Theiler (1982) 131–2, Watanabe (1988) 51–2, Whittaker (1990) 73–4.

thinkers earlier than the Stoics. In none of our exant sources is the definition of wisdom as knowledge of human and divine matters explicitly attributed to the Presocratic thinkers.[7] It cannot be found in Plato either, to whom I shall return later on in this section. It is also not in Aristotle's extant works.[8] What is more, not only is the formula 'knowledge of human and divine matters' absent from his writings, Aristotle also clearly separates knowledge of the divine from knowledge of the human, as for example in the *Nicomachean Ethics*, where Aristotle distinguishes between 'wisdom' (*sophia*) and 'practical wisdom' (*phronēsis*): wisdom concerns 'the most dignified things by nature' (1141b3),[9] as opposed to practical wisdom, which is concerned with 'human matters' (1141b8–9).[10] For Aristotle, wisdom is rather the theoretical 'knowledge of some [first] principles and causes'.[11] Also Xenocrates, head of Plato's Academy (d. 314 BCE, see Diogenes Laertius (on him, *infra*, p. 19) 4.14), another possible candidate, does not use the definition of wisdom as knowledge of human and divine matters.

7 See e.g. the index to DK *s.v.* σοφία.

8 According to Wilpert (1957) 156–8, and followed by Daiber (1980) 327, Aristotle in his *On Philosophy* would have used the definition of wisdom of knowledge as human and divine matters. But Philoponus (sixth century CE), *Commentary on Nichomachus' Introduction to Arithmetic* I α 8–46 Hoche, 402.1–4.12 Haase (Aristotle fr. 8 Ross, Aristocles of Messene vest. 1 Heiland, text 5 Chiesara), to which Wilpert and Daiber refer, does not give this definition, but rather offers an evolutionary account of the various conceptions of wisdom, ending, at ll. 41–2 Hoche, 404.6–7 Haase, with wisdom as the dealing with τὰ θεῖα καὶ ὑπερκόσμια καὶ ἀμετάβλητα παντελῶς, and defined as τὴν τοῦτων γνῶσιν κυριωτάτην σοφίαν ὠνόμασαν ('knowledge (*gnosis*) of divine and hypercosmic and unchangeable things'). Moreover, even this definition cannot be ascribed to Aristotle at all; only ll. 11–12 (εἰ καὶ φανότατά ἐστι κατὰ τὴν ἑαυτῶν οὐσίαν, ἡμῖν διὰ τὴν ἐπικειμένην τοῦ σώματος ἀχλὺν σκοτεινὰ δοκεῖ καὶ ἀμυδρά) can be traced back to Aristotle, that is, to his *Metaphysics* 993b7–11, explicitly referred to a little later on in ll. 33–40 Hoche. See further Jaeger (1934) 137 n. 1, Cherniss (1959) 38, Tarán (1966) 467–8, and (1969) 14 n. 70, Moraux (1984) 92 ff., Chiesara (2001) 58 n. 4 and esp. Haase (1965).

9 σοφία ἐστὶ καὶ ἐπιστήμη καὶ νοῦς τῶν τιμιωτάτων τῇ φύσει.

10 Only in a later, Syrian, tradition is Aristotle credited with the definition of wisdom as the knowledge of human and divine things. See for references and further discussion Baumstark (1922) 220–6, Furlani (1926) 102, Daiber (1980) 328.

11 *Metaphysics* 982a2 (cf. 982b9–10, 1003a26): ἡ σοφία περί τινας ἀρχὰς καὶ αἰτίας ἐστὶν ἐπιστήμη. On Aristotle's theoretical conception of wisdom as knowledge of the ultimate principles of what there is (i.e. what would come to be known as metaphysics) see e.g. Frede (2004) 20 (cf. 26): 'Wisdom ... thus includes knowledge of God, ... and deals with the divine.'

In the single account in which his notion of wisdom is reported, Xenocrates defines wisdom as 'the knowledge of the first causes and the intelligible substance', and presents it as the theoretical subdivision of 'thought' (*phronēsis*, here used in the general sense), alongside the subdivision of practical 'thought'.[12]

While this definition is thus absent in earlier thinkers than the Stoics, it does occur in other sources besides the Aëtius abridgment, in which it is either explicitly linked to the Stoics or presented in a clearly Stoic context. In one other source the definition is explicitly attributed to the Stoics. Church father Jerome (*c*. 345–420), in his *Commentary on the Letter to the Ephesians* at 1.9 (not in *SVF*) declares: 'The Stoics, too, maintain that wisdom and practical wisdom are different, saying that "wisdom is cognition of human and divine matters, and practical wisdom is cognition of matters that relate to mortals."'[13] The formulation is somewhat awkward, but Jerome presents practical wisdom here in good Stoic manner as a part of wisdom. In other sources, notably the later Stoic Seneca (4 BCE/1 CE–65), the sceptic Sextus Empiricus (presumably second century CE), but also Quintilian (35–90s) and Clement of Alexandria (*c*. 150–211/16), the definition is presented in Stoic contexts. In his 89th *Letter to Lucilius*, at 5 (*FDS* 2, LS 26G), Seneca discusses the distinction between philosophy as 'love of and striving for wisdom',[14] on the one hand, and wisdom as 'knowledge of human and divine matters', on the other.[15] Sextus Empiricus,

12 Clement of Alexandria, *Miscellanies* 2.24.1–2 (fr. 6 Heinze, fr. 177 Isnardi Parente and Dorandi) presents the Xenocrates passage as a gloss at σοφία ἐν στόματι πιστῶν at *Ecclesiasticus* 34.8, in a chapter in which he argues for faith as the starting point of knowledge: εἰκότως οὖν εἴρηται παρὰ τῷ Σολομῶντι 'σοφία ἐν στόματι πιστῶν', ἐπεὶ καὶ Ξενοκράτης ἐν τῷ Περὶ φρονήσεως τὴν σοφίαν ἐπιστήμην τῶν πρώτων αἰτίων καὶ τῆς νοητῆς οὐσίας εἶναι φησι, τὴν φρόνησιν ἡγούμενος διττήν, τὴν μὲν πρακτικήν, τὴν δὲ θεωρητικήν, ἥν δὴ σοφίαν ὑπάρχειν ἀνθρωπίνην. διόπερ ἡ μὲν σοφία φρόνησις, οὐ μὴν πᾶσα φρόνησις σοφία.

13 *sapientiam et prudentiam esse diversas, Stoici quoque opinantur, dicentes: 'sapientia est rerum divinarum humanarumque cognitio, prudentia vero tantum mortalium.'*

14 *sapientiae amor est et adfectatio.*

15 *divinorum et humanorum scientiam*. See also *Letter* 88.33: *magna et spatiosa res est sapientia: vacuo illi loco opus est: de divinis humanisque discendum est*. In connection with virtue see *Letter* 31.8: *perfecta virtus sit, aequalitas ac tenor vitae per omnia consonans sibi, quod non potest esse nisi rerum scientia contingit et ars per quam humana ac divina noscantur*, and *Letter* 74.29: virtue not without *scientia divinorum*

at *Against the Professors* 9.125 (*SVF* 2.1017), discusses the definition in the context of the Stoic arguments for the existence of the gods: 'If there are no gods, wisdom as knowledge of human and divine matters cannot exist either.'[16] In the same work, at 9.13 (*SVF* 2.36, *FDS* 5), he ascribes the distinction between philosophy and wisdom to 'those who philosophise in a dogmatic manner', by which he must have had the Stoics in mind: 'They judge a discussion of the gods to be absolutely essential. Hence they assert that philosophy is the exercise of wisdom and wisdom the knowledge of human and divine matters.'[17] Quintilian, *Institutions* at 1.10.5, describes the ideal orator as a sage, corresponding to a 'mortal god',[18] who ought not only to possess a 'grasp of heavenly and mortal matters', but also to be versed in (typically Stoic) logical puzzles as 'the horned' and 'the crocodile', in such a manner that he would not produce the smallest mistake.[19] Finally, Clement of Alexandria uses the definition very frequently, too, and almost often in a Stoic context.[20]

humanorumque. 'Matters human and divine' without reference to wisdom or virtue occur too, in e.g. in *Letter* 104.22 (see further below in relation to Chrysippus and Posidonius), *Letter* 110.8: *sed luscere . . . potest . . . si quis hanc humanorum divinorumque notitiam scientia acceperit*, and *To Helvia* 9.3: *humanorum divinorumque scientia*.

16 εἴγε μὴν μὴ εἰσὶ θεοί, ἀναιρεῖται σοφία, ἐπιστήμη οὖσα θείων τε καὶ ἀνθρωπείων πραγμάτων.

17 ὁ περὶ τῶν θεῶν λόγος πάνυ ἀναγκαιότατος εἶναι δοκεῖ τοῖς δογματικῶς φιλοσοφοῦσιν. ἐντεῦθεν τὴν φιλοσοφίαν φασὶν ἐπιτήδευσιν εἶναι σοφίας, τὴν δὲ σοφίαν ἐπιστήμην θείων τε καὶ ἀνθρωπίνων πραγμάτων.

18 On this Stoic conception see *infra* Section 2.2.3.

19 *nam et sapientem formantes eum qui sit futurus consummatus undique et, ut dicunt, mortalis quidam deus non modo cognitione caelestium vel mortalium putant instruendum, sed per quaedam parva sane, si ipsa demum aestimes, ducunt, sicut exquisitas interim ambiguitates: non quia* κερατίναι *aut* κροκοδίλιναι *possint facere sapientem, sed quia illum ne in minimis quidem oporteat falli*. Cf. 12.2.8. For the Stoic nature of *Institutions* 1.10.5 see already Spalding (1798) 212: '*Stoicorum autem in primis iste est sapiens*', Raubenheimer (1911) 11, Appel (1914) 39: 'Diese Definition beweist den Zusammenhang mit der Stoa', and Colson (1924) 122.

20 The definition occurs in a clearly Stoic context in *Miscellanies* 1.30.1 (*FDS* 6) in a discussion of the difference between wisdom and philosophy, at 6.54.1, where wisdom is *gnosis* of human and divine matters, and explained in terms of Stoic epistemology as 'a stable and unshakeable cognition', at 7.70.5, in relation to the Stoic doctrine that wisdom as knowledge of human and divine matters cannot be lost, at *The Teacher* 2.25.3 (*FDS* 9), from the definition it follows that wisdom defined as knowledge of human and divine matters is the 'expertise in life', too. The

Further evidence for the attribution of the definition to the Stoics is the apparent fondness of the founders of Stoicism for the expression 'human and divine matters'. The expression is attested for the immediate successors of Zeno (334–262) as the founder of the school, Cleanthes (331–230) and Chrysippus (d. 208–4, in the 143rd Olympiad, see Diogenes Laertius 7.184), as well as for the first-century BCE 'middle' Stoic Posidonius. Cleanthes holds – 'most ridiculously' according to the first-century BCE Epicurean Philodemus of Gadara, *On Music* 4.142.5–14 Delattre (*SVF* 1.486) – that philosophical discourse, in comparison with poetry and music, 'is sufficiently capable of expressing divine and human matters, but does not 'in its plain form' [*pseilou*, literally: 'in its nudity'] possess the appropriate words for the greatness of divine matters, whereas both epic and lyric poetry arrive as best they can at the truth of the contemplation of the gods'.[21] Chrysippus, in what is perhaps the best known among the fragments that have survived of his numerous writings, at the beginning of his book *On Law* (quoted by the early third-century CE lawyer Marcian in the first book of his *Institutions*, which is preserved in the *Digest* 1.3.2, *SVF* 3.314, LS 67R), declared that 'law is the king of all human and divine matters'.[22] Also Posidonius (c. 135–c. 51 BCE), in his book *On Style* (see Diogenes Laertius, at 7.60, fr. 44 Edelstein and Kidd), used the expression 'human and divine matters' in his definition of poetry as 'a representation [*mimēsis*] dealing with divine and human matters'. Finally, perhaps somewhat

definition occurs in a more general context in *Miscellanies* 6.133.5, 6.138.4 and at 6.160.2 as knowledge of human and divine 'goods'. At *Miscellanies* 1.35.3, 1.177.1 and 4.40.3 the formula 'knowledge of human and divine matters' appears, too, although without reference to wisdom. See further Stählin and Treu (1972) 171 (*ad The Teacher* 2.25.3), Malingrey (1961) 154–6.

21 τοῦ λ̣[ό]γου τοῦ τῆς φιλοσο/φίας ἱκανῶ̣ς μὲν ἐξαγγέλ/λειν δυναμένου τὰ θεῖα καὶ / ἀνθ[ρ]ώ[πι]ν̣[α], μὴ ἔχοντ̣ος δὲ / ψειλοῦ τῶν θείων μεγεθῶν / λέξεις οἰκείας, τὰ μέτρα καὶ / τά μέλη καὶ τοὺς ῥυθμοὺς / ὡς μάλιστα προσκινεῖσθαι / πρὸς τὴν ἀλήθειαν τῆς τῶν / θείων θ[ε]ωρίας.

22 *Chrysippus sic incipit libro quem fecit* Περὶ νόμου· 'ὁ νόμος πάντων ἐστὶ βασιλεὺς θείων τε καὶ ἀνθρωπίνων πραγμάτων· δεῖ δὲ αὐτὸν προστάτην τε εἶναι τῶν καλῶν καὶ τῶν αἰσχρῶν καὶ ἄρχοντα καὶ ἡγεμόνα, καὶ κατὰ τοῦτο κανόνα τε εἶναι δικαίων καὶ ἀδίκων καὶ τῶν φύσει πολιτικῶν ζῴων, προστακτικὸν μὲν ὧν ποιητέον, ἀπαγορευτικὸν δὲ ὧν οὐ ποιητέον.'

loosely, both Chrysippus and Posidonius are brought in connection with 'human and divine matters' by Seneca, *Letters* 104.22 (*FDS* 10): 'Live with Chrysippus, with Posidonius: they will give you a notion [*notitia*] of human and divine matters, they will bid you . . . to strengthen your mind and to rise in the face of threats.'[23] In summary: in absence of earlier attributions of the definition to the Stoics there is ample evidence that suggests that we should take the attribution to the early Stoics very seriously indeed.

A second, related, reason for doubting its attribution to the Stoics is that the definition, if not a commonplace, is said to go back to 'the ancients', an 'attribution' that can be found in the writings of Cicero (106–43 BCE). In for example *On Ends* 2.37 Cicero presents the definition as 'old and established' (*rite*), in *On Proper Functions* 2.5 he attributes it to 'the ancients' (*veteres*). In the *Tusculan Disputations* 5.7 he does so, too: 'And though we see that it [philosophy] is a very old notion we must admit that its name is of recent origin; for who can deny that wisdom itself at any rate is not only ancient in fact but in name as well? And by the cognition of things divine and human and the beginnings and causes of everything it gained its very beautiful name from the ancients.'[24]

If the attribution to the Stoics in the evidence discussed above had not already made us suspicious of this attribution to the 'ancients', it can be added that the Ciceronian usage of this expression has a specific origin, too. 'The ancients' is a favourite expression used by Antiochus of Ascalon (d. 69/68 BCE), one of Cicero's teachers. Antiochus used this expression to refer to Plato and his immediate followers, including

[23] *vive cum Chrysippo, cum Posidonio: hi tibi tradent humanorum divinorumque notitiam, hi iubebunt in opere esse nec tantum scite loqui et in oblectationem audientium verba iactare, sed animum indurare et adversus minas erigere.*

[24] *quam rem antiquissimam cum videamus, nomen tamen esse confitemur recens: nam sapientiam quidem ipsam quis negare potest non modo re esse antiquam, verum etiam nomine? quae divinarum humanarumque rerum, tum initiorum causarumque cuiusque rei cognitione hoc pulcherrimum nomen apud antiquos adsequebatur.* An echo of this passage can be found in Augustine, *Against the Academics* 1.16. Further uses are in *Varro* 9, where Cicero praises Varro, using the formulation in a rather general manner: *tu omnium divinarum humanarumque rerum nomina genera officia causas aperuisti*, and *On the Orator* 1.212.

Aristotle.[25] The strategy behind this move appears to have been motivated by his attempt to gain control over (the little that was left of[26]) Plato's Academy. Against his competitor Philo of Larissa's more sceptical interpretation of Plato's teachings Antiochus offered a harmonising, 'dogmatic' interpretation of Platonic and Aristotelian doctrines, thus defending a basic 'agreement between the ancients' (*consensus veterum*).[27] In fact, Antiochus went as far as to include the Stoics in this 'agreement': according to Antiochus, the Stoics, while agreeing in substance with the ancients, had merely introduced a new terminology.[28] Cicero's usage of the ancients is thus by no means proof that our definition should be attributed to earlier thinkers than the Stoics.[29] What is more, in other contexts, where his immediate source is not Antiochus, Cicero is clearly aware of the Stoic origin of the formulation,

[25] See the passages in which Antiochus is explicitly mentioned: Cicero, *On Ends* 5.14 (fr. 9 l. 57–8 Mette): *antiquorum sententiam Antiochus noster mihi videtur persequi, quam eandem Aristoteli fuisse et Polemonis docet*, *On Ends* 5.21 (fr. 9 l. 120 Mette): *antiqui, quos eosdem Academicos et Peripateticos nominamus*. Other occurrences of 'the ancients' that go back to Antiochus, too, include *On Ends* 5.23 (on the Stoics agreeing with the ancients), *On Ends* 5.53 (on the contrast between wisdom according to the ancients and wisdom according to us), and *Varro* 22 (on the unanimous view of ancient philosophy that the happy life consists in virtue alone). The following passages are from *On Ends* 4, which is often considered to be Antiochean, too (although here we cannot be sure, as Sedley (2012b) 334 warns): 8–9 (Zeno's contribution to dialectic was far less than by the ancients), 20 (on the Stoics criticising the ancients for calling the things good that are but preferred), 24 (on the Stoics agreeing with the ancients).

[26] See Polito (2012) 34–9.

[27] See Hirzel (1882) 646–7, Hoyer (1883) 2, Doege (1896) 9, Glucker (1978) 30, 64, 104, Dörrie (1987) 466–8, Görler (1990), Fladerer (1996) 43–54, Karamanolis (2006) 54–7, Bonazzi (2012) 308, Sedley (2012a) 2–3. The expression *consensus veterum* I took from Dörrie (1987) 461.

[28] See *On the Laws* 1.38: *ut Zenoni visum est, rebus non commutatis immutaverunt vocabula*. Cf. *Tusculan Disputations* 5.120: *cum ea re, non verbis ponderarentur, causam esse dissidendi* [sc. between Peripatetics and Stoics] *negabat*. Here, however, Cicero attributes this 'neutralising view' to the 'great Carneades', an attribution he presumably picked up from Antiochus, as Schofield (2012) 237–40 argues.

[29] However specific the usage in Cicero may be, it should be added that the early Stoics also used οἱ ἀρχαῖοι, too, in reference to Plato and his school: e.g. Zeno (*ap.* Stobaeus 1.136.24, *SVF* 1.65, LS 30A) denies the existence of what 'the ancients' called Ideas (or Forms), and Chrysippus, *On Lives* 4 (*ap.* Plutarch, *On Stoic Contradictions* 1035A, *SVF* 2.42, LS 26C, *FDS* 24) agrees with 'the ancients' on the tripartition of philosophy. For more (Chrysippean) examples and a full discussion see Brunschwig (1991) 84–7, repr. (1996) 236–41.

and does present the definition in Stoic contexts. Examples thereof are at *Tusculan Disputations* 4.57, in the Stoic context of the superiority of the sage, who is free from bad emotions, and also at *On Proper Functions* 1.153, in the context of the Stoic idea of the community or society of gods and men.[30] In short: in the Ciceronian passages the attribution to 'the ancients' of the definition of wisdom as human and divine matters is likely to go back to Antiochus of Ascalon, and should yet again not make us conclude that the definition was already explicitly formulated before the Stoics.

The third, and by far the most interesting reason for doubting the reliability of the attribution to the Stoics is the attribution of the definition to Plato, which can be found in Alcinous and Apuleius, authors of handbooks for students of Plato. Alcinous (first or second century CE?), in his *Handbook of Platonism*, at 1.1, presents the definition of wisdom as an afterthought in an otherwise Platonic passage, with the soul turning away from the body towards the intelligible: 'The following is a presentation of the principal doctrines of Plato. Philosophy is striving for wisdom, or the freeing and turning away of the soul from the body, when we turn towards the intelligible and what truly is; and wisdom is the knowledge of things human and divine matters.'[31] Apuleius (second century CE), in *On Plato and His Doctrines*, at 2.6, distinguishes among the virtues belonging to the highest part of the soul between, on the one hand, 'wisdom' (*sapientia*) as 'instruction in human and divine matters' and, on the other hand, 'practical wisdom' (*prudentia*) as 'the knowledge of understanding good and evil matters, and of the things that are called intermediate'.[32]

[30] Cf. *On Friendship* 20, where Cicero discusses friendship in relation to 'human and divine matters'.

[31] τῶν κυριωτάτων Πλάτωνος δογμάτων τοιαύτη τις ἂν διδασκαλία γένοιτο. φιλοσοφία ἐστὶν ὄρεξις σοφίας, ἢ λύσις καὶ περιαγωγὴ ψυχῆς ἀπὸ σώματος, ἐπὶ τὰ νοητὰ ἡμῶν τρεπομένων καὶ τὰ κατ' ἀλήθειαν ὄντα σοφία δ' ἐστὶν ἐπιστήμη θείων καὶ ἀνθρωπίνων πραγμάτων.

[32] *virtutes omnes cum animae partibus dividit et illam virtutem, quae ratione sit nixa et est spectatrix diiudicatrixque omnium rerum, prudentiam dicit atque sapientiam; quarum sapientiam disciplinam vult videri divinarum humanarumque rerum, prudentiam vero scientiam esse intellegendorum bonorum et malorum, eorum etiam quae media dicuntur.*

To these handbook authors could perhaps be added the Peripatetic Aristocles of Messene (first century CE[33]), who without reference to wisdom, in the seventh book of his *On Philosophy* (*ap.* Eusebius of Caesarea (*c.* 260–339), *Preparation for the Gospel* 11.3.6, fr. 1.6 Heiland, Chiesara) ascribes to Plato the doctrine that knowledge of human and divine matters is one.[34]

Remarkably enough, neither of these authors offers any further indication as to where this definition can be found in the Platonic corpus. In the modern literature attempts have been made to retrace the definition in Plato's writings.[35] Three passages have been suggested as a source, two from the *Republic*, and one in the *Laws*. But how close do we really get to the definition of wisdom as knowledge of human and divine matters in these passages? Let us look at each of them in turn.

In the first passage, in *Republic* 6, at 486A, Socrates notes that the mindset of the prospective philosopher-king 'should always reach out to the whole and all, both divine and human'.[36] As the philosopher-king is under discussion here, the notion of wisdom is obviously in the background (with wisdom indeed explicitly mentioned a page earlier on, at 485C), but with 'human and divine' in the singular, and without the mention of knowledge, it is still a stretch to distil the definition out of this passage. In the second passage, in *Republic* 10, at 598D–E, Plato criticises the pretensions of the poets that they 'know all types of expertise, and all human matters related to virtue and badness, and moreover the divine matters'.[37] Apart from the fact that in this passage the *definiendum* wisdom is missing, it is furthermore striking that Plato stresses the universality of the knowledge, when he speaks of 'all types of expertise', 'all human matters', where

[33] The dates are uncertain, see Chiesara (2001) xix.

[34] . . . Πλάτων μέντοι κατανοήσας ὡς εἴη μία τις ἡ τῶν θεῖων καὶ ἀνθρωπείων ἐπιστήμη.

[35] See Beaujeu (1973) 292, and esp. Männlein-Robert (2002).

[36] καὶ μήν που καὶ τόδε δεῖ σκοπεῖν, ὅταν κρίνειν μέλλῃς φύσιν φιλόσοφόν τε καὶ μή. – τὸ ποῖον; – μή σε λάθῃ μετέχουσα ἀνελευθερίας· ἐναντιώτατον γάρ που σμικρολογία ψυχῇ μελλούσῃ τοῦ ὅλου καὶ παντὸς ἀεὶ ἐπορέξεσθαι θείου τε καὶ ἀνθρωπίνου.

[37] οὐκοῦν, ἦν δ᾽ ἐγώ, μετὰ τοῦτο ἐπισκεπτέον τήν τε τραγῳδίαν καὶ τὸν ἡγεμόνα αὐτῆς Ὅμηρον, ἐπειδή τινων ἀκούομεν ὅτι οὗτοι πάσας μὲν τέχνας ἐπίστανται, πάντα δὲ τὰ ἀνθρώπεια τὰ πρὸς ἀρετὴν καὶ κακίαν, καὶ τά γε θεῖα.

this aspect is clearly missing in the definition of wisdom as knowledge of matters human and divine as it survived in the abridgement of Aëtius' treatise. The third and final passage from which the definition might have been derived can be found in the first book of the *Laws*. At 631B–C Plato makes a distinction between 'the good things' and 'the bad things', where '[the laws] bring about all good things. For the good things are of two kinds: human and divine. The former human things depend on the divine things, and if a city accepts the superior, it will also acquire the lesser but, if not, it will lose both.'[38] Here it is a stretch again: the other term in the *definiens* 'knowledge' is yet again absent, and no explicit connection with wisdom is on offer.[39]

The upshot, then, must be that neither of these Platonic passages can easily be regarded as the ultimate source for the definition of wisdom as knowledge of divine and human matters. As far as the later attribution of the definition to Plato in the Platonic manuals from the first century CE is concerned, for Platonists (perhaps under the influence of Antiochus) the above three passages may have been used to show that Plato already had the Stoic definition. As far as the attribution of the first definition to the Stoics is concerned, the Platonic material offers yet again no good reasons to doubt it.

1.2.2 Its meaning

Now that we have established that the definition was first formulated by the Stoics, we need to ask what it is that makes this definition specifically Stoic. By taking a closer look at the three elements of the definition, knowledge, human matters and divine matters, I submit, an answer can be found. In order

[38] πάντα γὰρ τἀγαθὰ πορίζουσιν. διπλᾶ δὲ ἀγαθά ἐστιν, τὰ μὲν ἀνθρώπινα, τὰ δὲ θεῖα· ἤρτηται δ' ἐκ τῶν θείων θάτερα, καὶ ἐὰν μὲν δέχηται τις τὰ μείζονα πόλις, κτᾶται καὶ τὰ ἐλάττονα, εἰ δὲ μή, στέρεται ἀμφοῖν.

[39] For the sake of completeness the remark in Eryximachos' speech in the *Symposium* 186B can be added here, in which 'human and divine matters' are mentioned: ὡς μέγας καὶ θαυμαστὸς καὶ ἐπὶ πᾶν ὁ θεὸς τείνει, καὶ κατ' ἀνθρώπινα καὶ κατὰ θεῖα πράγματα. ('How great and admirable the god is, and how the god stretches out over everything, both over human as well as divine matters.')

to do so, I will make a case for the correspondence between the three elements of the definition and the three so-called 'parts' of philosophy: logic, ethics and physics. The correspondence between elements and parts can be extended with regard to the manner in which the Stoics connect these parts: just as according to the Stoics the parts of philosophy are interconnected, so are the elements of wisdom. I will first deal with the connection between ethics and physics, which has drawn considerable attention in the modern literature. However, crucial for my interpretation of wisdom is the interconnectedness on the basis of logic, which in Stoicism includes theory of knowledge. I will end with a discussion of the Stoic notion of excellence or virtue, which offers an immediate parallel to my interpretation.

1.2.2a The parts of philosophy

The importance of the division of philosophy into three parts in the history of Western thought can hardly be overestimated.[40] The Stoics were among the first to have used it.[41] Our main evidence for the Stoic division survived in the compendium on the lives and doctrines of the philosophers by the otherwise unknown Diogenes Laertius (early third century CE?). However uncritically Diogenes Laertius may have dealt with his sources, book 7 of his compendium is the only systematic account on early Stoicism of substantial length that is still extant.[42] At 7.39 (*SVF* 2.37, *FDS* 1, LS 26B) Diogenes Laertius introduces the tripartition of philosophy as follows: 'They say that philosophical discourse has three parts: the physical, the ethical and the logical part.'[43]

40 See e.g. Kant, who in the first sentences of the *Groundwork of the Metaphysics of Morals* writes that 'this division suits the nature of the subject perfectly, and there is no need to improve upon it'. As we will see, Kant would strongly disagree with the Stoic view on how these parts are connected into a kind of 'Weltweisheit' (see the Introduction, p. 2). For 'philosophy' as the general term for academic discipline see Charlton (1985).

41 On Stoic tripartition see esp. Ierodiakonou (1993), cf. Hadot (1979), Annas (2007).

42 For Diogenes Laertius see Mejer (1978), on book 7 see Mansfeld (1986) and Hahm (1992).

43 τριμερῆ φασιν εἶναι τὸν κατὰ φιλοσοφίαν λόγον· εἶναι γὰρ αὐτοῦ τὸ μέν τι φυσικόν, τὸ δὲ ἠθικόν, τὸ δὲ λογικόν. The expression τὸν κατὰ φιλοσοφίαν λόγον is impossible to

The correspondence between the three parts of philosophy and the elements of the definition is already suggested in the Aëtius passage quoted in Section 1.2. In section [v] it is stated that philosophy can be divided into three parts: physical, ethical and logical. If philosophy can be divided in three parts, this tripartition must apply to wisdom, too. This already follows from the etymology of philosophy itself as exercise or love of wisdom.

This correspondence between elements and parts can be substantiated further by looking more closely at the objects of the exercise of wisdom, for which the Aëtius passage itself, but also a somewhat overlooked Stoic passage in Diogenes Laertius, are important. In the Aëtius passage, at [vi], the object of physics ('the physical part') is identified as the world and the things in it. Second, the object of ethics ('the ethical part') is human life, and finally the object of the logical part is reason. In Diogenes Laertius' account of Stoicism tripartition plays an important role, too: Diogenes Laertius uses it as the organisational principle of his presentation of Stoicism in book 7.[44] Surprisingly, however, tripartition is only mentioned there at 39, without Diogenes Laertius taking the trouble to explain it. This apparent 'omission' can easily be explained: Diogenes had already discussed tripartition in the introduction of his treatise, at 1.18. Although the tripartition of philosophy had already been developed in the Academy, and for the first time expressly formulated by Xenocrates,[45] this account of the tripartition most likely does go back to the Stoics, for two reasons, one negative, the other positive. The negative reason

translate. It literally means 'the tripartition of the *logos* according to the love of wisdom'. *Logos* can hence be understood blandly as discourse here, but also as substantive reason in the world.

44 On the organisation of the material in Diogenes Laertius book 7 see further Mansfeld (1986) and Hahm (1992).

45 According to Sextus Empiricus, *Against the Professors* 7.16 (Xenocrates, fr. 1 Heinze, *FDS* 20, fr. 1 Isnardi Parente and Dorandi) tripartition is 'implicitly' (δυνάμει) in Plato, 'explicitly' (ῥητότατα) only with later thinkers, including Xenocrates and his followers. If Cicero, *On Ends* 4.3–4 (*SVF* 1.45, *FDS* 252) is to be believed here (but then Antiochus could have made this up, cf. n. 25), Zeno may have taken over the tripartition from Polemo of Athens, one of Zeno's teachers, and given it his own 'Phoenician' twist (see Diogenes Laertius 7.25, and *infra* Section 4.2). See Dörrie and Baltes (1996) 206–9.

is that the tripartition of philosophy is neither Aristotelian nor Epicurean. Although in the *Topics*, at 105b19–29, Aristotle alludes to a division of premisses or problems into ethical, physical and logical kinds,[46] he prefers a division between theoretical and practical philosophy.[47] If Epicurus (341–271) already acknowledged a division of philosophy into three,[48] this tripartition is into physics, ethics and the introductory *kanonikon*, as he calls it.[49] The positive reason is that this passage contains the phrase 'on cosmos', without the definite article, which is at any rate typical of Stoic book titles, but is also their standard designation of a field of inquiry.[50] It is unfortunate that this is a feature that cannot easily be rendered in an English translation:

> Philosophy has three parts: physics, ethics and dialectic. Physics is the part concerned with [the] cosmos and the things in it; ethics is the part concerned with life and the things that relate to us; dialectic is the part that deals with the reasonings of both of these first two parts.[51]

Both the Aëtius passage, as well as Diogenes Laertius 1.18, can thus be used as evidence for Stoicism. In either account ethics

46 ἔστι δ' ὡς τύπῳ περιλαβεῖν τῶν προτάσεων καὶ τῶν προβλημάτων μέρη τρία· αἱ μὲν γὰρ ἠθικαὶ προτάσεις εἰσίν, αἱ δὲ φυσικαί, αἱ δὲ λογικαί.

47 See Karamanolis (2011) 133–7 for an overview of the relevant Aristotelian passages in the *Metaphysics* and the *Nicomachean Ethics*. For bipartition among the Peripatetics see e.g. the abridgment of Aëtius, at 874F (immediately continuing the passage containing the Stoic definition of wisdom): Ἀριστοτέλης δὲ καὶ Θεόφραστος καὶ σχεδὸν πάντες οἱ Περιπατητικοὶ διείλοντο τὴν φιλοσοφίαν οὕτως· ἀναγκαῖον τὸν τέλειον ἄνδρα καὶ θεωρητικὸν εἶναι τῶν ὄντων καὶ πρακτικὸν τῶν δεόντων and Diogenes Laertius 5.28: διττὸν εἶναι τὸν κατὰ φιλοσοφίαν λόγον, τὸν μὲν πρακτικόν, τὸν δὲ θεωρητικόν· καὶ τοῦ πρακτικοῦ τόν τε ἠθικὸν καὶ πολιτικόν, οὗ τά τε περὶ πόλιν καὶ τὰ περὶ οἶκον ὑπογεγράφθαι· τοῦ δὲ θεωρητικοῦ τόν τε φυσικὸν καὶ λογικόν, οὗ τὸ λογικὸν οὐχ ὡς ὅλου μέρος, ἀλλ' ὡς ὄργανον προσηκριβωμένον. For the difference between the Stoics and Peripatetics here see Ammonius (sixth century CE), *Commentary on Aristotle's Prior Analytics* 8.20–1 (*SVF* 2.49, LS 26E, *FDS* 28).

48 For Epicurean tripartition see Diogenes Laertius 10.30 (fr. 242 Usener): διαιρεῖται τοίνυν εἰς τρία, τό τε κανονικὸν καὶ φυσικὸν καὶ ἠθικόν, for Epicurean bipartition see Seneca, *Letter* 89.11 (fr. 242 Usener): *Epicurei duas partes philosophiae putaverunt esse, naturalem atque moralem: rationalem removerunt.*

49 See Diogenes Laertius 10.30 (fr. 35 Usener): τὸ μὲν οὖν κανονικὸν ἐφόδους ἐπὶ τὴν πραγματείαν ἔχει, καὶ ἔστιν ἐν ἑνὶ τῷ ἐπιγραφομένῳ Κανών.

50 See Mansfeld (1992) 392.

51 μέρη δὲ φιλοσοφίας τρία, φυσικόν, ἠθικόν, διαλεκτικόν· φυσικὸν μὲν τὸ περὶ κόσμου καὶ τῶν ἐν αὐτῷ· ἠθικὸν δὲ τὸ περὶ βίου καὶ τῶν πρὸς ἡμᾶς· διαλεκτικὸν δὲ τὸ ἀμφοτέρων τοὺς λόγους πρεσβεῦον.

is concerned with human life, physics with nature and dialectic with reason. The correspondence between the parts of philosophy and the elements of the definition of wisdom now becomes plausible. With ethics as the part concerned with life and the things that relate to us, human matters can easily be understood as a reference to ethics. With regard to physics as 'the part concerned with [the] cosmos and the things in it', the link with the divine matters in the definition of wisdom may at first seem more obscure than in the case of ethics. This is not so, though: according to standard Stoic doctrine nature or the cosmos is divine or even identified with god.[52] Dialectic and knowledge are perhaps at first sight less easy to connect. Some commentators have linked dialectic to human matters,[53] or to both human and divine matters.[54] But as already follows from the description of the object of logic in the Aëtius passage, 'dealing with reason', logic is a wide-ranging subject in Stoicism. For the Stoics logic encompasses dialectic and rhetoric, with dialectic broadly defined as the knowledge of what is true and false and neither.[55] The Stoics thus included the theory of knowledge in dialectic, even agreeing among themselves that the theory of knowledge should be 'placed first'.[56] We can thus conclude that a correspondence can be assumed between the three parts of philosophy on the one hand and the three elements in the definition of wisdom on the other.

This correspondence between parts and elements can be extended to the manner in which these parts of philosophy or elements of wisdom are related, to which I will devote the rest of my discussion of the first of the Stoic definitions of wisdom. Before moving on to the most important topics,

[52] See further Section 2.2.2c. [53] See the still valuable Ernesti (1739) *s.v. divinus*.

[54] Dougan and Henry (1934) 167.

[55] See Diogenes Laertius 7.41–2 (*SVF* 2.48, LS 31A, *FDS* 33), cf. the 'more detailed account' of logic by the little known Diocles of Magnesia *ap*. Diogenes Laertius, at 7.49 (*SVF* 2.52, LS 39A, *FDS* 255). For a 'map of [Stoic] logic' see Barnes (1999) 67 and Castagnoli (2010) 155.

[56] See Diocles of Magnesia's account (n. 55): ἀρέσκει τοῖς Στωικοῖς τὸν περὶ φαντασίας καὶ αἰσθήσεως προτάττειν λόγον, καθότι τὸ κριτήριον, ᾧ ἡ ἀλήθεια τῶν πραγμάτων γινώσκεται.

i.e. the interrelatedness of physics and ethics (in Section 1.2.2b), and its basis in knowledge (in Section 1.2.2c), we can already infer the importance that the Stoics attached to interrelatedness from the doctrine that according to some Stoics the integration should go even further. 'Some Stoics', according to Diogenes Laertius 7.40 (*SVF* 2.41, LS 26B, *FDS* 1), even state that 'no part prevails over the other: they are all mixed together'.[57] Even though the majority of the Stoics did not go as far as this, they stressed the interconnectedness of the parts of philosophy with several well-known images, for which Diogenes Laertius 7.39–40 is (yet again) our main evidence:

> They compare philosophy to a living being, likening logic to bones and sinews, ethics to fleshier parts, and physics to soul. They make further comparisons to an egg: logic is the outside, ethics is what comes next, and physics is the innermost part; or to a fertile field: the surrounding wall corresponds to logic, its fruit to ethics, and its land or trees to physics; or to a city which is well fortified and governed according to reason.[58]

The image in which the interconnectedness of the parts comes out most clearly is that of the living being, which is presumably the reason why a later (early first century BCE) Stoic, like Posidonius,[59] expressed a preference for it.

The different views within the Stoic sect on the 'correct order' of the parts can also be explained in relation to their interconnectedness. According to one source (Diogenes Laertius 7.40, *SVF* 2.43, LS 26B, *FDS* 1) Zeno and Chrysippus maintained that ethics is last, according to another (Plutarch, *On Stoic Contradictions* 1035A–F, *SVF* 2.42, *FDS* 24, LS 26C) Chrysippus maintained rather that physics comes last. Sextus Empiricus provides evidence for this apparent

[57] οὐθὲν μέρος τοῦ ἑτέρου ἀποκεκρίσθαι, καθά τινες αὐτῶν, φασιν, ἀλλὰ μεμίχθαι αὐτά.

[58] εἰκάζουσι δὲ ζῴῳ τὴν φιλοσοφίαν, ὀστοῖς μὲν καὶ νεύροις τὸ λογικὸν προσομοιοῦντες, τοῖς δὲ σαρκωδεστέροις τὸ ἠθικόν, τῇ δὲ ψυχῇ τὸ φυσικόν. ἢ πάλιν ᾠῷ· τὰ μὲν γὰρ ἔξω εἶναι τὸ λογικόν, τὰ δὲ μετὰ ταῦτα τὸ ἠθικόν, τὰ δ᾽ ἐσωτάτω τὸ φυσικόν. ἢ ἀγρῷ παμφόρῳ· τὸν μὲν περιβεβλημένον φραγμὸν τὸ λογικόν, τὸν δὲ καρπὸν τὸ ἠθικόν, τὴν δὲ γῆν ἢ τὰ δένδρα τὸ φυσικόν. ἢ πόλει καλῶς τετειχισμένῃ καὶ κατὰ λόγον διοικουμένῃ.

[59] See Sextus Empiricus, *Against the Professors* 7.19 (fr. 88 Edelstein and Kidd, LS 26D, *FDS* 20): ὁ δὲ Ποσειδώνιος . . . ζῴῳ μᾶλλον εἰκάζειν ἠξίου τὴν φιλοσοφίαν, αἵματι μὲν καὶ σαρξὶ τὸ φυσικόν, ὀστέοις δὲ καὶ νεύροις τὸ λογικόν, ψυχῇ δὲ τὸ ἠθικόν.

contradiction, too: in his *Outlines of Pyrrhonism* 2.13 (*FDS* 17) ethics is placed last in the order,[60] whereas in *Against the Professors* 7.22 (*SVF* 2.44, *FDS* 20) the last place is assigned to physics.[61] Adversaries of the Stoics, like the Platonist Plutarch, exploited these accounts by accusing the Stoics of inconsistency. This can easily be explained as an exaggeration. Rather, these different accounts (or these oscillating preferences) relate to a problem with which the Stoics struggled themselves, that is of how to teach a unified system of thought in the best possible manner.[62] For 'those new to Stoicism' (*tous neous*), according to Chrysippus as reported by Plutarch, it is best to start with logic, to continue with ethics and to finish off with physics,[63] whereas for those already versed in Stoic doctrine physics is the best starting point.[64] The different ways of presentation are thus anything but an inconsistency: they rather, yet again, reflect the interrelatedness of the parts of philosophy.

1.2.2b Ethics and physics

Thus far we have discussed interrelatedness of the parts of philosophy in connection with the doctrine that all parts are mixed, in connection with some images, and with the problem of the right order of the parts. Far more helpful for our purpose of getting to grips with the Stoic notion of wisdom is the interrelatedness of ethics and physics. This interrelatedness has been fiercely debated in the modern literature. The debate has focused on the question whether Stoic ethics can stand on its own feet, or whether it has to be understood in relation to

[60] οἱ Στωικοὶ τοίνυν καὶ ἄλλοι τινὲς τρία μέρη τῆς φιλοσοφίας εἶναι λέγουσι, λογικὸν φυσικὸν ἠθικόν.

[61] οἱ δὲ ἀπὸ τῆς Στοᾶς καὶ αὐτοὶ ἄρχειν μέν φασι τὰ λογικά, δευτερεύειν δὲ τὰ ἠθικά, τελευταῖα δὲ τετάχθαι τὰ φυσικά.

[62] For the order as a pedagogical problem see Ierodiakonou (1993) 70–1, Dufour (2004) 44–5, Sellars (2009) 81.

[63] See *On Stoic Contradictions* 1035A (*SVF* 2.42, *FDS* 24): ὁ Χρύσιππος οἴεται δεῖν τῶν λογικῶν πρῶτον ἀκροᾶσθαι τοὺς νέους δεύτερον δὲ τῶν ἠθικῶν μετὰ δὲ ταῦτα τῶν φυσικῶν, ὡς ἂν τέλος δὲ τούτοις τὸν περὶ θεῶν λόγον ἔσχατον παραλαμβάνειν.

[64] See Plutarch's quotes from several of Chrysippus' treatises (*On Gods*, *Physical Theses*, *On the Use of Reason*) in *On Stoic Contradictions* 1035B–E (*SVF* 3.326, 3.68, 2.50, LS 60A).

physics.[65] This question is particularly pressing with regard to the interpretation of the good life, or 'end' (*telos*) for short, which the Stoics formulated as 'living in consistency' or 'living in consistency with nature'. The pivotal point here is how to understand 'nature' in this formula. Does 'nature' refer here in a more restricted sense to human nature only, or does it refer in a broader sense to the nature of the whole, such that for the answer to the Stoics' main ethical question about the good life knowledge of the natural world is indispensable, too?

One of the more informative pieces of evidence, which any interpretation of the Stoic formula of the end needs to take into account, is the condensed report at Diogenes Laertius 7.87–8. This report offers formulations by the first five 'generations' of Stoics: Zeno, Cleanthes, Chrysippus, Diogenes of Babylon (*c.* 240–152) and Archedemus of Tarsus. For the sake of brevity I will restrict my discussion here to the first three heads of the Stoic school, and discuss their positions in turn, adding other evidence where it is available.

On Zeno, Diogenes Laertius in 87 (*SVF* 1.179, LS 63C) informs us thus: 'Therefore Zeno in his *On the Nature of Man* was the first to say that the end was to live in consistency with nature.'[66] In this account the word 'nature' occurs twice. In the book title 'nature' refers to man's nature, so it seems obvious to take it in that sense, too, when it occurs again. But there are several reasons to consider another meaning here.

[65] For the debate see, on the one hand, those who assign a role to physics: Long (1970–1), (1989), White (1979), Striker (1991), Cooper (1995), Inwood (1995), Betegh (2003), Vogt (2008), Boeri (2009), Liu (2009), and, on the other hand, those who offer a 'neo-Aristotelian' interpretation of the Stoic version of the end, in which cosmic nature plays no role: Engberg-Pedersen (1986), Irwin (1986), 208 n. 4, (1998), Annas (1993), (1995), (2007), Nussbaum (1994), Lukoschus (1999). Cf. Schofield (1999), who argued for Chrysippus as the initiator of the idea of the cosmic city (but see Laks (1994), broadening Schofield's thesis by arguing that Zeno had already endorsed the cosmic perspective), and Brunschwig (1991)/(1995), who argues for the cosmic perspective to constitute but one strain in Stoicism, next to the more 'Aristotelian' strain to be found in Cicero's *On Ends* 3, between which 'we need not choose' (1991) 95/(1995) 250). The moral relevance of Seneca's 'natural questions' in his eponymous treatise fits in here, too (for this topic, popular in recent scholarship, see e.g. Williams (2012), with further references on p. 11).

[66] διόπερ πρῶτος ὁ Ζήνων ἐν τῷ Περὶ ἀνθρώπου φύσεως τέλος εἶπε τὸ ὁμολογουμένως τῇ φύσει ζῆν.

Among the other evidence regarding Zeno on the end (collected in *SVF* 1.179–89), it is the first-century Stoic Epictetus, *Dissertations* 1.20.15–16 (*SVF* 1.182) – to be more precise, in his lectures as reported by his pupil Arrian – who explained that Zeno referred to 'the nature of the universe'. Epictetus contrasts the brevity of the doctrine on the end with the lengthy study needed to achieve the end (or – as it usually turns out – to find that one is still a long way from it) in 15: 'For what is the point of saying long-windedly that "the end is to follow the gods, and the essence of good consists in the proper use of impressions"?'[67] This description of the end is followed by a set of questions with regard to it, in 16: 'Say: "What, then, is god, and what is an impression? What is nature in nature of the parts, what is nature in nature of the universe?" It is now already long-winded.'[68] Although Epictetus presents these questions as Zenonian, i.e. originating from Zeno or at least in line with his thought,[69] the doubt can be formulated whether these questions were not added by Epictetus himself.[70] A different account is offered in the fifth-century anthology created by Stobaeus, at 2.75.12–6.6. Here Zeno's formulation of the end is the briefer 'to live in consistency',[71] which Zeno's successor Cleanthes, clarifying the formula, turned into the longer expression 'to live in consistency with nature'.[72] Zeno and Cleanthes can of course not both have been the first to use the formulation 'with nature,' so one of our sources must be incorrect. On the basis of the extant evidence with regard to 'nature' in Zeno's formulation of the end, we can thus only conclude that there is conflicting evidence whether Zeno had

[67] τί γὰρ ἔχει μακρὸν εἰπεῖν ὅτι 'τέλος ἐστὶ τὸ ἕπεσθαι θεοῖς, οὐσία δ' ἀγαθοῦ χρῆσις οἵα δεῖ φαντασίων';

[68] λέγε 'τί οὖν ἐστι θεὸς καὶ τί φαντασία; καὶ τί ἐστι φύσις ἡ ἐπὶ μέρους καὶ τί ἐστι φύσις ἡ τῶν ὅλων;' ἤδη μακρόν.

[69] See e.g. Stellwag (1933) 177, with further references esp. to Bonhöffer (1890) 10–11 and Bonhöffer (1894) 9, 163–4.

[70] See Schenkl (1916, who attributes only the part τέλος – φαντασίων to Zeno.

[71] 2.75.12 (*SVF* 1.179, LS 63B): τὸ ὁμολογουμένως ζῆν.

[72] 2.76.1–6 (*SVF* 1.552, LS 63B): οἱ δὲ μετὰ τοῦτον προσδιαρθροῦντες οὕτως ἐξέφερον 'ὁμολογουμένως τῇ φύσει ζῆν' ὑπολαβόντες ἔλαττον εἶναι κατηγόρημα τὸ ὑπὸ τοῦ Ζήνωνος ῥηθέν. Κλεάνθης γὰρ πρῶτος διδεξάμενος αὐτοῦ τὴν αἵρεσιν προσέθηκε 'τῇ φύσει' καὶ οὕτως ἀπέδωκε· 'τέλος ἐστὶ τὸ ὁμολογουμένως τῇ φύσει ζῆν'.

already included 'with nature' in it, and, even if we assume that he did, that there is no explicit evidence that he understood it as universal nature.[73]

Luckily, there is more evidence on Zeno's successors, Cleanthes and Chrysippus. According to Diogenes Laertius, at 7.87 (*SVF* 1.552, FS 63C), Cleanthes in his book *On Pleasure* agreed with Zeno on the formulation of the end. More information on Cleanthes' interpretation follows in a sort of afterthought to Diogenes' section on the end, in the first part of 7.89 (*SVF* 1.555, LS 63C). Diogenes reports that Cleanthes understands the end as living in accordance with 'common nature': 'Cleanthes takes common nature alone as that which one should be in accordance with, and not also the nature of the parts.'[74] The expression 'nature of the parts' here is the same as in Epictetus' *Dissertations* 1.20.15–16 with regard to Zeno, which might be proof for the early Stoic origin of Epictetus' last question. The expression 'common nature' is ambiguous: it can refer to the universe, but also to nature common to all beings. The contrast between common nature and nature of the parts, however, seems to exclude the interpretation 'common to all beings'. Cleanthes' *Hymn to Zeus* (*SVF* 1.537, LS 54I), the only complete surviving text by an early Stoic, offers confirmation, too, that Cleanthes understood the end to be in accordance with cosmic nature. According to the last two lines of the hymn, human beings best live in accordance with the common law that guides all: 'For neither men nor gods have any greater privilege than this: to sing forever in righteousness of a common law.'[75]

For Chrysippus we can move back to the Diogenes Laertius passage, at 7.89 (*SVF* 3.4, LS 63C), which immediately

[73] In favour of cosmic nature here were already Stellwag (1933) 209 and Rist (1977) 168. Inwood (1995) 654 points to Zeno's cosmological syllogism (in Sextus Empiricus, *Against the Professors* 9.108), but this only proves Zeno's interest in cosmological issues, not so much the role of the cosmos with regard to man.

[74] ὁ δὲ Κλεάνθης τὴν κοινὴν μόνην ἐκδέχεται φύσιν, ᾗ ἀκολουθεῖν δεῖ, οὐκέτι δὲ καὶ τὴν ἐπὶ μέρους.

[75] ἐπεὶ οὔτε βροτοῖς γέρας ἄλλο τι μεῖζον / οὔτε θεοῖς, ἢ κοινὸν ἀεὶ νόμον ἐν δίκῃ ὑμνεῖν. On Cleanthes' cosmological interpretation of nature see e.g. Wundt (1911) 245 n. 2, von Arnim (1921) 570, Long (1967) 61, Bloos (1973) 30, Pohlenz (1990) 117, Inwood (1995) 665, Thom (2005) 50, 70.

precedes Cleanthes' formulation: 'By the nature with which our life ought to be in accord Chrysippus understands both common nature and in a special sense human nature.'[76] Further evidence for the cosmic interpretation is in 87 (*SVF* 3.4, LS 63C), where Diogenes reports Chrysippus' formulation in his first book *On Ends* as 'living in accordance with experience of what happens by nature',[77] of which the following lines are a continuation, apparently as an 'explanation' and therefore presumably also to be attributed to Chrysippus: 'For our natures are parts of the nature of the whole.'[78] Diogenes continues thus: 'Therefore the end becomes to live in consistency with nature, that is to live according to the nature of oneself and according to the nature of the universe.'[79] 'The nature of oneself' can only refer to human nature. As Chrysippus was the only one who was said to have explicitly included human nature in his formulation of the end, this inference should also be ascribed to him, or at any rate considered to be in line with his interpretation of it.

On the basis of this discussion of the different formulations of the end, it can be concluded that it is likely that already Zeno, but more safely Cleanthes and at any rate Chrysippus referred to nature in the sense of cosmic nature. With regard to Zeno, the conjecture is somewhat shaky: Epictetus' account of Zeno's formulation suggests a cosmic interpretation, however. With regard to Cleanthes, the doxographical account in Diogenes Laertius may not offer an explicit affirmation of the end as living in harmony with cosmic nature, but his *Hymn to Zeus* leaves little room for doubt. With regard to Chrysippus, it is clear that the end is harmony with cosmic nature.

What does this conclusion imply for the interrelatedness of the parts of philosophy, or of the corresponding elements in

[76] φύσιν δὲ Χρύσιππος μὲν ἐξακούει, ᾗ ἀκολούθως δεῖ ζῆν, τήν τε κοινὴν καὶ ἰδίως τὴν ἀνθρωπίνην.

[77] τῷ κατ' ἐμπειρίαν τῶν φύσει συμβαινόντων ζῆν. The same formulation is attributed to Chrysippus by Stobaeus 2.76.8, as a clarification of Cleanthes' formulation: ὅπερ σαφέστερον βουλόμενος ποιῆσαι.

[78] μέρη γάρ εἰσιν αἱ ἡμέτεραι φύσεις τῆς τοῦ ὅλου.

[79] διόπερ τέλος γίνεται τὸ ἀκολούθως τῇ φύσει ζῆν· ὅπερ ἐστὶ κατά τε τὴν αὑτοῦ καὶ κατὰ τὴν τῶν ὅλων.

the Stoic definition of wisdom as knowledge of human and divine matters? It must imply that in terms of the parts of philosophy the Stoic position is that ethics cannot do without physics as knowledge of cosmic nature. This is the position that Chrysippus holds,[80] and even the one that Cicero presents in the final paragraphs of his book on the Stoic interpretation of the good life, in which he actually started out with human nature. According to Cato, Cicero's Stoic spokesperson in book 3 of *On Ends*, at 73 (*SVF* 3.282), the starting point for anyone who is to live in consistency with nature is the universe as a whole. He continues by stating that ethics cannot do without physics, that one cannot make correct judgements about good and evil unless one understands the whole of nature, or the life of the gods. One has to understand, too, that human nature ought to be in harmony with that of the universe.[81] In the terminology of the corresponding elements in the definition of wisdom this position can be rephrased as that human matters have to be understood in relation to divine matters.

1.2.2c Knowledge

In Section 1.2.2b we dealt with the interrelatedness of ethics and physics, or – in terms of the definition of wisdom – of human and divine matters. In order to arrive at a more profound understanding of this definition, I here submit that the interrelatedness of the elements in the definition of wisdom comes out even more clearly with regard to knowledge as the third element in the definition, or – in terms of the tripartition of philosophy – with regard to logic in the broad Stoic sense (see above, p. 22).

80 See Plutarch's quotes in *On Stoic Contradictions* 1035B–E (*SVF* 3.326, 3.68, LS 60A) from Chrysippus' *On Gods* 3: οὐ γὰρ ἔστιν εὑρεῖν τῆς δικαιοσύνης ἄλλην ἀρχὴν οὐδ᾽ ἄλλην γένεσιν ἢ τὴν ἐκ τοῦ Διὸς καὶ τὴν ἐκ τῆς κοινῆς φύσεως, and his *Physical Theses*: οὐ γὰρ ἔστιν ἄλλως οὐδ᾽ οἰκειότερον ἐπελθεῖν ἐπὶ τὸν τῶν ἀγαθῶν καὶ κακῶν λόγον οὐδ᾽ ἐπὶ τὰς ἀρετὰς οὐδ᾽ ἐπ᾽ εὐδαιμονίαν, ἀλλ᾽ <ἢ> ἀπὸ τῆς κοινῆς φύσεως καὶ ἀπὸ τῆς τοῦ κόσμου διοικήσεως.

81 *qui convenienter naturae victurus sit, ei proficiscendum est ab omni mundo atque ab eius procuratione. nec vero potest quisquam de bonis et malis vere iudicare nisi omni cognita ratione naturae et vitae etiam deorum, et utrum conveniat necne natura hominis cum universa.*

Let us first take a closer look at the Stoic definitions of knowledge, before dealing with each definition in relation to the other two elements in the definition of wisdom. The Stoics defined knowledge [*epistēmē*] in basically two ways, each with a different emphasis.[82] The fullest accounts of these variants are in two pieces of evidence, a short and a long one. The short piece is Diogenes Laertius, at 7.47 (*SVF* 2.130, LS 31B, *FDS* 33), which contains two definitions.[83] In the first definition knowledge is 'a secure cognition', in the second definition knowledge is 'a tenor that in the reception of impressions cannot be shaken by reason'. In the longer piece, Stobaeus 2.73.19–4.3 (*SVF* 3.112, LS 41H, *FDS* 385), four definitions are on offer:

Knowledge [*epistēmē*] is [1] a cognition [*katalēpsis*] that is secure and unshakeable by reason. [2] It is also a system of cognitions, like the knowledge of the part of logic as it exists in the sage. [3] It is also a system of such expert-like cognitions that has stability by itself, just as the virtues have. [4] It is also a tenor [*hexis*] that in the reception of impressions cannot be shaken by reason, which they say consists in tension and in power.[84]

The first and fourth definitions are (almost) identical to the two definitions in Diogenes Laertius. The second and third definitions in Stobaeus emphasise the systematic embeddedness of the secure and unshakeable cognition. With regard to these two definitions *epistēmē* there can also mean science, a systematic body of knowledge, like the science of logic. It is easy to understand why Diogenes left Stobaeus' second and third definitions out. In the first place the security of the cognition will imply that it is systematically embedded; the fact that it is systematically embedded makes it secure.[85] In the second place

[82] Other recent studies that stress the importance of both definitions of knowledge are Vogt (2008) 120–6 and (2012) 167–71, Liu (2009), Togni (2010).

[83] αὐτήν τε τὴν ἐπιστήμην φασὶν [1] ἢ κατάληψιν ἀσφαλῆ [2] ἢ ἕξιν ἐν φαντασιῶν προσδέξει ἀμετάπτωτον ὑπὸ λόγου.

[84] εἶναι δὲ τὴν ἐπιστήμην [1] κατάληψιν ἀσφαλῆ καὶ ἀμετάπτωτον ὑπὸ λόγου· [2] ἑτέραν δὲ ἐπιστήμην σύστημα ἐκ καταλήψεων [ἐξ ἐπιστημῶν, codd.] τοιούτων, οἷον ἡ τῶν κατὰ μέρος λογικὴ ἐν τῷ σπουδαίῳ ὑπάρχουσα· [3] ἄλλην δὲ σύστημα ἐξ ἐπιστημῶν τεχνικῶν ἐξ αὑτοῦ ἔχον τὸ βέβαιον, ὡς ἔχουσιν αἱ ἀρεταί· [4] ἄλλην δὲ ἕξιν φαντασιῶν δεκτικὴν ἀμετάπτωτον ὑπὸ λόγου, ἥν τινά φασιν ἐν τόνῳ καὶ δυνάμει κεῖσθαι. (For the text I leave out all Wachsmuth's emendations, with the exception of one; cf. Long and Sedley (1987) 2.258.)

[85] For the parallel with expertise see Section 1.3.2.

even with regard to the definition of knowledge as a science, the stress is still on the grasp: a science or a body of knowledge can only exist in as far as it is securely and unshakeably grasped, or – in Stobaeus' wordings – 'as it exists in the sage'.[86] In fact we are thus offered two variants of definitions of knowledge: the first one is knowledge as a secure cognition, to which in Stobaeus is added 'cannot be shaken by reason', and the second is knowledge as 'a tenor that in the reception of impressions cannot be shaken by reason', to which in Stobaeus is added that this condition of the soul is 'in tension and in power'.

The first variant is perhaps easiest to understand: knowledge for the Stoics is the secure, unshakeable grasp of an impression. The second variant contains the technical term 'tenor', which needs explanation. 'Tenor', as *hexis* is usually translated in Stoic texts,[87] is used in a general and in a specific sense. Tenor in its general sense refers to an enduring disposition. Such a disposition can either be invariable or not, that is, either is or is not capable of increasing and decreasing.[88] Tenor

[86] If not securely and unshakeably grasped, a science is just a set of empty 'principles' (θεωρήματα). Training is needed for a θεώρημα in order to become a cognition. For the relation between θεώρημα and cognition see e.g. *Anecdota Graeca Parisiensa* 171.25–30 (*SVF* 3.214, referred to at *FDS* 398): πᾶσα δὲ τέχνη σύστημα ἐκ θεωρημάτων συγγεγυμνασμένων· καὶ κατὰ μὲν τὰ θεωρήματα ὁ λόγος· κατὰ δὲ τὴν συγγυμνασίαν τὸ ἔθος· φύσει δὲ πάντες πρὸς ἀρετὴν γεννώμεθα, and Stobaeus 2.67.13–16 (*infra* n. 98). Further occurrences of θεώρημα in our sources are in Chrysippus, *On Lives* 4 *ap*. Plutarch, *On Stoic Contradictions* 1035A (*SVF* 2.1008, *FDS* 24, in the context of the transmission of 'speculations' as Cherniss translates *ad loc*.), in a book title of Chrysippus, *On the Principles of Syllogisms*, in one book, *ap*. Diogenes Laertius 7.195 (*SVF* 2.15, *FDS* 194), Sextus Empiricus, *Against the Professors* 8.280 (*SVF* 2.223, *FDS* 1031, on the principles or *praecepta*, as Fabricius (1718) *ad loc*. translates it, that characterise an expertise), Chrysippus, *On Excellences* 1, *ap*. Diogenes Laertius 7.125 (on the 'principles' that the excellences have in common), Cicero, *On Fate* 11 (*SVF* 2.954, *FDS* 473, on the principles of divination, to which Mayet (2010) 82–3 attaches a discussion of the difference between θεώρημα and cognition in some non-Stoic sources).

[87] ἕξις goes back to ἔχειν, which basically means 'to have' or 'to hold'. The standard translation has become the Latinised 'tenor', where the basic meaning might be lost sight of. 'Holding' is an interesting alternative, proposed by Bett (2012) 20 n. 65.

[88] On tenor and character see Simplicius (sixth century CE), *Commentary on Aristotle's Categories* 237.29–31 (*SVF* 2.393, LS 47S): καὶ γὰρ τὰς μὲν ἕξεις ἐπιτείνεσθαί φασι δύνασθαι καὶ ἀνίεσθαι· τὰς δὲ διαθέσεις ἀνεπιτάτους εἶναι καὶ ἀνανέτους, and also Seneca, *Letter* 66.7–9: *nec minor fit aut maior ipsa. decrescere enim summum bonum non potest nec virtuti iri retro licet; . . . quid accedere perfecto potest? nihil; Letter* 124.23: *hanc tu ad suum finem hinc evoca, <sine> in quantum potest plurimum crescere.*

in its specific sense is used to refer to a variable or not yet invariable disposition. This tenor is thus opposed to an 'invariable tenor', for which the Stoics sometimes also used yet another technical term, 'character' (*diathesis*).[89] Whereas in Stobaeus' fourth definition it is left open whether the second variant can be understood in terms of a stable disposition, there is some indication in the passage itself that the Stoics had 'character' in mind, where the stability of knowledge is mentioned, and the virtues are given as examples thereof. A further indication can be found in Plutarch, *On the Common Notions* 1061C (*SVF* 3.213): 'Yet in the sage every cognition and memory, being secure and stable, is by itself knowledge and a great or even the greatest good',[90] and in Stobaeus 2.112.1–5 (*SVF* 3.548, LS 41G, *FDS* 89): 'The wise man never supposes anything weakly, but rather securely and stably, therefore he does not opine either ... Opinions are alien to his character.'[91] The second variant of their definition of knowledge thus makes clear that for the Stoics knowledge is also a matter of having an enduring, and at any rate as far as the virtues are concerned stable disposition, which is not to be shaken by reason.

The relation between the two variants of the definitions can be captured in several ways. A difference can be formulated in terms of focus: in the first definition the focus is on the act of knowing or on the 'grasp' within a systematic body of knowledge, which will make it secure, in the second definition the focus is on the state or disposition of the person who knows.[92] The difference can also – in a now fashionable manner – be formulated in terms of different types of epistemologies. The first definition would fit in with what is referred to as 'traditional' epistemology, with its focus on beliefs and the

[89] The translation 'character' is Long and Sedley's, and is now widely accepted. They furthermore provide a diagram at LS, vol. 1, 376, in which the distinctions are set out. For virtue as character see further at the end of this section as well as Section 2.2.3a.

[90] καίτοι πᾶσα κατάληψις ἐν τῷ σοφῷ καὶ μνήμη τὸ ἀσφαλὲς ἔχουσα καὶ βέβαιον εὐθύς ἐστιν ἐπιστήμη καὶ ἀγαθὸν μέγα καὶ μέγιστον.

[91] μηδὲν δ' ὑπολαμβάνειν ἀσθενῶς, ἀλλὰ μᾶλλον ἀσφαλῶς καὶ βεβαίως, διὸ καὶ μηδὲ δοξάζειν τὸν σοφόν. ... ταύτας [sc. δόξας] δ' ἀλλοτρίους εἶναι τῆς τοῦ σοφοῦ διαθέσεως.

[92] Nussbaum (1995) 36, Liu (2009) 263 n. 20.

appropriate justification thereof,[93] the second definition with the 'new' 'virtue' epistemology, with its focus on the disposition of the knower.[94] What unites both Stoic definitions of knowledge, the 'cognitional' and the 'dispositional' definition, is the emphasis on the unshakeability by reason. (In this respect Stoic epistemology is a far cry from the modern versions of epistemology just mentioned.) The relation between the two types of knowledge must be one of dependence: the secure grasp is possible on the basis of the enduring disposition.[95]

Let us now take a closer look at these two variants in relation to the interrelatedness of the elements of wisdom. The first variant of the definition of knowledge can easily be understood here, with wisdom as the secure cognition of human and divine matters, and thus of ethics combined with physics. It is important to stress here that for the Stoics the interrelatedness did not imply omniscience. They did not maintain that the sage's wisdom would be universal knowledge, covering 'the complete structure of the universe', as has sometimes been maintained.[96] The Stoics rejected omniscience as a characteristic of the sage,[97] as the following three passages make clear. In the first passage, Stobaeus 2.67.13–16 (*SVF* 3.654), the rejection of omniscience is formulated in so many words thus: 'Only the sage will be a good diviner, poet, rhetorician, dialectician and critic: but not all these things together, because it is necessary to acquire for

93 Note, however, that for the Stoics the focus is in fact on (the justification of) knowledge rather than on belief, as for them 'belief' (δόξα, but in the literature on Stoicism usually translated as 'opinion') is but a kind of ignorance. See *infra* Section 2.2.2b.

94 See e.g. Battaly (2008), Crisp (2010). (I owe these references to Ryan Hanley.)

95 Cf. Liu (2009) 263.

96 See Christensen (1962) 86, Mackenzie (1988) 348–51, Liu (2009), whose interpretation that 'for the Stoics, wisdom is the comprehensive knowledge of all things' (248) sits uneasily with the dispositional interpretation she offers later on (263–4). This association of wisdom and omniscience is perhaps all too common. See e.g. Aquinas' *Commentary on Aristotle's Metaphysics*, at 1.2.43: *ut ille sapiens dicatur, qui scit omnia etiam difficilia per certitudinem et causam, ipsum scire propter se quaerens, alios ordinans et persuadens.*

97 Cf. Frede (1996) 16–17 (without reference to the evidence), Vogt (2008) 120–6 (who mainly relies on Stobaeus).

these things some principles.'[98] The sage will not already possess the relevant insights, which entails that he will not be omniscient. As a sage, however, he can *acquire* the appropriate 'principles' (*theōrēmata*), if he decides to foretell, to write poems, etc.[99] In the second passage, in *Letter* 109, Seneca deals with the question whether sages need to help each other. According to Seneca sages help each other in acting and thinking. With regard to the latter, he states in 3: 'For even in the case of the wise man there will also remain something to discover, something towards which his mind may make new ventures.'[100] A little bit further on, in 5, Seneca makes the point explicit. He explains how one sage helps the other, that is among others by bringing 'joy' (*gaudium*, or *chara* in Greek), one of the 'good passions' (*eupatheiai* in Greek) that go with being a sage (see further Section 2.4), as well as by transmitting knowledge of things to each other: 'For a sage does not know everything.'[101] In the third and final passage, *Letter* 88.33–45, Seneca makes the point in a normative manner, in a protreptic passage directed at the sage-to-be: since wisdom is a large thing, and the number of things to be learned vast, one must get rid of all superfluous things. According to Seneca the sage is thus not a man of learning, who knows all kinds of superfluous things. Seneca gives the negative example of the scholar Apion, who knows all kinds of irrelevant things in relation to Homer.

Rather than omniscience, the Stoics bring wisdom into connection with a more restricted set of secure cognitions, that is with the traditional Delphic maxim of 'know thyself'.[102]

98 μόνον δέ φασι τὸν σοφὸν καὶ μάντιν ἀγαθὸν εἶναι καὶ ποιητὴν καὶ ῥήτορα καὶ διαλεκτικὸν καὶ κριτικόν, οὐ πάντα δέ, διὰ τὸ προδεῖσθαι ἔτι τινὰ τούτων καὶ θεωρημάτων τινῶν ἀναλήψεως.

99 Cf. e.g. Dougan and Henry (1934) 167, Kerferd (1978), Menn (1995) 29 n. 35.

100 *semper enim etiam sapienti restabit, quod inveniat et quo animus eius excurrat.*

101 *non enim omnia sapiens scit*. Gummere in his Loeb-translation takes up the point of omniscience in the continuation of the sentence, but this is misleading: *etiam si sciret* does not mean 'even if he were all-knowing', but rather 'even if he were to know x'.

102 See also Wilkins (1917) 66, who speaks of a 'tendency of the Stoics to center all their philosophy around γνῶθι σαυτόν', Courcelle (1974) 22–3, Gerson (1990) 144, who loosely remarks: 'The Stoic sage is not one who has attained esoteric knowledge regarding a remote and superior being, but rather one who has acquired a

Traditional as it may be, the Stoics give it their own twist. Here they bring in the other elements of the definitions of wisdom, or the three parts of philosophy. Cicero's three eulogies of wisdom serve as our main evidence, although their status as evidence for early Stoicism is somewhat controversial.[103] In the first of Cicero's eulogies, *On Ends* 3.73 (*SVF* 3.282), self-knowledge is referred to somewhat in passing, but the relation with physics is unequivocally made. Cato, the Stoic character in Cicero's dialogue, makes it clear that without physics the force of old maxims such as 'know thyself' cannot be acknowledged: 'Without physics no one can see what the force is – and it is the greatest possible – of the old precepts of wisdom, which order "yield to the times", "follow the gods", "know thyself" and "nothing in excess."'[104] In the second of the eulogies, *Tusculan Disputations*, at 5.70, the maxim 'know thyself' is placed centre stage, and related to the three parts of philosophy again: 'In a soul that deals with such subjects [i.e. the three parts of philosophy], and thinks about them night and day, the cognition prescribed by the Delphic god exists, such that the mind knows itself and is aware of its connection with the divine mind, from whence it is filled with an insatiable joy.'[105] And thirdly, in *On the Laws*, at 1.58, Cicero deals with this connection between wisdom and self-knowledge in even more detail: wisdom, 'the mother of all good things', is self-knowledge, developed on the basis of the

perhaps equally difficult self-knowledge.' Kühn (2009), an otherwise fascinating study on self-knowledge in Plotinus and his predecessors, discusses Stoic self-knowledge only in relation to the non-sage (see e.g. 36).

103 The Stoicism of book 3 of *On Ends* is obvious, however, and the passage from book 5 of the *Tusculan Disputations* is Stoic too; see Forschner (1995). The passage in *On the Laws* is disputed as evidence for Stoicism (e.g. by Boyancé (1963) and (1975), who maintains that the passage would rather go back to Antiochus of Ascalon), but both its structure (comparable to the Stoic eulogies in *On Ends* and the *Tusculan Disputations*) and its details (wisdom, the tripartition, world citizenship) are clearly Stoic. Dyck (2004) 222 does not take a position here.

104 *quaeque sunt vetera praecepta sapientium, qui iubent tempori parere et sequi deum et se noscere et nihil nimis, haec sine physicis quam vim habent – et habent maximum – videre nemo potest.*

105 *haec tractanti animo et noctes et dies cogitanti existit illa <a> deo Delphis praecepta cognitio, ut ipsa se mens agnoscat coniunctamque cum divina mente se sentiat, ex quo insatiabili gaudio compleatur.*

discovery of reason within oneself. In the next three sections wisdom is presented from the viewpoint of the three parts of philosophy: the sage's perfected reason makes him realise that he is both a good person (in 59), and a citizen of the world (in 60–1). This self-knowledge ('in this perception and understanding of nature how he will know himself'[106]) is fortified by the sage's ability to distinguish between truth and falsehood and to argue correctly (in 62). Outside the Ciceronian corpus, there is another interesting piece of evidence, too: emperor Julian (331–363), *Orations* 6.6, at 185D–6A, also presents self-knowledge as the central Stoic doctrine, and connects it with physics and ethics:

> That they [Julian refers to 'the students of the man from Citium' in 185C, i.e. Zeno and his followers] made 'know thyself' into the main point of their philosophy, you may believe, if you will, not only from the things which they brought up in their writings, but even more so by the end of their philosophy: for they made the end living in consistency with nature, which cannot be achieved if one does not know who one is, and of what nature one is; for someone who does not know who he is, will surely not know what he ought to do.[107]

Wisdom as knowledge in the cognitional sense thus turns out to be the Stoic interpretation of the traditional maxim 'know thyself', which the Stoics brought into connection with the other elements in the definition of wisdom, or with the three parts of philosophy. Wisdom is thus the secure cognition (or set of cognitions) of one's own human nature as part of the nature of the whole.

We can now move on to the other 'dispositional' definition of knowledge, and discuss this in relation to the two other elements in the definition of wisdom. The thrust of the Stoic position is perhaps best expressed like this: the sage's disposition is a special part of the force that pervades nature as a

[106] 61: *in hoc conspectu et cognitione naturae, … quam se ipse noscet.*

[107] ὅτι δὲ τὸ 'γνῶθι σαυτὸν' κεφάλαιον τίθενται φιλοσοφίας, οὐ μόνον ἐξ ὧν κατεβάλλοντο ξυγγραμμάτων ὑπὲρ αὐτοῦ τοῦτου πεισθείης ἄν, εἴπερ ἐθέλοις, ἀλλὰ πολὺ πλέον ἀπὸ τοῦ τῆς φιλοσοφίας τέλους· τὸ γὰρ ὁμολογουμένως ζῆν τῇ φύσει τέλος ἐποιήσαντο, οὗπερ οὐχ οἷόν τε τυχεῖν τὸν ἀγνοοῦντα τίς καὶ ὁποῖος πέφυκεν· ὁ γὰρ ἀγνοῶν ὅστις ἐστίν, οὐκ εἴσεται δήπουθεν ὅτι πράττειν ἑαυτῷ προσήκει.

whole.[108] With regard to nature as a whole, the Stoics, in line with earlier thinkers like Heraclitus (around 500 BCE) and Plato, considered the cosmos an ensouled living being.[109] This cosmos is pervaded and controlled by an active principle, referred to as force or breath (*pneuma*), which in its purest form the Stoics identified among other things with reason as well as Zeus.[110] In contrast to Plato, they understood this active principle as corporeal.[111] The force or breath dilutes itself throughout the world, manifesting itself in its weakest form in inanimate things, but ever more strongly in plants, animals and human beings.[112] In terms of reason, perfect human beings are of the same kind as the cosmic force in its undiluted, purest form of reason, which makes them 'share' or 'participate' in cosmic nature in the most powerful way.[113]

[108] For similar treatments of the evidence, both stressing the special nature of the sage as well as his relation to the nature of the whole, see among the older literature Aall (1896) 136–7, Wundt (1911) 250–1, and more recently Horn (2006) 354–5, Vogt (2008) 134–48, Liu (2009) 257–63.

[109] See e.g. (Antipater of Tarsus (second century BCE), *On Cosmos* 8 *ap.*) Diogenes Laertius 7.139 (*SVF* 2.634): οὕτω δὴ καὶ τὸν ὅλον κόσμον, ζῷον ὄντα καὶ ἔμψυχον καὶ λογικόν, Arius Didymus (perhaps to be identified with the Stoic philosopher who consoled Augustus' wife Livia on the death of her son on campaign in Germany in 9 CE, see Seneca, *To Marcia* 4–5) *ap.* Eusebius of Caesarea, *Preparation for the Gospel* 15.15.1–2 (fr. 29 Diels, *SVF* 2.528): ὅλον δὲ τὸν κόσμον σὺν τοῖς ἑαυτοῦ μέρεσι προσαγορεύουσι θεόν· τοῦτον δὲ ἕνα μόνον εἶναί φασι καὶ πεπερασμένον καὶ ζῷον καὶ ἀΐδιον καὶ θεόν.

[110] On reason and Zeus see e.g. Diogenes Laertius 7.88 (*SVF* 3.4, LS 63C): ὁ ὀρθὸς λόγος διὰ πάντων ἐρχόμενος, ὁ αὐτὸς ὢν τῷ Διί, καθηγεμόνι τούτῳ τῆς τῶν ὄντων διοικήσεως ὄντι, Church father Tertullian (c. 160–240), *Apology* 21.10 (*SVF* 1.160): *apud vestros quoque sapientes* λόγον, *id est sermonem atque rationem, constat artificem videri universitatis. hunc enim determinat factitatorem, qui cuncta in dispositione formaverit, eundem et fatum vocari et deum et animum Iovis et necessitatem omnium rerum.* See further Section 2.2.3c.

[111] Aristocles of Messene, *On Philosophy* 7 *ap.* Eusebius of Caesarea, *Preparation for the Gospel* 15.14.1 (*SVF* 1.98, LS 45G, Aristocles of Messene fr. 3 Heiland, Chiesara): στοιχεῖον εἶναί φασι τῶν ὄντων τὸ πῦρ, καθάπερ Ἡράκλειτος, τούτου δ' ἀρχὰς ὕλην καὶ θεόν, ὡς Πλάτων. ἀλλ' οὗτος ἄμφω σώματά φησιν εἶναι, καὶ τὸ ποιοῦν καὶ τὸ πάσχον, ἐκείνου τὸ πρῶτον ποιοῦν αἴτιον ἀσώματον εἶναι λέγοντος ('They [the Stoics] say that fire is the element of all that exists, as for Heraclitus. It has as its principles god and matter, like Plato. But Zeno says that they are both bodies, the passive and the active, whereas for Plato the first active cause is incorporeal.')

[112] On this *scala naturae* see further *infra* Section 2.2.3c.

[113] See Arius Didymus *ap.* Eusebius, *Preparation for the Gospel* 15.15.5 (fr. 29 Diels, *SVF* 2.528, LS 67L), which describes the community of gods and human beings as participating in reason or natural law: κοινωνίαν δ' ὑπάρχειν πρὸς ἀλλήλους διὰ τὸ λόγου μετέχειν, ὅς ἐστι φύσει νόμος, ps.-Plutarch, *On Homer* 2.119 describes (perfect)

This implies that the 'consistency' (*homo-logia*) of the wise person with nature, which we encountered already in Section 1.2.2b in relation to the Stoic definitions of the good life, should thus not only be understood in the sense of having cognitions that are consistent with cosmic order, or that follow or imitate the plan of the nature of the whole,[114] but also in the sense of having the same nature: the disposition of the sage is of the same perfectly rational nature as the cosmic force.

Wisdom is thus a special kind of knowledge about one's special place in the world, based on a special disposition. This disposition can be described as the perfect tenor of 'character' (*diathesis*) that no longer allows a more or less anymore.[115] It is out of this disposition of character that the sage understands and does everything well. He can thus acquire knowledge of other subjects, which are not essential to his wisdom, such as e.g. of divination, for which he will have to learn the 'principles' (*theōrēmata*) thereof.[116] This acquired knowledge is characterised as a tenor in the general sense, as in Diogenes Laertius 7.47 or Stobaeus 2.74.2, although only the sage, out of his perfect disposition of character, will be able to acquire such a tenor of e.g. divination perfectly.

This understanding of wisdom as knowledge – in terms of a secure cognition as well as a perfect disposition – can now also be related to the Stoic notion of 'excellence' (*aretē*), by which I will round off this reconstruction of wisdom.[117] As with

human beings as ruling the one cosmos alongside the gods, sharing in natural justice: τὸ δὴ ἕνα μὲν εἶναι τὸν κόσμον, συμπολιτεύεσθαι δὲ ἐν αὐτῷ θεοὺς καὶ ἀνθρώπους δικαιοσύνης μετέχοντας φύσει.

114 For these formulations in the standard interpretation of consistency see e.g. White (1979), Menn (1995), Betegh (2003) 291, Boeri (2009) 190, Cooper (2012) 166–83.

115 See above p. 31.

116 See the Stobaeus passage quoted above, n. 98. For θεωρήματα see n. 86.

117 A parallel can be drawn with *eudaimonia*, too, which has the religious connotations its modern translation 'happiness' lacks. The sage is *eu-daimon*, as he has appropriated his *daimon*, which Zeus as part of himself has given to each human being. In other words: the sage has perfected his reason as part of the reason that pervades the world. See on the human *daimon* for the early Stoics Diogenes Laertius 7.151 (*SVF* 2.1102): φασὶ δ' εἶναι καί τινας δαίμονας ἀνθρώπων συμπάθειαν ἔχοντας, ἐπόπτας τῶν ἀνθρωπείων πραγμάτων, and on the relation between the human *daimon*, Zeus, and reason Epictetus 1.14.12 and esp. Marcus Aurelius (121–80) *Meditations* 5.27: συζῇ δὲ θεοῖς ὁ συνεχῶς δεικνὺς αὐτοῖς τὴν ἑαυτοῦ ψυχὴν ἀρεσκομένην

knowledge, the Stoics understood excellence both in cognitional and in dispositional terms, and they furthermore placed human excellence, as a character, in the wider context of the nature of the whole.

Before moving on to the excellence of the sage, a preliminary remark on the translation of *aretē* as excellence should be made here. The standard modern translation of *aretē* as '(moral) virtue' is often less appropriate, as it suggests a restriction of its usage to ethics. The Stoics also used the term in a broader sense, and did not restrict its usage to the moral virtues. The traditional Greek understanding of *aretē* as 'excellence' thus often fits them better.[118] The most general Stoic definition of *aretē* as 'perfection', which survived in Diogenes Laertius, at 7.90 (*SVF* 3.197), shows that clearly: 'Excellence is in a general sense the perfection for each thing <. . .> like of a statue.'[119] A perfect statue can thus be called excellent, and so can a human being. The excellence of a human being, again according to Diogenes Laertius, at 7.94 (*SVF* 3.76), consists in 'the natural perfection of a rational being as a rational being'.[120]

The Stoics used this notion of excellence with regard to the perfect human being in two more specific senses, too. It is here that the parallel with knowledge and wisdom comes in. The first specific sense is in terms of cognitions, the other is in terms of a disposition. The variant in terms of cognitions is somewhat implicit, but can already be found in the eulogies of wisdom we have already encountered above. According to Cicero, *On Ends*, at 3.72–3 (*SVF* 3.281–2), the sage has the excellences of logic, and physics, without which the moral excellences are impossible. Logic as an excellence, according to Cicero, provides a method of reasoning that guards against

μὲν τοῖς ἀπονεμομένοις, ποιοῦσαν δὲ ὅσα βούλεται ὁ δαίμων, ὃν ἑκάστῳ προστάτην καὶ ἡγεμόνα ὁ Ζεὺς ἔδωκεν, ἀπόσπασμα ἑαυτοῦ. οὗτος δέ ἐστιν ὁ ἑκάστου νοῦς καὶ λόγος.

118 See Chantraine (1999) 107.

119 ἀρετὴ δ᾽ ἡ μέν τις κοινῶς παντὶ τελείωσις <. . .> ὥσπερ ἀνδριάντος. Cf. Galen, *On the Doctrines of Plato and Hippocrates* 5.5.39 (*SVF* 3.257): ἡ δ᾽ ἀρετὴ τελειότης ἐστὶ τῆς ἑκαστου φύσεως, ὡς αὐτὸς [sc. Chrysippus] ὁμολογεῖ.

120 τὸ τέλειον κατὰ φύσιν λογικοῦ {ἢ} ὡς λογικοῦ.

assenting to incorrect impressions, as well as protecting and preserving the acquired knowledge of ethics. Physics is an excellence, too: without an explanation of the natural world justice towards other human beings and piety towards the gods is impossible. In the *Tusculan Disputations*, at 5.68–72, these excellences of physics, ethics and logic, are described in terms of cognitions, too, as the 'threefold product of the human mind'.[121]

The 'dispositional' definition of excellence is in Diogenes Laertius, at 7.89 (*SVF* 3.39, LS 61A). The brevity (or opacity) of this definition is difficult to surpass: 'Excellence is consistent character.'[122] Plutarch, *On Moral Virtue* 441C (*SVF* 1.202, LS 61B) has a longer version on offer, in which excellence is described as both character and 'reason ... itself': 'All of them agree that excellence is a certain character and power of the governing principle of the soul that is brought into being by reason; or that it itself is reason, consistent, stable and unshakeable.'[123] When we look more in particular to the Stoic definitions of specific moral excellences ('virtues'), we find that some of these are defined in terms of character, too.[124] (The other moral excellences are defined as knowledge, and as knowledge is either defined as a secure cognition or – in the context of the virtues – as a character, they are indirectly secure cognitions or character, too.)

The excellence of the sage is thus either a cognition of his own nature or his being in a state of character, but in either case related to the nature of the whole, as Chrysippus in the first book of his *On Ends* according to Diogenes Laertius 7.87 (*SVF* 3.4, LS 63C) reminds us (see above nn. 77 and 78): 'Living according to excellence is equivalent to living according to

[121] *triplex ille animi fetus*. See Forschner (1999) 179, 185.

[122] τήν τ' ἀρετὴν διάθεσιν εἶναι ὁμολογουμένην.

[123] κοινῶς δ' ἅπαντες οὗτοι τὴν ἀρετὴν τοῦ ἡγεμονικοῦ τῆς ψυχῆς διάθεσίν τινα καὶ δύναμιν γεγενημένην ὑπὸ λόγου, μᾶλλον δὲ λόγον οὖσαν αὐτὴν ὁμολογούμενον καὶ βέβαιον καὶ ἀμετάπτωτον ὑποτίθενται.

[124] See the 'catalogues' of the moral virtues in Diogenes Laertius 7.92–3 (*SVF* 3.265) and (if indeed Stoic) ps.-Andronicus, *On Emotions* (*SVF* 3.266–8). Stobaeus 2.59.3–60.8, 2.60.24–2.6 (*SVF* 3.262, 264, LS 61H) has a clear preference for defining moral virtues as knowledge.

experience of what happens by nature: for our own natures are parts of the nature of the whole.'[125]

The conclusion of this long section is thus that according to the Stoics wisdom is both a (set of) cognition(s) relating to cosmic and human nature, and also, more fundamentally, the character by which the perfectly rational nature of the sage is part of or tied in with the cosmic active principle in its purest form of reason. Out of this disposition, the sage will be able to understand and act well in any given circumstance.

1.3 The second definition

1.3.1 Two sources

The second definition of wisdom explicitly survived in the corpus of writings of the physician Galen (129–199?), but can be distilled from the Aëtius passage, too. The definition of wisdom as 'fitting expertise' is presented in the following manner in ps.-Galen's *On the History of Philosophy*, at 5, 602.19–3.2 Diels:

> Others defined philosophy as the exercise of fitting expertise of the best life for human beings, saying that philosophy is exercise, and calling wisdom fitting expertise, which is also a cognition of human and divine matters.[126]

In this text the definition of wisdom as fitting expertise is simply presented on an equal footing with the first Stoic definition, as cognition or knowledge of human and divine matters. The order of presentation of the two definitions, with fitting expertise here presented first, is obviously motivated by the author's focus on philosophy rather than wisdom. Modern commentators have thus rightly stressed the independence of the ps.-Galenic treatise here.[127] The second definition can be

[125] πάλιν δ' ἴσον ἐστὶ τὸ κατ' ἀρετὴν ζῆν τῷ κατ' ἐμπειρίαν τῶν φύσει συμβαινόντων ζῆν, ὥς φησι Χρύσιππος ἐν τῷ πρώτῳ Περὶ τελῶν· μέρη γάρ εἰσιν αἱ ἡμέτεραι φύσεις τῆς τοῦ ὅλου.

[126] τὴν φιλοσοφίαν ... οἱ δὲ ἄσκησιν ἀνθρώποις ἀρίστης ζωῆς ἐπιτηδείας τέχνης ὡρίσαντο, ἄσκησιν μὲν τὴν φιλοσοφίαν εἴποντες, ἐπιτηδείαν δὲ τέχνην τὴν σοφίαν ὀνομάσαντες, ἥ τίς ἐστι κατάληψις θείων τε καὶ ἀνθρωπίνων πραγμάτων.

[127] See Diels (1879) 246: *c. 5 philosophiae definitiones proponuntur. quarum mediam* [our definition] *Stoicorum esse Plut. Plac. prooem. 2 confirmatum habemus. neque tamen inde eam manasse credam*, followed by Überweg and Praechter (1926) 5, and Mansfeld and Runia (1997), who acknowledge that the 'text contains some extra

read in our Aëtius passage, too. In order to do so we need to dwell on the term 'philosophy', which had become an ambiguous notion, at least since Plato. In the earliest occurrences of the word, as in Herodotus' *Histories* at 1.30,[128] or in Heraclitus,[129] philosophy is used in the sense of 'loving wisdom', with the 'wisdom lover' already in possession of wisdom. Plato introduced the meaning 'striving towards wisdom', which would finally overshadow the traditional one.[130] The Stoics appear to have had a preference for the traditional meaning. The traditional meaning already occurs in the 'exercise' in ps.-Galen. However, it most often appears in the Chrysippean formulation of 'dealing with right reason'.[131] The other meaning of striving towards wisdom occurs, too.[132] In the Aëtius passage philosophy can be read in either sense. If we look at [i] and [ii] alone, the difference between wisdom and philosophy

material' (151), otherwise describing ps.-Galen's treatise as a 'shoddy epitome of an epitome [i.e. of Aëtius' *Placita*]' (330).

128 Croesus, addressing the 'wise' Solon: Ξεῖνε Ἀθηναῖε, παρ' ἡμέας γὰρ περὶ σέο λόγος ἀπῖκται πολλὸς καὶ σοφίης [εἵνεκεν] τῆς σῆς καὶ πλάνης, ὡς φιλοσοφέων γῆν πολλὴν θεωρίης εἵνεκεν ἐπελήλυθας· νῦν ὦν ἐπειρέσθαι σε ἵμερος ἐπῆλθέ μοι εἴ τινα ἤδη πάντων εἶδες ὀλβιώτατον.

129 Fr. 35 DK (= Clement of Alexandria, *Miscellanies* 5.140.6). On the traditional meaning in the fragment see Burkert (1960) 172, Albert (1989) 19, Wohlfart (1991) 21, Schäfer (2007) 220.

130 See *Lysis* 218A, *Symposium* 204A and *Phaedrus* 278D. Among the literature on Plato's new meaning see Gauss (1937), Pérez Ruiz (1959), Burkert (1960), Malingrey (1961) 46–55, Albert (1989), Dörrie and Baltes (1996) 22–38, 231–56, Schäfer (2007), 220–3.

131 See *PHerc 1020* col. 1 ll. 14–15 (*FDS* 88), Sextus Empiricus, *Against the Professors* 9.13 (*FDS* 5), Isidorus of Pelusion (d. *c.* 435 CE), *Letters* 5.558 (*FDS* 2B).

132 For the occurrence of the 'Platonic' meaning in Stoicism see e.g. Seneca, *Letter* 89.4 (*FDS* 2) and Philo of Alexandria, *On the Preliminary Studies* 79 (*FDS* 4). Modern scholars tend to focus on this meaning in Stoicism, often in terms of 'exercise': see esp. Hadot (1989) 594, (1995) 210–16 and (2002), cf. Hülser (1987) *ad FDS* 2–5 (translating *epitēdeusis* as 'Streben'). Cf. Horn (2002) 31–49 for a typology of kinds of exercise. The exceptions here are Wilckens (1959) 473, who characterises philosophy as 'praktischer Vollzug der Weisheit', and Sellars (2009) 82–4, who interprets the Stoic notion of philosophy as both the desire for wisdom as well as the cultivation of wisdom. 'Cultivation' is somewhat infelicitous, in as far as it suggests that wisdom needs to be cared for on a regular basis, which would go against the Stoic doctrine that the perfect disposition, once acquired, cannot be lost (although Chrysippus, different from Cleanthes (Diogenes Laertius 7.127, 128, *SVF* 1.568–9), was prepared to admit that in the exceptional circumstances of drunkenness or melancholy the sage could lose his wisdom (see Diogenes Laertius 7.127, *SVF* 3.237)).

can be understood as the contrast between the perfect disposition of wisdom, on the one hand, and the striving for that state, on the other. Here we thus find the 'Platonic' reading of striving for wisdom, that is, practising our way towards the fitting expertise. In [vi] this meaning of striving seems to be on offer again, where the inclusive 'we' suggests that the Aëtius passage is referring to those not yet perfect or wise. The other meaning, loving or acting out of wisdom, can be read, too. For in [iii] the passage continues on the level of perfection or excellence, of which in [iv] he offers its most general subdivision into three kinds of excellences. In combination with [iii] and [iv], then, the contrast between [i] and [ii] can also be read as the contrast between wisdom, on the one hand, and philosophy as the acting out of wisdom, on the other. This reading of philosophy as the exercise of wisdom continues in [v]. If this reading is correct, and the Aëtius passage ambiguously offers us the Stoic usage of 'philosophy' in these two meanings, it also offers us in [ii] – however implicit – the second definition of wisdom as fitting expertise.

1.3.2 Its meaning

The expression, which I translated with 'fitting expertise' is peculiar, but has not received much discussion.[133] Long and Sedley suggest taking *epitēdeios* in its sense of 'useful', which is the second meaning in LSJ, and read the expression '*epitēdeios* expertise' as a shorthand for 'expertise of what is really useful'.[134] This may well be what the Stoics had in mind. However, this still leaves the question unanswered as to what it is that makes wisdom really useful, and also, as Long and Sedley remark, why the Stoics decided to use this adjective, rather than the more familiar *sumpherōn* or *ōphelimos*.

133 Modern translations, without further discussion, include Hülser *ad FDS* 15: 'geeignet', Inwood and Gerson (2008) 9: 'suitable', Mansfeld and Runia (2009) 63: 'required'.

134 See LS, vol. 2, 163 (followed by Brunschwig in the French translation of LS, see Brunschwig and Pellgrin (2001) vol. 2, 7): 'The expression is awkward. We interpret ἐπιτηδείου as shorthand for περὶ τοῦ ἐπιτηδείου.'

A somewhat more substantial answer is suggested by Seneca, who compares the usefulness of various types of expertise in connection with the distinction between knowing how and knowing why. In *Letter* 88.26–7 he contrasts the expertise of the sage with the expertise of the geometer. According to Seneca the geometer only knows how, whereas the sage also knows why. The geometer describes, whereas the sage can give the causes.[135] This distinction between knowing how and knowing why can also explain a similar difference offered in Diogenes Laertius 7.132–3 between 'physicists' (*phusikoi*) and 'scientists' (*hoi apo tōn mathēmatikōn*). The latter only describe the cosmos, whereas the former not only describe it, but also deal with questions such as what the essence of the cosmos is, whether it has a beginning or not, whether it is ensouled or not, whether it is destructible or indestructible and whether it is governed by providence, etc. Here the ordinary types of expertise are thus presented as a sort of 'organon' of wisdom,[136] with wisdom as the supreme, more useful, expertise that explains and gives the causes. The problem with this distinction between knowing how and knowing why is that it is often considered as an interpretation developed by Posidonius,[137] and that it would thus not give further information as to how the early Stoics might have explained their second definition of wisdom.

Here I would like to offer another interpretation as to why the Stoics chose to connect *epitēdeios* with expertise, or why they preferred *epitēdeios* over *sumpherōn* or *ōphelimos*.[138] According to LSJ, the first meaning of *epitēdeios* is 'fit', which is etymologically connected with the adverb *epitēdes*. *Epitēdes* occurs already in *Iliad* 1.142 and *Odyssey* 15.28, in the meaning 'of set purpose, advisedly'.[139] From 'of set purpose' the

135 See further Reinhardt (1954) 644, Kerferd (1978) 130, Kidd (1978) 7–15.
136 Kidd (1978) 10. 137 See Duhot (1989) 64–7, LS, vol. 1, 161.
138 Cf. the (brief) interpretation by Lachenaud (2003) 193: 'Ce qui est bien adapté à son objectif, le souverain bien ou la nature', with reference to *aptus* as Cicero's Latin translation in *Lucullus* 31 (see *infra* n. 158).
139 Cf. Chantraine (1999) 361: 'à dessein, à cette fin', Frisk (1960) 544: 'mit Vorbedacht, absichtlich'.

adjective 'fit', as that which has achieved its purpose was derived, as well as the denominative verb, *epitēdeuō*, 'to deal with', and *the nomen actionis*, *epitēdeusis*, 'dealing with'. How can this first meaning of 'fit' be understood in relation to wisdom as fitting expertise? In what way can wisdom as expertise said to be fitting? An answer can be formulated if we first look at the two Stoic definitions of expertise, and secondly at the application of expertise, which the Stoics did not restrict to human activities. I propose that wisdom turns out to be a fitting expertise if it somehow fits nature, which has an expert-like structure, too. I will present the evidence for this interpretation in three steps, the first one dealing with the two Stoic definitions of expertise, the second with expertise applied to nature and the third with how the sources combine the two.

The first step is that the Stoics formulated two definitions of expertise, similar to the two definitions of knowledge we have already encountered above.[140] Both definitions of expertise can be found in the *Commentary on the Gorgias* 12.1 (*SVF* 1.73, *FDS* 392, LS 42A) by the sixth-century Platonist Olympiodorus, in the context of the question with which the discussion in Plato's *Gorgias* begins: whether rhetoric is an expertise. The first of the Stoic definitions is that expertise is a system of cognitions: 'Zeno says that "expertise is a system of cognitions unified by training towards some useful end in life."'[141] That this definition indeed goes back to Zeno himself is confirmed in other evidence. According to Sextus Empiricus, *Against the Professors* 7.373 (*FDS* 403), Chrysippus spoke of expertise as 'a system and a collection of cognitions',[142] and in a passage in a work entitled *Introduction*, at 14, 44.5–6 (*FDS* 393A), by David, presumably a student of Olympiodorus, the definition

140 Discussions of the Stoic definitions of expertise include Sparshott (1978), Ioppolo (1980) 280–1, Mansfeld (1983), Sellars (2009) 68–75 (who discusses the systematic definition only).

141 Ζήνων δέ φησιν ὅτι 'τέχνη ἐστὶ σύστημα ἐκ καταλήψεων συγγεγυμνασμένων πρός τι τέλος εὔχρηστον τῶν ἐν τῷ βίῳ'. In reading συγγεγυμνασμένων rather than συγγεγυμνασμένον I follow von Arnim's silent emendation *ad loc.*, made explicit by Mansfeld (1983) 57, as it should be the cognitions rather than the system that are unified by training.

142 οἱ περὶ τὸν Χρύσιππον . . . σύστημα καὶ ἄθροισμα καταλήψεων.

is cited anonymously, but has 'by experience' added to it.[143] This extra clause Chrysippus also used in his definition of the end, while clarifying Zeno's as well as Cleanthes' definitions.[144] This makes it likely that not only is the definition in David's *Introduction* by Chrysippus, but also that Olympiodorus' attribution of the definition to Zeno is reliable.[145] The second definition of expertise is also in Olympiodorus immediately after the first definition, at 12.2 (*SVF* 1.490, *FDS* 392):

> Cleanthes, then, says that an expertise is 'a tenor that accomplishes everything methodically'. But this definition is considered to be incomplete, for nature is also a tenor that does methodically all it does. Accordingly Chrysippus, after adding the phrase 'with impressions', said 'an expertise is a tenor that proceeds methodically with impressions'.[146]

In the *Scholia on Dionysius Thrax* 118.13–16 (*SVF* 1.72, *FDS* 410) this definition is ascribed to Zeno, too: 'Zeno says that "expertise is a tenor capable of doing something methodically", that is doing something according to a certain way and method.'[147] Although again doubts about the attribution to Zeno have been raised,[148] Chrysippus' variation is yet a further example of the process of clarification of an earlier formulation by the earliest heads of the Stoic school.

The second step: the Stoics applied expertise to nature, too. To be more precise, they described nature as an expert-like fire, as in Diogenes Laertius 7.156 (*SVF* 1.171): 'They maintain that nature is an expert-like fire, progressing methodically to

143 τέχνη ἐστὶ σύστημα ἐκ καταλήψεων ἐμπειρίᾳ συγγεγυμνασμένη πρός τι τέλος εὔχρηστον τῶν ἐν τῷ βίῳ.

144 See e.g. the clarifications of Zeno's formula of the end in Stobaeus 2.75.12–6.6 (LS 63B, *FDS* 794A): 'To Zeno's "living accordingly" Cleanthes added "with nature", and Chrysippus, wishing to clarify this further, expressed it in this way: "living according to the experience of the things happening by nature"', discussed in Section 1.2.2b. More examples of this procedure of clarification are conveniently listed by Schofield (1999) 81 n. 29.

145 Mansfeld (1983) 64.

146 Κλεάνθης τοίνυν λέγει ὅτι 'τέχνη ἐστὶν ἕξις ὁδῷ πάντα ἀνύουσα'. ἀτελὴς δ' ἐστιν οὗτος ὁ ὅρος, καὶ γὰρ ἡ φύσις ἕξις τίς ἐστιν ὁδῷ πάντα ποιοῦσα· ὅθεν ὁ Χρύσιππος προσθεὶς τὸ 'μετὰ φαντασιῶν' εἶπεν ὅτι 'τέχνη ἐστὶν ἕξις ὁδῷ προιοῦσα μετὰ φαντασιῶν'.

147 ὁ Ζήνων, λέγων 'τέχνη ἐστὶν ἕξις ὁδοποιητική [ὁδῷ ποιητική' – Festa (1932–5) 110, Mansfeld (1983) 62], τουτέστι δι' ὁδοῦ καὶ μεθόδου ποιοῦσά τι.

148 E.g. Pearson (1891) 27, von Arnim *ad SVF* 1.72, Festa (1932–5) 41, Isnardi Parente (1966) 288, Ioppolo (1980) 280–1.

come into being.'[149] In Cicero's Latin version, in *On the Nature of the Gods* at 2.57 (*SVF* 1.171), the origins of the description are assigned to Zeno: 'Zeno defined nature as an expert-like fire, proceeding to bringing things into being in a certain way.'[150] Incidentally, the same definition is applied to god. See the abridgment of Aëtius, at 881F (= 1.7.33, *SVF* 2.1027): 'The Stoics make clear that god is thinking, an expert-like fire proceeding methodically to bring order into being methodically.'[151] The identification of nature and god is standard Stoic doctrine. So we can safely assume that the Stoics held this doctrine from the very beginning.

I now move on to the third step: the relation between human expertise and nature as an expert-like fire. Here Olympiodorus is yet again our main source. According to his account, at 2.2 (*FDS* 393), 'the philosopher adds "with impressions" in contrast to nature, for nature also proceeds in a certain way and order, but not together with impressions'.[152] In this passage Olympiodorus does not make it explicit to whom he refers, but it is likely that by 'the philosopher' Chrysippus must have been meant, as in 12.2. In a parallel passage, acclaimed 'a new fragment of Chrysippus',[153] David, *Introduction* 14, 43.33–4.5 (*FDS* 393A), presents the combination of nature and expertise thus:

> 'With impressions' is added because of nature; for nature is also a tenor (since she has her being in things that have it, as in a human being, a stone, in

[149] δοκεῖ δὲ αὐτοῖς τὴν μὲν φύσιν εἶναι πῦρ τεχνικόν, ὁδῷ βαδίζον εἰς γένεσιν. See also ps.-Galen, *Medical Definitions* 95, 19.371 Kühn (*SVF* 2.1133): φύσις ἐστὶ πῦρ τεχνικὸν ὁδῷ βαδίζον εἰς γένεσιν, and Clement of Alexandria, *Miscellanies* 5.100.4 (*SVF* 2.1134): πῦρ μὲν οὖν τεχνικὸν ὁδῷ βαδίζον εἰς γένεσιν τὴν φύσιν ὁρίζονται οἱ Στωικοί. The Armenian translation of Philo of Alexandria, *On God* 82 Siegert must have read τεχνικὸν ὁδῷ βαδίζον εἰς γένεσιν in Philo's lost Greek original, too (see Siegert (1980–92) *ad loc.* and at 100–1).

[150] *Zeno igitur naturam ita definit ut eam dicat ignem esse artificiosum ad gignendum progredientem via.* The relation between the formulation in Greek and Cicero's translation was already noted by e.g. Ritter, Preller and Wellmann (1913) no. 494 n. a, Hahm (1977) 200, Mansfeld (1983) 61, Pohlenz (1990) 36.

[151] οἱ Στωικοὶ νοερὸν θεὸν ἀποφαίνονται, πῦρ τεχνικόν ὁδῷ βαδίζον ἐπὶ γένεσιν κόσμου.

[152] τέχνη γάρ ἐστι μέθοδος ὁδῷ καὶ τάξει μετὰ φαντασίας προιοῦσα· τὸ δὲ 'μετὰ φαντασίας' προσέθηκεν ὁ φιλόσοφος πρὸς ἀντιδιαστολὴν τῆς φύσεως, καὶ ἡ φύσις γὰρ ὁδῷ καὶ τάξει πρόεισιν, ἀλλ' οὐ μετὰ φαντασίας.

[153] Mansfeld (1983) 57.

a piece of wood) and moves methodically in its course (for she proceeds according to a pattern), but not 'with impressions' like expertise. For the expert, who uses reason when he wants to make something, first makes an imprint of what he wants to make, then by this means creates it; but nature does nothing of that kind, for she does not first make an imprint of what she wants to make.[154]

David more often quotes an author without naming him; as we saw, a little way further on, in *Introduction* 14, 44.5–6 (*FDS* 393A), citing a variant of the other description of expertise, he also does not tell us what his underlying source is. It thus is likely that the passage in David's *Introduction* can serve as confirmation of Olympiodorus' account in 2.2.

Elsewhere this relationship between expertise and nature is extended to the nature of living beings, or of beings with a soul. In Diogenes Laertius, at 7.156 (*SVF* 2.774), the description of nature as an expert-like fire is followed by a description of the human soul: 'For they hold that nature is an expert-like fire, proceeding methodically to come into being, which is a breath in fiery and expert-like form; and the soul is a nature with impressions.'[155] If this translation is based on a correct reading of this muddled passage,[156] then what applies to nature as a whole also applies to the human soul, with the distinction that the human soul is a nature that receives impressions.

How the Stoics combined human expertise and the expert-like structure of nature is suggested by Cicero in his exposition of Zenonian doctrine in *On the Nature of the Gods*, at 2.57 (*SVF* 1.171): 'What in the processes of our types of expertise is done by the hand, is done with far more expertise by nature, that is as I said by that expert-like fire, which is the teacher of

[154] 'μετὰ φαντασίας' δὲ πρόσκειται διὰ τὴν φύσιν· καὶ γὰρ ἡ φύσις ἕξις ἐστίν (ἔχει γὰρ τὸ εἶναι ἐν τοῖς ἔχουσιν αὐτήν, οἷον ἐν ἀνθρώπῳ, ἐν λίθῳ, ἐν ξύλῳ) καὶ ὁδῷ βαδίζει (κατὰ γὰρ τάξιν προέρχεται), ἀλλ' οὐ μετὰ φαντασίας ὥσπερ ἡ τέχνη· καὶ γὰρ ὁ τεχνίτης κεχρημένος τῷ λόγῳ, ἡνίκα βούλεται τι ποιῆσαι, πρότερον διατυποῖ ἐν ἑαυτῷ ὃ βούλεται ποιῆσαι καὶ εἶθ' οὕτως ἀποτελεῖ αὐτό, ἡ δὲ φύσις οὐδὲν τοιοῦτον ποιεῖ· οὐδὲ γὰρ προδιατυποῖ ἐν ἑαυτῇ ὃ βούλεται κατασκευάσαι.

[155] δοκεῖ δὲ αὐτοῖς τὴν μὲν φύσιν εἶναι πῦρ τεχνικόν, ὁδῷ βαδίζον εἰς γένεσιν, ὅπερ ἐστὶ πνεῦμα πυροειδὲς καὶ τεχνοειδές· τὴν δὲ ψυχὴν αἰσθητικὴν.

[156] After αἰσθητικὴν von Arnim in *SVF ad loc.* inserted φύσιν, although this 'animal' φύσιν needs to be carefully distinguished from cosmic φύσιν at the beginning of the sentence. Perhaps that is why Gigante (1998) 539 n. 179 added ἕξιν.

the other kinds of expertise.'[157] Here human expertise and cosmic nature's expertise are presented as closely connected notions. Like human nature, cosmic nature proceeds in an expert-like way. If, furthermore, as Cicero states, cosmic nature is more expert-like than ordinary human kinds of expertise, then the obvious inference is that the expert-like structure of nature can be discovered by human nature. The result of that discovery can be described in Stoic terminology – and that brings us finally back to the second definition of wisdom – as the *epitēdeios* expertise, as the sage's expertise that fits the expert processes in nature. If this interpretation is indeed correct, we have found yet another way in which wisdom can be properly characterised as *epitēdeios* expertise. Wisdom is not only the most useful of the kinds of expertise, it also fits the expert-like structure of the universe.[158] The fittingness of human expertise and the expert-like structure of nature can thus be put on par with the Stoic formulation of the end as consistency of human and cosmic reason, respectively. Reformulated in terms of the two definitions of expertise, in terms of cognitions the sage's wisdom consists in cognitions structured in an expert-like way reflecting the expert-like structure of nature, whereas in terms of dispositions the sage's wisdom consists in his particular disposition that makes him part of the expert-like structure of nature.

1.4 Conclusion

The two definitions of wisdom, as knowledge of human and divine matters and as fitting expertise, turn out to be remarkably similar. The Stoics understood both definitions in terms of cognitions as well as in terms of a disposition: as we have seen,

[157] *quodque in operibus nostrarum artium manus efficiat id multo artificiosus naturam efficere, id est, ut dixi, ignem artificiosum, magistrum artium reliquarum.*

[158] *Aptissimus* may well have been Cicero's translation of ἐπιτήδειος, as suggested by Lachenaud (2003) 193. See *Lucullus* 31: *ad rerum igitur scientiam vitaeque constantiam aptissima cum sit mens hominis amplectitur maxime cognitionem et istam* κατάληψιν, *quam ut dixi verbum e verbo exprimentes conprehensionem dicemus, cum ipsam per se amat (nihil enim est ei veritatis luce dulcius) tum etiam propter usum.*

the sage's knowledge or expertise is either a cognition of human nature as a part of cosmic nature, or else his disposition in the cosmos. The second definition also runs parallel to the first definition in terms of the interrelatedness of knowledge, cosmic and human nature or, for that matter, of the interrelatedness of dialectic, physics and ethics.

If we look back at the Aëtius passage with which we started out in Section 1.2, it can now be rephrased as follows, along the lines of both variants of the definitions of wisdom as knowledge. In the definition of knowledge as a (set of) secure cognition(s) [i] wisdom deals with the relationship between divine and human nature, and [ii] philosophy is the use thereof (or the attempt to find it). This (set of) cognition(s) can also be described as a special expertise dealing with cosmic nature, human behaviour, and reason. In the definition of knowledge as an enduring disposition [i] wisdom is the perfectly rational disposition of the sage in the world, and [ii] philosophy is the use of this disposition (or the striving for this disposition). This cognition or disposition is an expertise that fits the expert-like or rational structure of the world. [iii] This expertise can furthermore be characterised as an excellence. [iv] This excellence can be considered in three general ways, from the point of view of physics (that is of how one's reason is part of the reason that governs the world), of ethics (that is of how the human mind acts in accordance with it) and of logic (that is of how the mind deals properly with reason itself). [v–vi] The activity that goes with the exercise of (or the search for) this expertise is called physics when we investigate the world and the things in the world, ethics when we occupy ourselves with human life, and logic (or dialectic) when we deal with reason as such.

CHAPTER 2

THE CHANGE

2.1 Introduction

In this chapter I will elucidate the Stoic conception of wisdom further by concentrating on one small, but important, aspect: the moment of becoming wise. As I will show, the change to wisdom can help us to understand that wisdom is, above all, a disposition of a very special nature, which enables the sage to do well everything he does.

The change to wisdom has drawn little attention in the scholarly literature. The best, although rather brief, description is still to be found in an essentially nineteenth-century handbook,[1] but valuable observations were offered by Rist and, more recently, by Bénatouïl and Liu.[2] Otherwise it was rejected as an early Stoic doctrine,[3] played down,[4] dealt with in passing,[5] described as a by-product of the Stoic theory of progress,[6] perfunctorily characterised – after the ancient critics of the Stoics – as notorious,[7] bizarre,[8] and (incorrectly in an important way, as we shall see) compared to Paul's Road to Damascus experience, to Augustine's *tolle lege* experience,[9] or to the experience of a blinded man who has his bandages removed.[10]

The lack of attention may be explained by the pitiful state of our sources, which is particularly precarious here. A snippet in Clement of Alexandria's *Miscellanies* 4.6.28.1 (*SVF* 3.221)

[1] Zeller and Wellmann (1923) 261–2.
[2] Rist (1969) 90–3, Bénatouïl (2005) 21, 24, Liu (2009) 262.
[3] Reinhardt (1921) 421 (ascribing the doctrine to Posidonius), Heitmann (1940) 36.
[4] See Pembroke (1971) 121, and Vimercati (2011) 591, who describes it as a 'novità rispetto alla tradizionale dicotomia saggio-stolto'.
[5] Described as a 'crisis' in Inwood (1984) 174.
[6] Luschnat (1958) 195, 204, Roskam (2005) 29.
[7] Sedley (1977) 93.
[8] Mignucci (1999) 163, Veyne (2005) 683.
[9] Bickel (1957) 98.
[10] Passmore (2000) 80.

illustrates the matter: 'The turn towards the divine the Stoics say happens as a result of a change, when the soul changes to wisdom.'[11] Becoming wise is here described as a 'change' (*metabolē*). Clement connects it with a 'turn towards' (*metastrophē*) the divine. Clement's is but a miscellaneous remark (in keeping with the title of his work), and needs to be put into context in order to make sense of it. What kind of change will the Stoics have had in mind? How, if at all, does 'turn towards the divine' fit in?

Fortunately, two somewhat longer pieces of evidence that deal with becoming wise can be found in the Plutarchean corpus. The first passage is but a side topic in Plutarch's *How a Man May Become Aware of his Progress in Virtue* [hereafter, *Progress*], at 75C–F (*SVF* 3.539, *FDS* 1233, LS 61S (part)). Despite its familiarity I print it here, with my own subdivisions for ease of reference:

[i] The sage changes in a moment or a second of time from the lowest possible inferiority to an unsurpassable character of virtue; [ii] and all his vice, of which he has not over a long time succeeded in removing even a small part, he instantaneously flees forever. [iii] Yet, you doubtless know that, on the other hand, those who say these things make for themselves much trouble and great difficulties over the doctrine of the man who has not noticed, who has not yet grasped that he has become wise, but is ignorant and hesitates to believe that his advancement, which has been effected by the gradual and long-continued process of getting rid of some things and adding others, has, as on a journey, unnoticed and quietly brought him to virtue. [iv] But if there were such a swiftness and magnitude of the change that the man who was the very worst in the morning should have become best in the evening, [v] or should the change so come about that he who was a fool when he fell asleep should awake wise, and could say, having dismissed from his soul yesterday's gross stupidities and false conceptions: 'False dreams, goodbye! You are nothing' – [vi] who would fail to recognise that a great difference like this had been generated in his own self, and that practical wisdom had all at once poured forth its beams? For it seems to me more likely that anyone who, like Caeneus, was made man from woman in answer to prayer, would fail to recognise that make-over, [vii] than that anyone moderate, wise and brave, from being cowardly, foolish and weak-willed,

[11] τὴν δὲ μεταστροφὴν τὴν ἐπὶ τὰ θεῖα οἱ μὲν Στωικοὶ ἐκ μεταβολῆς φασὶ γίνεσθαι μεταβαλλούσης [after Von Arnim; the mss. have γενέσθαι μεταβαλούσης] τῆς ψυχῆς εἰς σοφίαν.

[viii] and having changed from a bestial to a divine life, [ix] should for a single moment not notice what had happened to him.[12]

As the title already indicates, the treatise and indeed this passage concentrate not so much upon the moment of change as such as upon moral progress in general, and this from the perspective of the unawareness that goes with it.

In the other, longer passage in the *Synopsis of the Treatise 'The Stoics talk More Paradoxically than the Poets'* [hereafter, *Synopsis*], becoming a sage is the central topic. Nothing from this passage, or indeed from the *Synopsis* as a whole, has ended up in any of the collection of Stoic fragments, like *SVF* or *FDS*. This neglect may partly have been caused by the obscurity of the treatise,[13] partly by the extravagant doctrines it contains.[14] Of the latter cause the first chapter of the *Synopsis* is a splendid example. The Stoic sage is compared with Pindar's description of Caeneus, king of the Lapiths. The sage and Caeneus have unvulnerability in common: but where Caeneus,

[12] [i] ἀκαρεὶ χρόνου καὶ ὥρας ἐκ τῆς ὡς ἔνι μάλιστα φαυλότητος εἰς οὐκ ἔχουσαν ὑπερβολὴν ἀρετῆς διάθεσιν μεταβαλὼν ὁ σοφός, [ii] ἧς οὐδ᾽ ἐν χρόνῳ πολλῷ μέρος ἀφεῖλε κακίας, ἅμα πᾶσαν ἐξαίφνης ἀποπέφευγε. [iii] καίτοι ἤδη ταῦτά γε λέγοντας οἶσθα δήπου πάλιν πολλὰ παρέχοντας αὑτοῖς πράγματα καὶ μεγάλας ἀπορίας περὶ τοῦ διαλεληθότος, ὃς αὐτὸς ἑαυτὸν οὔπω κατείληφε γεγονὼς σοφός, ἀλλ᾽ ἀγνοεῖ καὶ ἀμφιδοξεῖ τῷ κατὰ μικρὸν ἐν χρόνῳ πολλῷ τὰ μὲν ἀφαιροῦντι τὰ δὲ προστιθέντι γιγνομένην τὴν ἐπίδοσιν καθάπερ πορείαν τῇ ἀρετῇ λαθεῖν ἀτρέμα προσμίξασαν. [iv] εἰ δέ γε ἦν τάχος τοσοῦτον τῆς μεταβολῆς καὶ μέγεθος, ὥστε τὸν πρωὶ κάκιστον ἑσπέρας γεγονέναι κράτιστον, [v] ἢ ἂν οὕτω τινὶ συντύχῃ τὰ τῆς μεταβολῆς, καταδαρθόντα φαῦλον ἀνεγρέσθαι σοφὸν καὶ προσειπεῖν ἐκ τῆς ψυχῆς μεθεικότα τὰς χθιζάς ἀβελτερίας καὶ ἀπάτας 'ψευδεῖς ὄνειροι, χαίρετ'· οὐδὲν ἦτ᾽ ἄρα' – [vi] τίς ἂν ἀγνοήσειεν ἑαυτοῦ διαφορὰν ἐν αὑτῷ τοσαύτην γενομένην καὶ φρόνησιν ἀθρόον ἐκλάμψασαν; ἐμοὶ μὲν γὰρ δοκεῖ μᾶλλον ἄν τις, ὡς ὁ Καινεύς, γενόμενος κατ᾽ εὐχὴν ἀνὴρ ἐκ γυναικὸς ἀγνοῆσαι τὴν μετακόσμησιν, [vii] ἢ σώφρων καὶ φρόνιμος καὶ ἀνδρεῖος ἐκ δειλοῦ καὶ ἀνοήτου καὶ ἀκρατοῦς ἀποτελεσθεὶς [viii] καὶ μεταβαλὼν εἰς θεῖον ἐκ θηριώδους βίον [ix] ἀκαρὲς διαλαθεῖν αὑτόν.

[13] The treatise is after all only three Teubner pages long. Furthermore, its authorship is disputed, as the title does not occur in the Lamprias catalogue, the ancient list of Plutarch's writings. However, the title *The Stoics Talk More Paradoxically than the Poets* occurs in it as no. 79, and our treatise indeed qualifies as a *synopsis* rather than an *epitome* or summary by giving a flavour of the main text offering some examples out of it (on this distinction see Casevitz and Babut (2004) 97). It thus seems likely that Plutarch is at least the author of the separate passages, the style and language of which have been characterised by Cherniss (1976) 607 as thoroughly Plutarchean.

[14] Ziegler (1951) 760 described it as an exaggeration that should not be taken seriously and Pohlenz (1939) 2 (cf. Pohlenz and Westman (1959) 59) as a piece of writing that was to be read aloud in a banquet to amuse Plutarch's friends.

although unwounded, finally had to disappear underground in his battle against the Centaurs,[15] so the sage remains invulnerable, even when 'wounded, in pain, on the rack', etc.

In what follows I will present and discuss the material on the moment of becoming a sage in the *Synopsis*, see whether it can be taken seriously by looking for Stoic parallels in *Progress* and elsewhere, and – even more importantly – deal with the question whether and how the evidence fits the Stoic system of thought. I will restrict myself to the *Synopsis* at first, thus leaving the doctrine of unawareness as it occurs in *Progress* (and indeed elsewhere) for later (Section 2.3).

2.2 The characteristics in the *Synopsis*

As the title already indicates, the author of the *Synopsis* tries to show that what the Stoics talk about is even more absurd than what can be found in works of fiction.

In its Chapter 2 a comparison is offered between the Stoic sage-to-be and the depiction of Iolaus by Aeschylus and Euripides. In order to kill Eurystheus, who chased Heracles' children, old Iolaus, Heracles' nephew, got his strength and youth back from Zeus and Hebe, whereas

> [2.1] the sage of the Stoics, though yesterday he was most ugly and at the same time most vicious, today all of a sudden has changed to virtue, [2.2] and from being a wrinkled and sallow and, as Aeschylus says 'lumbago-ridden, wretched, pain-distraught elder', has become seemly, of godlike form and good-looking.[16]

In Chapter 3 the Stoic sage is compared to Homer's Odysseus. At three crucial moments on his journey back home to Ithaca Athena gives him better looks: when after his shipwreck he has to present himself to the king of the Phaeacians (6.229–35), and twice at Ithaca, when he presents himself to his son

[15] Pindar's description 'survived' as fr. 128F 7–9 Maehler. (Casevitz and Babut (2004) 103 have a typo here.) Our main Greek source is Apollonius of Rhodes, *Argonautica* 1.59–64.

[16] [2.1] ὁ δὲ τῶν Στωικῶν σοφὸς χθὲς μὲν ἦν αἴσχιστος ἅμα καὶ κάκιστος τήμερον δ' ἄφνω μεταβέβληκεν εἰς ἀρετὴν, [2.2] καὶ γέγονεν ἐκ ῥυσοῦ καὶ ὠχροῦ καὶ κατ' Αἰσχύλον 'ἐξ ὀσφυαλγοῦς κὠδυνοσπάδος λυγροῦ / γέροντος' εὐπρεπὴς θεοειδὴς καλλίμορφος.

(16.172–6), and finally to his wife (23.156–62). The chapter picks up on the notion of 'wrinkled' in [2.2]. In the first sentence Odysseus is said to have had his wrinkles removed by Athena, whereas the Stoic sage has not: nevertheless the sage should not be considered ugly. The second and last sentence is badly connected with the preceding one. Yet again an apparently absurd doctrine is expressed in it. The lover will turn away from the person he loves, once that person has become a sage: 'like beetles preferring bad smell and avoiding perfume' lovers prefer to be together with persons who are very ugly, and turn away when these persons '[3] change by wisdom into good looks and beauty'.[17] The reaction of these non-sages may surprise, as it surprised Plutarch in the parallel passage of *On Common Notions* 1073A–B (*SVF* 3.719).[18]

Chapter 4 of the *Synopsis* picks up on 'most vicious' from [2.1]:

[4.1] Among the Stoics the man who is most vicious in the morning, if so it happens to be, is virtuous in the afternoon, [4.2.1] and having fallen asleep [a] unstable, ignorant, [b] unjust and licentious, [c] and even, by Zeus, a slave, [d] poor and without means, [4.2.2] he gets up the very same day, having become [a] a king, [b] rich and blessed as well as [c] moderate, just, [d] stable and holding no opinions, [4.3.1] not having grown a beard yet or pubic hair in a body young and soft, [4.3.2] but having got, in a soul that was feeble and soft and unmanly and not stable, [a] perfect insight, [b] the highest practical wisdom, [c] a character equal to the gods, [d] unopining knowledge and [e] an unshakeable tenor, [4.4.1] and this not by any previous diminution of depravity, [4.4.2] but instantaneously, one could almost say, by having become from the most vicious of wild beasts some hero or *daimon* or god. [4.5] For, if one has received virtue from the Stoa, it is possible to say: 'Ask, if there's anything you wish, all will be yours.' It brings wealth, it comprises kingship, it gives luck, it makes men prosperous and free from all other wants as well as self-sufficient, though they have not a single drachma of their own.[19]

[17] [3] ὅταν εἰς εὐμορφίαν καὶ κάλλος ὑπὸ σοφίας μεταβάλωσιν.

[18] The absurdity is perhaps explained in Stobaeus 2.105.1–2 (*SVF* 3.682): μόνον δὲ προτετράφται τὸν σοτφὸν καὶ μόνον προτρέπειν δύνασθαι ('only the sage can be attracted [by other sages], and only he can attract [other sages]').

[19] [4.1] ὁ παρὰ τοῖς Στωικοῖς κάκιστος, ἂν οὕτω τύχῃ, πρωὶ δείλης ἄριστος, [4.2.1] καὶ καταδαρθὼν [a] ἔμπληκτος καὶ ἀμαθὴς καὶ [b] ἄδικος καὶ ἀκόλαστος καὶ [c] ναὶ μὰ Δία δοῦλος καὶ [d] πένης καὶ ἄπορος [4.2.2] αὐθημερὸν ἀνίσταται [a] βασιλεὺς καὶ [b] πλούσιος καὶ ὄλβιος γεγονώς, [c] σώφρων τε καὶ δίκαιος καὶ [d] βέβαιος καὶ ἀδόξαστος, [4.3.1] οὐ γένεια φύσας οὐδὲ ἥβην ἐν σώματι νέῳ καὶ ἁπαλῷ, [4.3.2] ἀλλ' ἐν ἀσθενεῖ καὶ ἁπαλῇ ψυχῇ

Here, as well as in [2] and [3], and in *Progress*, in [i], [iv], [v] and [viii], the standard term to describe what happens to someone who becomes a sage is the same as used by Clement: change. Otherwise these passages seem to offer a rather mixed bag of characterisations associated with becoming a sage. In what follows I will, therefore, organise its contents by discussing three features: the change as instantaneous (Section 2.2.1), as between opposite states (Section 2.2.2) and as radical (Section 2.2.3).

2.2.1 *Instantaneous*

A first feature of the change as described in the *Synopsis* is the apparent speed with which it occurs. In [2] the suddenness of becoming a sage is put centre stage. Being compared to Iolaus, who from being weak suddenly changes into being young, strong and prepared for battle, the sage of the Stoics also suddenly changes from a state of vice and ugliness to a state of virtue and beauty. In [4] the suddenness is mentioned again. In [4.1] the change occurs between morning and afternoon; in [4.2] between the moment of going to bed and waking up. The suddenness can also be found in the implicit contrast expressed in the simile of [4.3.1] and [4.3.2]: other than the youth who slowly grows a beard and gets pubic hair [4.3.1], the sage-to-be suddenly has perfect intelligence, etc. [4.3.2].[20] This implicit contrast between [4.3.1] and [4.3.2] is explained in [4.4.1] and [4.4.2]: the change happens suddenly without any previous alleviation.

In *Progress* the swiftness of the change is recorded in comparable variety: 'in a moment or a second of time' in [i], 'instantaneously' in [ii], 'morning' and 'evening' in [iv], and

καὶ ἀνάνδρῳ καὶ ἀβεβαίῳ, [a] νοῦν τέλειον, [b] ἄκραν φρόνησιν, [c] ἰσόθεον διάθεσιν, [d] ἀδόξαστον ἐπιστήμην καὶ [e] ἀμετάπτωτον ἕξιν ἐσχηκώς [4.4.1] οὐδὲν ἐνδούσης πρότερον αὐτῷ τῆς μοχθηρίας, [4.4.2] ἀλλ' ἐξαίφνης, ὀλίγου δέω εἰπεῖν, ἥρως τις ἢ δαίμων ἢ θεὸς ἐκ θηρίων τοῦ κακίστου γενόμενος. [4.5] ἐκ τῆς Στοᾶς γὰρ λαβόντα τὴν ἀρετὴν ἔστιν εἰπεῖν: 'εὖξαι εἴ τι βούλει· πάντα σοι γενήσεται.' πλοῦτον φέρει, βασιλείαν ἔχει, τύχην δίδωσιν, εὐπότμους ποιεῖ καὶ ἀπροσδεεῖς καὶ αὐτάρκεις, μίαν οἴκοθεν δραχμὴν οὐκ ἔχοντας.

[20] Cf. Cherniss (1976) *ad loc.*

'falling asleep' and 'awaking' in [v]. In yet another piece of evidence Plutarch, *On Common Notions* 1062B (not in *SVF*, LS 61U, *FDS* 1235), the time span is 'a little later', as the sage has 'now become both prudent and supremely happy when a little earlier he was utterly wretched and foolish'.[21] In the *Synopsis* we thus find a characteristic that is confirmed in other sources.

2.2.2 *The opposite states*

A second feature of the change as described in the *Synopsis* is that it is a change between opposite states. In Chapter 2 Plutarch begins with the ugliness and badness of the sage-to-be. He thereupon tells us that the badness of the sage-to-be is transformed into virtue with the newly born sage. He thereafter returns to the former state of the sage-to-be as the ugliest being, who is transformed into a being that is seemly, godlike in form and good-looking.

Chapter 4 offers an ever-richer variety of changes. After the introductory [4.1], which is a repetition of [2], in [4.2] the state before and the state after the change are characterised by two sets of opposite states, which – based on their positions in the text – could be described as internal and external, respectively. In the internal set of opposites, [4.2.1c–d] and [4.2.2a–b], the state before is characterised as one of a slave, a pauper, someone without means, and the state after as one of a king, a rich and blessed man. The pair of opposites here are in fact two: in [4.2.1c] and [4.2.2a] slave and king are opposed, in [4.2.1d] and [4.2.2b] poor and rich. In the external set, [4.2.1a–b] and [4.2.2c–d], we find two subsets of opposites. In the first subset the state before is in [4.2.1a] characterised as unstable and ignorant, and the state after in [4.2.2d] as stable and having nothing to do with holding opinions. In the second subset the change is described from unjust and licentious [4.2.1b] to just and moderate [4.2.2c]. In [4.4.2] another set of opposites is added: the sage-to-be changes from the most vicious of wild

[21] μικρῷ πρόσθεν ἀθλιώτατος ὢν καὶ ἀφρονέστατος νῦν ὁμοῦ φρόνιμος καὶ μακάριος γέγονεν.

beings into a hero, a *daimon* or a god. The change leads to an encompassing state of positive qualities, enumerated in [4.3.2] and appropriately illustrated in [4.5]. According to [4.3.2] next to [a] perfect insight and [d] unopining knowledge, the sage has [b] the highest practical wisdom, and [e] an 'unshakeable tenor', and [c] a 'character equal to the gods'. In [4.5] wealth and kingship are repeated, and the gifts of good fortune[22] and self-sufficiency are added. The quotation at the beginning of [4.5] – from Menander, the fourth-century BCE writer of (so-called New comedies, and preserved in a longer version by Stobaeus at 4.743.8, fr. 838.6 Kassel and Austin – offers an apt introduction to this list of good things, since the sage, on the basis of his virtuous disposition, will have them all.

These bewildering sets of states can most easily be classified on the basis of the Stoic tripartition of philosophy into ethics, logic (or dialectic) and physics, which we encountered in Chapter 1, and to which I will now turn.

2.2.2a *Ethics*

Most of the states are to be placed within the ethical part of philosophy. The states are presented in terms of virtue (or moral excellence) and vice in general as well as in terms of specific virtues and vices. The states in terms of the virtues and vices *in general* are to be found in *Synopsis* [2] and [4.1]. In either passage the state of the sage-to-be changes from vice to virtue. *Progress* contains a similar account: in [i] and [ii] the change is from vice to a state of virtue, in [iv] the change is from worst to best. The states in terms of the specific virtues and vices are in [4.2.1b] and [4.2.2c]. Before he changed to wisdom the sage was unjust and licentious, after the change he is moderate and just. In *Progress* [vii] we also find the change described in relation to two specific virtues. As in the *Synopsis* the virtue of moderation occurs again; here the other specific virtue is bravery: whereas the inferior person is a coward, the sage is brave. The contrast between sage and

[22] Referred to by the words τύχη and πότμος.

inferior person as a contrast between virtue(s) and vice(s), respectively, is well known.[23]

Two expressions in the *Synopsis* can be understood as implicit references to the virtuous state of the sage. The expressions are in [4.3.2]: 'unshakeable tenor' and a 'character equal to the gods'.[24] In *Progress* [i] Plutarch makes the relation explicit, when he speaks of the character of virtue. This is soundly Stoic. As I discussed in Section 1.2.2c, the Stoics defined virtue as a stable disposition or 'character'. Character is a special kind of tenor, one that cannot be intensified and relaxed. Virtue as a character is thus also 'unshakeable tenor'.

Other variants of the change from one extreme state to the other to be found in the *Synopsis* can be discussed under the heading of ethics, too. These variants include the change from ugliness to beauty in [2], from slavery to kingship in [4.2.1c] and [4.2.2a] and from poverty to wealth in [4.2.1d] and [4.2.2b]. All these variants are yet again soundly Stoic. The beauty of the sage and the ugliness of the inferior person are mentioned in e.g. Cicero, *On Ends* 3.75 (*SVF* 1.221, 3.591), although implicitly in the expression that only the sage is beautiful.[25] A similar implicit usage can be seen with regard to the kingship of the sage, but here we find the contrast with the slavery of the inferior person explicitly, too.[26] The wealth

[23] See the passages assembled in *SVF* 3.657–684.

[24] On 'equal to the gods' see *infra* Section 2.2.2c.

[25] Further evidence on the beautiful sage is in Cicero, *In Defence of Murena* 61 (*SVF* 1.221), *Lucullus* 136 (*SVF* 3.599), Philo of Alexandria, *Questions and Answers on Genesis* 4.99 (*SVF* 3.592).

[26] The implicit usage can e.g. be found in Plutarch, *On Common Notions* 1060B (not in *SVF*), *On the Tranquillity of Mind* 472A (*SVF* 3.655). Further evidence on 'the sage as king': Cicero, *On Ends* 3.75 (*SVF* 3.591): the sage has a better claim to the title of king than Tarquinius; Philo of Alexandria, *On Dreams* 2.244, 'a doctrine laid down by those who occupy themselves with philosophy', *On the Change of Names* 152 (*SVF* 3.620), where the doctrine is ascribed to Moses, *On Sobriety* 57 (*SVF* 3.603), and *On the Migration of Abraham* 197 (*SVF* 3.621); other sources include: Lucian (b. *c.* 120 CE), *Philosophers for Sale* 20 (*SVF* 3.622), Clement of Alexandria, *Miscellanies* 2.4.19.4 (*SVF* 3.619), the Platonist Proclus (fifth century CE), *Commentary on Plato's Alcibiades* 165.1 Cousin (*SVF* 3.618), Olympiodorus, *Commentary on Plato's First Alcibiades* 55.23–6.1 Creuzer (*SVF* 3.618). The explicit contrast between the sage and the inferior person can be found at Stobaeus 2.102.11 (*SVF* 3.615), 2.108.26 (*SVF* 3.617) and Diogenes Laertius 7.122 (*SVF* 3.617, LS 67M).

of the sage and the poverty of the inferior person (cf. *Synopsis* at [4.5] and 1058C) are explicitly contrasted at Stobaeus 2.101.14–20 (*SVF* 3.593); the implicit distinction that only the sage is rich (and hence all non-sages are poor) is also a Stoic commonplace.[27]

The *Synopsis* makes it abundantly clear (if only because of its title) that it is not according to common sense that the sage is a king, rich, or beautiful, or the inferior person a slave, poor, or ugly. With regard to beauty the sage may be hunch-backed, toothless and one-eyed, he is nevertheless not ugly or misshapen or unhandsome of face (see 1058A). Nor is it according to common sense that the sage is king, or that the sage is rich. On the contrary: he may not even possess a drachma of his own [4.5], he may beg his bread from others, may analyse logical arguments for pay, and pay rent and buy his bread by borrowing or asking alms of those who have nothing (see 1058C). For the Stoics, these values of beauty, power and wealth in their commonsense interpretations are of no importance, but are all to be understood in terms of virtue.[28] In the

The last passage apparently contains information from Chrysippus' lost *On the Fact that Zeno Used Terms in Their Proper Significations*, in which 'kingship being answerable to no one' is attributed to the sage and denied to the inferior person.

27 Further evidence on the sage as being rich includes Plutarch, *On Stoic Contradictions* 1043E (*SVF* 3.153), *On Common Notions* 1060B, *On the Tranquillity of Mind* 472A (*SVF* 3.655), Cicero, *In Defence of Murena* 61 (*SVF* 1.221), *On the Paradoxes of the Stoics* 6 (not in *SVF*), *Lucullus* 136 (*SVF* 3.599), *On Ends* 3.75 (*SVF* 3.591): richer than Crassus, Philo of Alexandria, *On Sobriety* 56 (*SVF* 3.603): the sage is even πάμπλουτος, Lucian, *Philosophers for Sale* 20 (*SVF* 3.622), the Aristotelian commentator Alexander of Aphrodisias (around 200 CE), *Commentary on Aristotle's Topics* 134.13–16 (*SVF* 3.594), 147.12–17 (*SVF* 3.595), Sextus Empiricus, *Against the Professors* 11.170 (*SVF* 3.598), Clement of Alexandria, *Miscellanies* 2.4.19.4 (*SVF* 3.619), Proclus, *Commentary on Plato's Alcibiades* 165.2 Cousin (*SVF* 3.618), Olympiodorus, *Commentary on Plato's First Alcibiades* 56.1–3 Creuzer (*SVF* 3.618).

28 The beauty of the sage is explained in Cicero, *On Ends* 3.75 (*SVF* 3.591): it is the beauty of the sage's virtuous soul that counts. The wealth of the sage is explained in the same manner: only virtue makes one rich and self-sufficient, independent from fortune, for which see Cicero, *On Ends* 3.75 (*SVF* 3.591), Philo of Alexandria, *On Noah's Work as a Planter* 69 (*SVF* 3.596), Stobaeus 2.101.23–2.3 (*SVF* 3.626, LS 60P). The paradox of the sage as king was according to Diogenes Laertius 7.122 (*SVF* 3.617) explained by Chrysippus as being that the sage alone has knowledge of good and bad, which is one of the definitions of the virtue of practical wisdom (see e.g. Plutarch, *On Common Notions* 1066D (*SVF* 2.1181), Diogenes Laertius 7.92 (*SVF* 3.265), Stobaeus 2.59.5–6 (*SVF* 3.262), ps.-Andronicus, *On Emotions* 2.1

Synopsis, however, and as a matter of course in a treatise entitled *[Synopsis of the Treatise] 'The Stoics talk More Paradoxically than the Poets'*, the paradoxes are exploited to the full.

2.2.2b Logic

In the *Synopsis* becoming a sage is expressed from the perspective of logic, too. That is, if logic is understood in the broad sense, as the Stoics did, as dialectic and rhetoric, with dialectic broadly defined as the knowledge of what is true and false and neither, and thus included their epistemology.[29] Plutarch's description of the transition in epistemological terms is short. He uses the opposition between 'unstable and ignorant' in [4.2.1a] on the side of the inferior person and 'stable and holding no opinions' in [4.2.2d] on the side of the sage.

'Stable' and 'holding no opinions' used with regard to the sage are well-established Stoic notions. Although the expression 'holding no opinions' (in fact, one word in Greek: *adoxastos*) is associated with Aristo, Zeno's pupil and later rival, this rival attached most importance precisely to this 'Stoic doctrine', as it is called in Diogenes Laertius 7.162 (*SVF* 1.347, *FDS* 139). What is more, the conviction that the sage does not hold opinions is a well-known Stoic doctrine.[30] 'Stable' can also be placed in an epistemological context, as in one of the variants of the Stoic definitions of knowledge (see Section 1.2.2c). 'Ignorant' (*amathēs*) used with

Glibert-Thirry (*SVF* 3.266), Sextus Empiricus, *Against the Professors* 9.162 (*SVF* 3.274), 11.170 (*SVF* 3.598), Simplicius, *Commentary on Aristotle's Categories* 389.19 (*SVF* 2.174, *FDS* 945)).

29 See my discussion above, in Section 1.2.2a.

30 Most of the evidence is collected in *SVF* 1.54: Cicero, *In Defence of Murena* 61, *Lucullus* 113 (*FDS* 339), Lactantius (*c.* 240–320), *Institutions* 3.4 (*SVF* 3.553, *FDS* 377), Augustine, *Against the Academics* 2.11 (*FDS* 338, 376), Stobaeus 2.112.2 (*FDS* 89, see also 2.113.10–1, *SVF* 3.548, *FDS* 89). Other evidence includes *PHerc. 1020*, fr. In ll. 12–3 (*SVF* 2.131, *FDS* 88), Cicero, *Varro* 42 (*SVF* 1.53, *FDS* 256), Diogenes Laertius 7.121 (*SVF* 1.54, 3.549, *FDS* 176, 196, 375A), the Sphaerus anecdote in Diogenes Laertius 7.177 (*SVF* 1.625, *FDS* 196), Chrysippus' book title *Demonstrations for the Doctrine that the Sage Will not Hold Opinions* in 7.201 (*SVF* 2.17, *FDS* 194), Sextus Empiricus, *Against the Professors* 7.157 (*SVF* 3.550), 7.409. See further Tsekourakis (1974) 30, Ioppolo (1980) 29, Vogt (2012) 158–66.

regard to the inferior person does not, as far as I am aware, occur in Stoic texts. *Amathēs*, however, will in Greek often be used as the standard adjective in relation to the noun 'ignorance' (*agnoia*) and the verb 'to be ignorant' (*agnoeō*). For the Stoics, ignorance or to be ignorant *is* one of the distinctive characteristics of the inferior person: every inferior person is ignorant,[31] whereas the sage is not.[32] 'Unstable' seems the equivalent of 'weak' (*asthenēs*): ignorance is changeable and weak assent, only to be found in the non-sage.[33]

In these few words Plutarch may have intended to offer a characterisation of the state before and after the change on two epistemological levels: one level referring to the epistemological state of the inferior person and sage as such, i.e. in terms of 'unopining' vs. 'ignorant', respectively, the other being an explanation of these states, i.e. in terms of 'unstable' vs. 'stable', respectively. The inferior person is ignorant, because he deals with his perceptions in an unstable manner, or – in the technical expression used by the Stoics – has weak cognitions. The sage has knowledge that has nothing to do with holding opinions, since he has stable cognitions.

2.2.2c *Physics*

At first sight the *Synopsis* does not seem to contain a description of the change in terms of physics. What we do find, however, is a change to the divine. As the Stoics considered theology a part of physics,[34] the change can thus be discussed in relation to physics. In the *Synopsis* three references to the divine or the gods can be found. In [2] the sage is described as 'of godlike form'. Here one could perhaps say that this reference should not be taken literally. After all, the context is a

31 Sextus Empiricus, *Against the Professors* 7. 434 (*SVF* 3.657) presented by Sextus as a Chrysippean doctrine.

32 *PHerc. 1020* Ox Ld ll. 1–2 (*SVF* 2.131, *FDS* 88): μηδὲν ἀγνοεῖν τὸν σοφόν.

33 Stobaeus 2.111.20–2.2 (*SVF* 3.548, LS 41G, *FDS* 89): τὴν γὰρ ἄγνοιαν μεταπτωτικὴν εἶναι συγκατάθεσιν καὶ ἀσθενῆ. μηδὲν δ' ὑπολαμβάνειν ἀσθενῶς, ἀλλὰ ἀσφαλῶς καὶ βεβαίως, διὸ καὶ μηδὲ δοξάζειν τὸν σοφόν.

34 According to Chrysippus *ap.* Plutarch, *On Stoic Contradictions* 1035A (*SVF* 2.42, LS 26C, *FDS* 24) physics is the final part.

description of the beauty of the sage, and 'divine' could simply, metaphorically, reinforce that claim. However, in [4.4.2] and [4.3.2] reference is yet again made to the gods. In [4.4.2] the change is from beast to hero, *daimon* or god, in [4.3.2c] a 'character equal to the gods' is ascribed to the newly born sage. In *Progress* [viii] the change is from a bestial to a divine life.

Should we thus after all take these expressions literally? And if so, how? Let us begin with the phrase 'a character equal to the gods' in [4.3.2c]. The most obvious interpretation of this phrase is that sages are *like* the gods. This interpretation appears to be confirmed by the passage in Clement with which I started, and by a variety of passages, in which the sage is declared to be either as happy as the gods,[35] or as virtuous (or excellent) as the gods[36] or as Zeus.[37]

[35] See Stobaeus 2.98.19–9.2 (*SVF* 3.54): καὶ <ἐκείνων> τὴν εὐδαιμονίαν μὴ διαφέρειν τῆς θείας εὐδαιμονίας (μηδὲ τὴν ἀμεριαίαν ὁ Χρύσιππός φησι διαφέρειν τὴς τοῦ Διός εὐδαιμονίας) <καὶ> κατὰ μηδὲν αἱρετωτέραν εἶναι μήτε καλλίω μήτε σεμνοτέραν τὴν τοῦ Διὸς εὐδαιμονίαν τῆς τῶν σοφῶν ἀνδρῶν (for the reading see von Arnim's introduction to *SVF* 1, xliii: only the bracketed part can safely be ascribed to Chrysippus (followed by Viano (1999), but not by Pomeroy (1999)), Cicero, *On the Nature of the Gods* 2.153: *quae contuens animus accipit* [Davies: *accedit ad*] *cognitionem deorum, e qua oritur pietas, cui coniuncta iustitia est reliquaeque virtutes, e quibus vita beata existit, par et similis deorum, nulla alia re nisi immortalitate (quae nihil ad bene vivendum pertinet), cedens caelestibus*, Origen, *Against Celsus* 6.48 (*SVF* 3.248): τὴν αὐτὴν ἀρετὴν λέγοντες ἀνθρώπου καὶ θεοῦ οἱ ἀπὸ τῆς Στοᾶς φιλόσοφοι μὴ εὐδαιμονέστερον λέγωσιν εἶναι τὸν ἐπὶ πᾶσι θεὸν τοῦ ἐν ἀνθρώποις κατ' αὐτοὺς σοφοῦ, ἀλλ' ἴσην εἶναι τὴν ἀμφοτέρων εὐδαιμονίαν.

[36] Proclus, *Commentary on Plato's Timaeus* 2.106F, p. 351.11–14 (*SVF* 1.564, *SVF* 3.252): οἱ δὲ ἀπὸ τῆς Στοᾶς καὶ τὴν αὐτὴν ἀρετὴν εἶναι θεῶν καὶ ἀνθρώπων εἰρήκασιν, Alexander of Aphrodisias, *On Fate* 211.13–7 (*SVF* 3.247) in his criticism of Stoic doctrine: οὐ γὰρ τὰς αὐτὰς ἀρετὰς οἷον τε λέγειν εἶναι τῶν τε ἀνθρώπων καὶ τῶν θεῶν. οὔτε γὰρ ἄλλως ἀληθὲς τὸ τὰς τῶν τοσοῦτον ἀλλήλων κατὰ τὴν φύσιν διεστώτων τὰς αὐτὰς τελειότητας τε καὶ ἀρετὰς λέγειν, οὔθ' οἱ πρὸς αὐτῶν περὶ αὐτῶν λεγόμενοι λόγοι εὔλογόν τι ἐν αὑτοῖς ἔχουσιν, Cicero, *On the Laws* 1.25 (*SVF* 1.564, *SVF* 3.245): *iam vero virtus eadem in homine ac deo est, neque alio ullo in genere* [Davies; *ingenio* – codd.] *praeterea*, Seneca, *On Constancy* 8.2: *sapiens autem vicinus proximusque dis consistit, excepta mortalitate similis deo*, *Letters* 59.14: [*sapiens*] *cum dis ex pari vivit*, Clement of Alexandria, *Miscellanies* 7.88.5–6 (*SVF* 3.250) οὐ γὰρ καθάπερ οἱ Στωικοὶ, ἀθέως πάνυ τὴν αὐτὴν ἀρετὴν ἀνθρώπου λέγομεν καὶ θεοῦ, Origen, *Against Celsus* 4.29 (*SVF* 3.249): ἡ αὐτὴ ἀρετὴ ἀνθρώπου καὶ θεοῦ, Themistius, *Orations* 2.27C (*SVF* 1.564, *SVF* 3.251): in the context of the reliability of oracles the Stoics say that τὴν αὐτὴν ἀρετὴν καὶ ἀλήθειαν ἀνδρὸς καὶ θεοῦ.

[37] Plutarch, *On Common Notions* 1076A (*SVF* 3.246): against the common conception that men and gods differ in excellence Chrysippus maintained that οὐδὲ τοῦτο περίεστιν αὐτοῖς [θεοὶς]· ἀρετῇ τε γὰρ οὐχ ὑπερέχειν τὸν Δία τοῦ Δίωνος ὠφελεῖσθαι θ'

However, the expression in [4.3.2c] and the confirmation in these other sources sit uneasily with the other expression on the divine in the *Synopsis*, 'from the most vicious of wild beasts some hero or *daimon* or god' in [4.4.2], or for that matter in *Progress* [viii]. The expression in [4.4.2] goes a step further, as the sage is not *like* a god or Zeus any more, he *is* divine. Are we dealing with a deliberate exaggeration here?

Yet again there is evidence outside the Plutarchean texts for the reading that sages *are* divine. Stobaeus 2.68.3 (*SVF* 3.604) records that the sage is the only priest, as for a priest it is not only necessary to be experienced in the regulations concerning sacrifices, prayers, etc., but also 'to be inside divine nature'.[38] Furthermore, Sextus Empiricus, *Against the Professors* 7.423, emphatically conveying the doctrine as Stoic, tells us that the Stoics have described the sage as divine, this time because of the sage's ability to distinguish between truth and falsehood:

> according to them [i.e. the Stoics] the sage possesses an infallible criterion, which makes him in all respects divine because he never holds opinions, that is assents to what is false, wherein lies the height of unhappiness and the ruin of the inferior person.[39]

It may, of course, be maintained that the expression 'to make him in all respects divine' should not be given too much weight

ὁμοίως ὑπ' ἀλλήλων τὸν Δία καὶ τὸν Δίωνα, σοφοὺς ὄντας, Chrysippus, *On Motion* 3 *ap.* Plutarch, *On Stoic Contradictions* 1038C–D (*SVF* 3.256): τοῖς ἀγαθοῖς . . . κατ' οὐδὲν προεχομένοις ὑπὸ τοῦ Διός, Seneca, *Letters* 73.13: *Iuppiter quo antecedit virum bonum? diutius bonus est: sapiens nihilo se minoris aestimat quod virtutes eius spatio breviore cluduntur*, *Natural Questions* Praef. 6: *effugisti vitia animi? . . . multa effugisti, te nondum. virtus enim ista quam adfectamus magnifica est non quia per se beatum est malo caruisse, sed quia animum laxat et praeparat ad cognitionem caelestium, dignumque effecit qui in consortium <cum> deo veniat*. More passages can be found in Lipsius (1604) bk 3, ch. 14.

38 καὶ <τοῦ> ἐντὸς εἶναι τῆς φύσεως τῆς θείας. Some interpreters, however, have rendered the Greek more freely as 'to have knowledge of the divine nature.' Among the defenders of the strong reading may be counted Pomeroy (1999) n. 51. Among the more liberal interpreters are Inwood and Gerson (1997) 208/(2008) 128, who translate 'to be intimate with the nature of divinity' and Viano (1999) 42, who gives 'saper penetrare <nel> profondo della natura divina'.

39 ἀπλανὲς γὰρ εἶχε κριτήριον κατ' αὐτοὺς ὁ σοφός, καὶ κατὰ πάντα ἐθεοποιεῖτο διὰ τὸ μὴ δοξάζειν, τουτέστι ψεύδει συγκατατίθεσθαι, ἐν ᾧ ἔκειτο ἡ ἄκρα κακοδαιμονία καὶ ἡ τῶν φαύλων διάπτωσις.

here, and is simply used metaphorically, as an expression of the sage's excellence.[40]

Further evidence for the sage as divine is ascribed to Cleanthes in the (admittedly not always very reliable) doxography by bishop Epiphanius (fourth century), *On Faith* 9.41 (*SVF* 1.538),[41] who is reported to have said that 'those who are possessed by the divine are initiates' [*telestai*].[42] Although the connection with wisdom is not obvious, the Stoics sometimes refer to the sage as 'initiated'; Chrysippus brought initiation into relation with perfection, and hence, we may infer, identified the initiated with the perfected.[43] In Greek the words 'initiation' (*teletē*) and 'fulfilment' (*teleutē*) only differ by one letter, which will not have escaped Chrysippus. The relation of the sage to the divine is thus that he is filled with the divine, and hence 'fulfilled' (to preserve the etymological association in the translation). Cleanthes would thus have said that sages are divine.

Moreover, Diogenes Laertius 7.119 (*SVF* 3.606), giving an overview of the sages' qualities, informs us that

> they are divine; for they have god in themselves as it were, but the inferior person is godless. The word 'godless' has two senses: the first sense is 'opposite to divine', the other sense is 'one who denies the divine'. In this latter sense the term does not apply to every inferior person.[44]

As 'godless' in the latter sense of being an atheist 'does not apply to every inferior person' (as in the Greek world most people will have honoured the (Olympian) gods), by contrast

[40] Only Fabricius (1718) *ad loc.* seems to have taken the expression seriously by giving a reference to Lipsius (1604) bk 3, ch. 14 (see n. 37).

[41] On the reliability see Diels (1879) 175, 177, followed by Pourkier (1992) 96–9.

[42] τοὺς κατόχους τῶν θείων τελεστὰς ἔλεγε. The manuscripts have τελετάς, but all modern editors, starting with Lobeck (1829) 130 (overviews in Holl and Dummer (1985) *ad loc.* or Watanabe (1988) 171–2) change it into τελεστάς.

[43] The main source is the *Great Etymological Dictionary s.v.* τελετή p. 751.16–22, col. 2108 Gaisford (*SVF* 2.1008, *FDS* 650), which I will discuss further in Section 2.3. Other sources on this connection include Plutarch, *On Stoic Contradictions* 1035A from Chrysippus' *On Lives* 4 (*SVF* 2.42, *FDS* 24, LS 26C), and Seneca, *Letters* 90.28, 95.64.

[44] θείους τ' εἶναι· ἔχειν γὰρ ἐν ἑαυτοῖς οἱονεὶ θεόν. τὸν δὲ φαῦλον ἄθεον. διττὸν δὲ τὸν ἄθεον, τόν τ' ἐναντίως τῷ θείῳ λεγόμενον καὶ τὸν ἐξουθενητικὸν τοῦ θείου· ὅπερ οὐκ εἶναι περὶ πάντα φαῦλον.

'godless' in the former sense will apply to every inferior person, who will hence be 'the opposite of the divine man'. The conclusion must thus be that the sage is a divine man.[45]

What we find is that the two ways in which the sage is related to the divine in the *Synopsis* (and in *Progress*) are *both* reflected in other sources on Stoicism. The Stoics would explain this apparent contradiction with reference to their allegorical interpretation of popular religion. On the one hand, they would of course have admitted that the sage would surely never become a god as in the popular rites. He would at best be *like* these gods. On the other hand, they would have pointed out that the divinities of traditional religion should in fact be understood as parts of the cosmos. In *On Piety*, a treatise written by the Epicurean Philodemus, in which some information about Chrysippus' first book *On Gods* (*SVF* 2.1076) is given,[46] we find a particularly telling example of this allegorical method, which at the same time is linked with a description of men becoming divine. It should already be noted that the title of the work lacks the definite article, and that therefore the traditional translation of *On the Gods* is at least inaccurate. It may seem a small point, but the absence of the article suggests that the book deals with a wider phenomenon than the traditionally acclaimed set of Olympian gods.[47] This suggestion is confirmed by what Philodemus tells us about its contents. Chrysippus explains in allegorical fashion that not only the Olympian gods such as Zeus, Ares and Hephaistos are to be 'assimilated' to, respectively, reason that rules over everything, war or the principle of order and disorder, and fire, but also that the sun and moon are gods. What we thus seem to have is an interpretation of the gods of traditional religion in terms of natural phenomena and an interpretation of natural phenomena in terms of the divine.

[45] Cf. du Toit (1997) 94–6.

[46] The standard edition of this text is Henrichs (1974), although parts of it, in improved readings, can now also be found in Obbink (2002). Our text (no. 5 in Obbink's numbering) is on 199–200.

[47] A similar phenomenon can be discerned with regard to the book title *On Cosmos*. See Section 1.2.2a.

Philodemus ends his summary of Chrysippus' *On Gods* 1 with the remark (col. 6.14–16 Henrichs): 'He says also that men change into gods.'[48] Unfortunately, Philodemus does not elaborate.[49] Notwithstanding the lack of further information, in this context of reinterpreting traditional religion it seems unlikely that Chrysippus is talking about traditional deification of human beings for services to (parts of) mankind, such as the examples in conformity with popular usage given by Cicero in *On the Nature of the Gods* 3.49–50. It seems rather more likely that he is talking about a man becoming a divine sage. The description of the sage in the *Synopsis* as having a character equal to the popular gods and even transforming into a god is thus wholly in line with the Stoic position.

The description of the change in physico-theological terms in [4.4.2] and [viii] seems to run into trouble, however, from a Stoic point of view. The description of the change from beast to god is not Stoic, as the Stoics would object to an immediate change between an animal and a perfect human being (or god, for that matter). The important point for the Stoics is that human beings should first develop reason, before they can take on the next step to perfection.[50] (I will return to this in Section 2.2.3c). Nevertheless, this objection is rebutted if we understand 'beast' here in a metaphorical sense, as referring to a most immoral human being. The adjective 'most vicious' that Plutarch actually uses in combination with 'beast' makes this suggestion as referring (in an exaggerated way) to a very

48 κ̣α̣[ὶ ἀν]θρώπους εἰς θεο̣[ύ]ς̣ φησι μεταβάλλε̣ι[ν.] Henrich's reading (silently returning to the reading by Gomperz (1866) 80 of the apographs) is different from μεταβαλεῖν in Diels (1879) 574b15–16 (without acknowledgement) or in *SVF* 2.1076.

49 Nor does the parallel account in Cicero, *On the Nature of the Gods* 1.39 (*SVF* 2.1077, LS 54B): *iam vero Chrysippus … magnam turbam congregat ignotorum deorum …; atque etiam homines eos qui immortalitem esse consecuti.*

50 Also in a more technical sense the combination of most vicious and beast is not meaningful for the Stoics, as 'vicious' can only be applied to human beings, who due to the fact that they possess reason, are able to make a choice between good and bad. See e.g. Alexander of Aphrodisias, *Ethical Questions* 121.32–2.4 (*SVF* 3.537): children and animals are neither just nor unjust. Only if they become rational, *can* they become good. This implies that human beings, once having become rational, are *not yet* good and hence are inferior. Cf. Philo of Alexandria, *On the Creation* 73 (*SVF* 3.372), Diogenes Laertius 7.129 (*SVF* 3.367), Cicero, *On Ends* 3.67 (*SVF* 3.371).

immoral person rather likely. Taking the phrase in [4.4.2] as a metaphor we yet again find the *Synopsis* (and *Progress*) a reliable (although hostile) source on Stoicism.

2.2.3 *The radical change*

A third feature of becoming wise is the radicalism of the change. In the *Synopsis* the change is not only characterised under its temporal aspect as sudden, it is moreover characterised as a change from the one extreme state to the other, most clearly in [4.4.1]: 'and this not by any previous diminution of depravity'. In *Progress* the radicalism comes out well in [ii]: over a long time the sage-to-be has not succeeded in removing even a small part of his vice; only at the moment of change does he leave vice behind forever.

This radicalism is yet again perfectly Stoic and can be found formulated in general terms, and in terms of the parts of philosophy – in general terms in a central passage in the last part of Arius Didymus' exposition of Stoic ethics in Stobaeus.[51] It is central because it forms the introduction to the long description of the qualities of the sage, which are in most cases accompanied by a short reference to the absence of these qualities in the inferior person.[52] At 2.99.3–5 (*SVF* 1.216, LS 59N) we read:

> Zeno and the other Stoic philosophers after him hold that there are two kinds of human being, the virtuous and the inferior, and that the class of the virtuous use the virtues during their whole life, and that the inferior use the vices.[53]

From this distinction it follows, as Stobaeus 2.99.7–8 has it, that to sages and inferior persons belong, respectively, 'doing everything they undertake rightly and doing everything wrongly'.[54]

[51] Chapter 11 in Wachsmuth's edition.
[52] Cf. Viano (2005) 346.
[53] ἀρέσκει γὰρ τῷ Ζήνωνι καὶ τοῖς ἀπ᾿ αὐτοῦ Στωικοῖς φιλοσόφοις δύο γένη τῶν ἀνθρώπων εἶναι, τὸ μὲν τῶν σπουδαίων, τὸ δὲ τῶν φαύλων· καὶ τὸ μὲν τῶν σπουδαίων διὰ παντὸς τοῦ βίου χρῆσθαι ταῖς ἀρεταῖς, τὸ δὲ τῶν φαύλων ταῖς κακίαις.
[54] τὸ μὲν ἀεὶ κατορθοῦν ἐν ἅπασιν οἷς προστίθεται, τὸ δὲ ἁμαρτάνειν.

As with my discussion of the opposed states in Section 2.2, I will discuss the radical nature of the change from the organisational principle of tripartition, too.

2.2.3a *The radical change in ethics*

With the Stobaeus passage we have in fact already moved on towards the distinction in ethics. The radicalism was not only expressed in the doctrine that the sage does everything well and the inferior person everything badly. It is in fact already implied in the Stoic definition of virtue as a character, discussed in Chapter 1.[55] As a character, virtue does not admit of degrees, so the change to virtue must be radical. The radicalism comes out more clearly in formulas such as 'there is nothing in between virtue and vice', and 'all mistakes are equal'. The Stoics were happy to exploit these 'paradoxes' by the use of various images.[56] The formula 'there is nothing in between virtue and vice' was explained by the images of the stick and the unfinished verse. Just as a stick is either straight or crooked, justice is an all-or-nothing affair. There is neither a more just nor a less just. The same goes for the other virtues.[57] According to Stobaeus 2.65.7–11 (*SVF* 1.566) Cleanthes compared human beings who have natural impulses to virtue to an unfinished verse: like the metre of the verse not being brought to completion, human beings who have not brought their natural impulses to completion are not good, either.[58]

[55] For virtue as character see the end of Section 1.2.2c.

[56] Cicero was interested in these Stoic paradoxes too. See his *On the Paradoxes of the Stoics*, esp. 20–6 (referred to at *SVF* 1.224).

[57] Diogenes Laertius 7.127 (*SVF* 3.536, LS 61I): μηδὲν μεταξὺ εἶναι ἀρετῆς καὶ κακίας· ὡς γὰρ δεῖν φασιν ἢ ὀρθὸν εἶναι ξύλον ἢ στρεβλόν, οὕτως ἢ δίκαιον ἢ ἄδικον, οὔτε δὲ δικαιότερον οὔτ᾽ ἀδικώτερον, καὶ ἐπὶ τῶν ἄλλων ὁμοίως.

[58] ἀρετῆς δὲ καὶ κακίας οὐδὲν εἶναι μεταξύ. πάντας γὰρ ἀνθρώπους ἀφορμὰς ἔχειν ἐκ φύσεως πρὸς ἀρετήν, καὶ οἱονεὶ τὸν τῶν ἡμιαμβείων λόγον ἔχειν κατὰ τὸν Κλεάνθην· ὅθεν ἀτελεῖς μὲν ὄντας εἶναι φαύλους, τελειωθέντας δὲ σπουδαίους. The expression τὸν τῶν ἡμιαμβείων λόγον has been interpreted by Pomeroy (1999) 109 n. 38 as a reference to comedy. In comedy a series of iambic dimeters is used to conclude a scene. If the dimeters are only halfway finished, the scene is not completed, and the laughter will not follow. Another interpretation is that the expression refers to an unfinished account in a specific type of metre (e.g. the iambic trimeter described by Aristotle, *Poetics* 1449a24 as best suited to natural speech). This interpretation is not only simpler,

The formula 'all mistakes are equal', already ascribed to Zeno and his pupil Persaeus (*c.* 306–*c.* 243) (at Diogenes Laertius 7.120, *SVF* 1.224, 1.450), was illustrated with the images of the pilgrim, the blind and the drowning. According to Chrysippus in his fourth book *Ethical Questions* (see Diogenes Laertius 7.120, *SVF* 3.356), just as it does not matter whether the pilgrim is a hundred or a few miles away from Canopus (a sanctuary in the Nile delta which flourished in the third century BCE), as they are both not in Canopus, so it does not matter whether one makes a big or a small mistake: in either case, one is not virtuous.[59] The other two images are attested by Plutarch, at *On Common Notions* 1063A (*SVF* 3.539, LS 61T): just as the blind person who is going to recover his sight a little bit later is, until the recovery, still blind,[60] and just as it does not matter whether the person is drowning when he is one foot or a hundred feet under water, it does not matter whether one makes a big or small moral mistake: one is equally vicious and inferior.

2.2.3b The radical change in logic

In logic, or more specifically in epistemology as a part of it,[61] we find a similar radical approach.[62] It is knowledge that counts; everything else, whether it is called opinion or ignorance, does not. Presenting it as the cardinal point in Zeno's epistemology (or perhaps even in Zeno's contribution to philosophy in general – the context leaves that open), Cicero, *Varro* 42 (*SVF* 1.53, 1.60 (part), LS 41B, *FDS* 256) informs us that Zeno 'removed error, rashness, ignorance, opinion, and conjecture from virtue and wisdom, and in a word, everything

but also in line with Cleanthes' interest in metre, rhythm and melody, not just as such, but also with respect to divine things, for which the most important piece of evidence is Philodemus, *On Music* 4.142.5–14 Delattre (esp. ll. 10–14: 'epic and lyric poetry arrive as best as they can at the truth of the contemplation of the gods'), already discussed in Section 1.2.1.

59 On the image see further Rolke (1975) 162–3. It also occurs in the doxographical *PMilVogliano 1241*, ll. 11–19 (in the revised reading by Decleva Caizzi and Funghi (1991) 132). In the papyrus reference is made to a 'city' (ἄστυ) rather than Canopus.

60 Cicero, *On Ends* 3.48 (*SVF* 3.530) uses the image of a puppy about to be born.

61 See above Sections 1.2.2a and 2.2.2b.

62 See esp. Meinwald (2005).

foreign to stable and consistent assent'.[63] The same radical distinction had been expressed a little earlier, at *Varro* 41 (*SVF* 1.60, LS 41B, *FDS* 256), in terms of the definitions of knowledge and ignorance, which are presented as complementing each other: knowledge as sense-perception so grasped as not to be disrupted by reason; ignorance as otherwise.

This simple binary picture seems to be complicated by two other accounts, which suggest a less clear-cut picture: the famous image of Zeno's hands and the account of Stoic epistemology in Arcesilaus' critique of it. In the hand simile in Cicero, *Lucullus* 145 (*SVF* 1.66, LS 41A, *FDS* 369) Zeno is said to have compared the open palm of his hand with an impression, the fingers of his hand a bit contracted with assent to the impression, his fingers made into a fist with a cognition and the tight and forceful gripping of his other hand over the fist with knowledge. This simile can, of course, be understood in a developmental sense, as offering a description of the various phases in the process of gaining knowledge, together with a mnemonic device to get to grips with Stoic terminology (note that the setting seems to be one of a lecture, or of a conversation at least). This interpretation should not obscure, however, that the passage is also used to get the point across that only the sage has knowledge. For this is how Cicero introduces the simile in the dialectical setting of the *Lucullus*: 'You deny that anyone knows anything, except the sage. And this Zeno demonstrated with gestures.'[64]

In the other problematic passage, Sextus Empiricus, *Against the Professors* 7.151 (*SVF* 2.90, LS 41C, *FDS* 370), in the context of his overview in 7.89–260 of the various epistemological theories since Thales, the Stoics make a surprise appearance in the discussion of the theory of the sceptical Arcesilaus, head of Plato's Academy in the third century BCE. (The account of Stoic epistemology proper is at the end,

[63] *errorem autem et temeritatem et ignorantiam et opinationem et suspicionem, et uno nomine omnia quae essent aliena firmae et constantis adsensionis, a virtute sapientiaque removebat.*

[64] *at scire negatis quemquam rem ullam nisi sapientem. et hoc quidem Zeno gestu conficiebat.*

227–60.) But as Arcesilaus' theory, Sextus explains, was only formulated in response to the Stoics, Stoic doctrine needs to be introduced, too. In his therefore multi-layered account Sextus informs us that according to Arcesilaus 'they [sc. the Stoics] say there are three things that are linked together, knowledge, opinion, and cognition stationed between them'.[65] This passage might be taken as a description of three successive epistemological phases, in which opinion becomes cognition, and cognition becomes knowledge. However, Meinwald pointed rightly to the usage of 'linking' or – as it can also be translated – 'yoking'.[66] If this image of the yoke between two oxen is taken seriously, cognition is not an intermediate stage in between opinion or knowledge, but rather functions as a yoke in between opinion and knowledge: if it is used badly, it is opinion, if well, it is knowledge. Yet again this passage would thus confirm the radical opposition of the inferior person and the sage, that we have so far encountered, and henceforward the radical change from the state of ignorance to the state of knowledge.

2.2.3c *The radical change in physics*

Finally, the radical character of the change can be expressed in physical terms. This is best approached by the Stoic theory of the taxonomy of natural kinds that, as I mentioned in Section 1.2.2c, is the result of the force or breath, which dilutes itself throughout the world. The basic tenets of this hierarchical scheme of nature, or *scala naturae*, are clear, although our sources offer different versions, especially where the lowest and highest levels are concerned.[67] The lowest level (level 1)

[65] τρία γὰρ εἶναί φασιν ἐκεῖνοι τὰ συζυγοῦντα ἀλλήλοις, ἐπιστήμην καὶ δόξαν καὶ τὴν ἐν μεθορίῳ τούτων τεταγμένην κατάληψιν.

[66] Meinwald (2005) 15–16.

[67] Complete taxonomies are offered by Cicero, *On Proper Functions* 2.11, Philo of Alexandria, *Allegorical Interpretation* 2.22–3 (*SVF* 2.458, LS 47P, with the highest kind supplied in vol. 2 only); cf. Philo of Alexandria, *On the Eternity of the World* 75 (*SVF* 2.459), *On the Creation* 73 (*SVF* 3.372, although Runia (2001) *ad loc.* doubts its specifically Stoic character: 'The passage is sufficiently general to be subscribed to by Stoics, Platonists and Aristotelians.'). A complete taxonomy is implied in a passage on kinds of movement by Simplicius, *Commentary on*

is referred to as that of 'tenor' (*hexis*), as the power of holding together, for which stones are the standard examples.[68] At the second level (level 2), which the Stoics call 'nature' (*phusis*), the power of holding together is supervened by the capacity to grow and to generate, as can be found in plants. The third level (level 3) is the level of the 'soul', which brings the power to perceive and to act, as can be found in animals. The fourth level (level 4) is the level of mature human beings, whose souls have a rational faculty, or as it is usually called, 'commanding-faculty' (*hēgemonikon*).[69] Finally, a fifth level (level 5) can be ascribed to gods and sages alike,[70] and is characterised by 'mind' (*nous*) or virtue (or excellence, for that matter).[71] Reason on level 4 differs from reason on level 5, succinctly characterised by Seneca, *Letter* 92.27, as 'reason which is capable of being perfected' (*ratio consummabilis*) and 'reason brought to perfection' (*ratio consummata*), respectively.

As the higher levels supervene on the lower levels, a human being will not only have the peculiar characteristic of reason, but also the characteristics that belong to the level of tenor (to be found in bones and sinews[72]), *phusis* and soul. The higher level is said to guide the lower level, e.g. reason guiding perception: a rational being perceives the world in a totally

Aristotle's Categories 306.14–27 (*SVF* 2.499), although the passage is contaminated with Aristotelian terminology. The taxonomy without the lowest – inanimate – kind is given in Cicero, *On the Nature of the Gods* 2.33–6 (referred to at *SVF* 1.529), and used by Cleanthes according to Sextus Empiricus, *Against the Professors* 9.88 (*SVF* 1.529). The taxonomy without the highest kind (for reasons that will become apparent *infra* Section 2.4) is offered by Clement of Alexandria, *Miscellanies* 2.20.110–1 (*SVF* 2.714), Origen, *On Principles* 2.1.2–3 (*SVF* 2.988, LS 53A; cf. Origen, *On Prayer* 6.1 (*SVF* 2.989), as with Simplicius in a passage on the kinds of movement). For the *scala naturae* see e.g. Inwood (1985) 21–6, Bénatouïl (2002).

68 It has sometimes been doubted whether Zeno already introduced level 1, but it seems likely: according to Themistius, *Commentary On the Soul* 35.32–4 (*SVF* 1.158) the Zenonians, as the Stoics are called here, unanimously held this opinion.

69 See e.g. Aëtius 903A (= 4.21.1; *SVF* 2.836, LS 53H).

70 Gods and sages is in Cicero, *On Proper Functions*, *On the Nature of the Gods*, mind in Philo of Alexandria, *Allegorical Interpretation* and virtue in Philo of Alexandria, *On the Eternity of the World*, *On the Creation* and Simplicius (as referred to in n. 67).

71 See also Section 4.4, n. 80.

72 See Diogenes Laertius 7.139 (*SVF* 2.634, LS 47O): δι' ὧν μὲν γὰρ ὡς κέχρηκεν, ὡς διὰ τῶν ὀστῶν καὶ τῶν νεύρων· δι' ὧν δὲ ὡς νοῦς, ὡς διὰ τοῦ ἡγεμονικοῦ.

different manner from a non-rational being, i.e. he perceives it by means of reason, he accepts or rejects impressions by using substantive conceptions about the world.[73]

The taxonomical accounts do not deal with possible transitions between the levels. However, the Stoics *were* interested in them, especially where human beings are concerned. Best known are the Stoic descriptions of two of these transitions: the transition from the level of *phusis* to the level of soul, and the transition from the level of soul to the level of the soul becoming rational. The moment of getting a soul occurs at birth: when the foetus leaves the womb, its breath, which till that point is still characterised as *phusis*, becomes chilled by air and tempered, which brings about the change to the level of soul (like Plato, at *Cratylus* 399D–E, and Aristotle, at *On the Soul* 405b28–9, before them, the Stoics preserve the etymological link between 'soul' (*psuchē*) and 'cold' (*psuchros*) here).[74] The transition to the next level starts at the age of about seven years and ends at the age of about fourteen, when the body starts emitting seminal fluids.[75] In either case, the change is described as a physical process.

However hard it may be to reconcile these instances of power and the qualities of cold and warm,[76] if not already because of the state of our evidence, and however tentative my reconstruction here can thus only be, these accounts at least make clear that the Stoics relate the changes between

[73] On the rational being that perceives rationally or has rational impressions see Diogenes Laertius 7.51 (*SVF* 2.87, LS 39A, *FDS* 255); on the definition of a rational impression see Sextus Empiricus, *Against the Professors* 8.70 (*SVF* 2.187, LS 33C, *FDS* 699). See also the late Stoic philosopher (around 100 CE) Hierocles, *Elements of Ethics* 1.5–33 (LS 53B).

[74] The sources are conveniently assembled in *SVF* 2.806, esp. Plutarch, *On Stoic Contradictions* 1052E–F (*FDS* 680), *On Common Notions* 1084D–E, to which can be added Hierocles, *Elements of Ethics* 1.25–6 (LS 53B): φύσις ἐμβρύου πέ̣π̣ον[ος] ἤ̣δη γεγονότ̣[ο]ς οὐ βραδύνε̣[ι τ]ὸ μ(ετα)βα[λ]λεῖν εἰς ψυχὴν ἐμ̣[πε]σοῦσα τῷ π̣[(ερι)έχον(τι).

[75] See Aëtius 900B (= 4.11.4; *SVF* 2.83, LS 39E), 909C (= 5.23.1; *SVF* 2.764). Cf. the Platonist Iamblichus (*c*. 250–325), *On the Soul ap*. Stobaeus 1.317.21–4 (*SVF* 1.149, *SVF* 2.835). The completion at the age of fourteen is already ascribed to Zeno in the *Old Scholia on Alcibiades* 1.121E (*SVF* 1.149), and is ascribed to Diogenes of Babylon too at Diogenes Laertius 7.55 (*SVF* 3 Diogenes of Babylon, fr. 17). See further e.g. Long (1982) 50 (repr. (1996) 246), Frede (1994) 56–63.

[76] Cf. e.g. Hatzimichali (2011) 112 n. 73.

the natural kinds to qualities such as cold and warm. They distinguished four of these basic qualities (cold, warm, moist and dry) and identified these qualities with the four elements (air, fire, water and earth, respectively).[77] The former two elements were considered to be the active qualities or elements: fire was thought to expand, and air to contract.[78] The latter two were considered to be passive, to be acted upon by the active elements.[79] The natural kinds are hence explained as combinations of the active elements of air and fire, which in different quantities pervade bits of combinations of the passive elements water and earth. (Presumably the lowest kind is characterised by the active element air going through (contracting) the passive elements of water and air.[80]) The Stoics call this combination of fire and air (or of warm and cold) 'breath' (*pneuma*).[81] The changes may hence have been understood as changes in the composition of these elements within these bodies.

The change to wisdom is of a different nature than the other changes that befall human beings earlier on. For evidence, we may look at the Stoic definitions of soul, which is defined in two distinct ways. First, soul is defined as a mixture of the elements of fire and air in sources as varied as Galen,[82] Alexander of Aphrodisias (around 200 CE)[83] and Macrobius (around 400 CE).[84] Second, soul is defined as fire (or warmth), without the mention of air (or coldness, for that matter). This definition of soul as fire is attributed to Zeno by Cicero,

77 See e.g. Diogenes Laertius 7.137 (*SVF* 2.580, LS 47B, cf. LS 1, 287).

78 See e.g. Galen, *On the Natural Faculties* 2.7 (*SVF* 2.406, LS 47E).

79 See e.g. Nemesius (around 400 CE), *On the Nature of Man* 5.52.18–9 (*SVF* 2.418, LD 47D).

80 The tenor of iron, stone, or silver is air according to Chrysippus in his *On Tenors* and *Physical Questions* 1 *ap*. Plutarch, *On Stoic Contradictions* 1053F–4B (*SVF* 2.449, LS 47M).

81 For breath as a mixture of air and fire (or of cold and hot) see e.g. Galen, *On the Doctrines of Hippocrates and Plato* 5.3.8 (*SVF* 2.841, LS 47H), Alexander of Aphrodisias, *On Mixture* 224.14 (*SVF* 2.442, LS 47I).

82 *The Soul's Dependence on the Body (Quod animi mores)* 4.45.22–3 (*SVF* 2.787).

83 *On the Soul* 26.16–7 (*SVF* 2.786).

84 *Commentary on the Dream of Scipio* 1.14.20 (attributed to Boëthus, *SVF* 3 Boëthus of Sidon, fr. 10).

Tusculan Disputations 1.19 (*SVF* 1.134),[85] and to the Stoics in general by Plutarch, Alexander of Aphrodisias and Plotinus' pupil Porphyry (third century CE), and in the *Scholia on Lucan's Civil War*.[86] The definition of soul as warmth also occurs several times.[87] As fire corresponds to the quality of warmth (as we have seen), this is not surprising.[88]

How can these different definitions of the soul be accounted for? If we look more carefully at the passages that offer the definition of soul as fire or warmth, we find that this definition is related to excellence or the divine.[89] It thus seems reasonable to suppose that the soul in its highest state is characterised as fire or warmth, and that the first definition of the soul is a description of it in its non-virtuous, that is inferior, state. Unlike the changes at birth or in the period of puberty, which are explained in terms of combinations of fire and air, the change to wisdom should thus apparently be understood as a physical change to the level of fire only.[90] This change does not

[85] Hahm (1977) 159 appears overcautious when he states that 'we do not know know whether Zeno tried to integrate the notions of fire and pneuma', By defining soul as fire, as well as warm breath, Zeno must have integrated the notions. The question is rather: exactly how did Zeno do that?

[86] In Plutarch, *On the Face of the Moon* 926C (*SVF* 2.1045) the soul is described as swift and fiery (and a divine thing, traversing instantaneously in its flight all heaven and earth and sea); in Alexander of Aphrodisias, *Supplement to On the Soul* 115.6 (*SVF* 2.785) the soul is either fire or a breath consisting of fine particles (there is no need to consider the first view Heraclitean and the second Stoic, as Mansfeld (1990) 3109 n. 220 suggests: as ll. 8 and 11 make clear, fire and breath are simply put on a par. Hence the soul as fire is simply explained as breath); in Porphyry, *On the Soul ap.* Eusebius of Caesarea, *Preparation for the Gospel* 15.11.4 (*SVF* 2.806) the soul is thinking fire (immediately followed by an account of its birth, in a set of 'scandalous' views on the soul), as in *Scholia on Lucan's Civil War* 9.7 (*SVF* 2.775), see further n. 88.

[87] Zeno, *On Soul ap.* Diogenes Laertius 7.157 (*SVF* 1.135): soul as warm breath; Aëtius 898D (= 4.3.3; *SVF* 2.779): soul as breath, thinking and warm; Stobaeus 2.64.22–3 (*SVF* 3.305): soul as breath, which is warm.

[88] The definition of the soul offered by Nemesius, *On the Nature of Man* 2.16.17 (*SVF* 2.773) as the kind of breath that is 'warm as well as thoroughly fiery' (ἔνθερμον καὶ διάπυρον) is hence pleonastic, from a Stoic point of view.

[89] Stobaeus 2.64.22–3 (*SVF* 2.305), *Scholia on Lucan's Civil War* 9.7 (*SVF* 2.775): according to the scholiast virtue in Lucan's phrase *quos ignea virtus innocuos vita* means virtue of the soul, as the Stoics call the soul fire, Plutarch, *On the Face of the Moon* 926C (*SVF* 2.1045).

[90] The role of fire is obscured by the fact that the Stoics distinguished between ordinary, consuming, fire and 'creative' (τεχνικὸν) fire. See on this distinction Arius Didymus *ap.* Stobaeus 1.213.17–20 (Arius Didymus fr. 33 Diels, *SVF* 1.120, LS

only involve the elimination of the cold (after all, this might still imply gradualism[91]), it also involves a radical transformation: undiluted, the human soul (or its commanding faculty, for that matter) consisting of pure fire will have become 'in a sense identical with' or rather part of the divine active principle in the world.[92] Seneca characterises this kind of radical change, brought about 'after many additions' (*post multa incrementa*, *Letter* 118.16), and unique to human beings,[93] as a change in 'property' (*proprietas*, *Letter* 118.13).[94]

A well-known phrase ascribed to Cleanthes in Plutarch's summary of Cleanthes' *Physical Treatises*, at *On Stoic Contradictions* 1034D (*SVF* 1.563), may also be understood in this context of the change to wisdom as a change to fire only. According to Cleanthes 'tension is a stroke of fire'.[95] In his *Hymn to Zeus* l. 10–11 (*SVF* 1.537, LS 54I) he had used the

46D), Cleanthes according to Cicero, *On the Nature of the Gods* 2.40–1 (*SVF* 1.504), Aëtius 881F–2A (= 1.7.33; *SVF* 2.1027, LS 46A), and Clement of Alexandria, *Selections from the Prophets* 26.3 as (i) the change from the element of consuming fire to the principle of technical fire (see e.g. Lapidge (1973) 270, White (2003) 134), or (ii) – if fire is already technical fire on the lower levels (see Sharples (1984) 232), less or in a lesser amount with regard to plants, but more on the level of animals as in Stobaeus 1.213.19–20 – as the change to the level of pure technical fire.

91 Cf. Seneca, *Letter* 66.9: *crescere posse imperfectae rei signum est*. Note that we are a long way from Aristotelian (or Hippocratic or Galenic) notions of correct ratios or balances here, as in e.g. *SVF* 2.789, where the second part is not Stoic, but rather Galen himself.

92 Sharples (1984) 232, who for god as the active principle refers to Stobaeus 1.35.9 (*SVF* 1.157): Ζήνων ὁ Στωικὸς νοῦν κόσμου πύρινον [θεὸν ἀπεφήνατο], and see also e.g. Aëtius 881F (= 1.7.33; *SVF* 2.1027, LS 46A): god as νοερός, πῦρ τεχνικὸν, ὁδῷ βαδίζον ἐπὶ γενέσει κόσμου.

93 See *Letters* 66.11: *una inducitur humanis virtutibus regula*.

94 Seneca in *Letter* 118.16 gives the fascinating example of the archway: only the addition of the closing stone transforms two rows of stones into a solid archway. (The source for the example is perhaps already Hecato, Panaetius' pupil, for which see Diogenes Laertius 7.90 (fr. 6 Gomoll): τῆς ψαλίδος οἰκοδομίᾳ τὴν ἰσχὺν ἐπιγίνεσθαι.) On the origin and afterlife of the 'qualitative change' see esp. Schmidt (1960) 112–15/(1988) 392–404. Bénatouïl (2005) 21 suggests a role for coldness here: like the change to (or birth of) the soul the change to wisdom might be understood in terms of chilling, which in either case would bring a kind of firmness of the soul. However, apart from the fact that there is no support for this parallel in the sources (as Bénatouïl himself acknowledges), the firmness of the commanding faculty seems rather the result of the qualitative change to fire only and to consist in the commanding faculty having become part of the fiery divine active principle in the world.

95 πληγὴ πυρὸς ὁ τόνος ἐστί.

same phrase referring to the strokes of the obviously fiery thunderbolts with which Zeus accomplishes all works of nature.[96] These lines in the hymn in the fashion of traditional popular religion may be translated in terms of Stoic physics as follows: fire plays an active role in the formation of nature as a whole. In the soul this stroke of fire, in the formulation extant in Plutarch, is at some point apparently 'enough for fulfilling what comes in one's path'.[97] If so, 'it is called strength and might'.[98] Plutarch explains Cleanthes' doctrine of strength and might with a quotation from Cleanthes' *Physical Treatises*, in which Cleanthes states that this strength and power manifest themselves as virtues.[99] Cleanthes thus seems to describe a state in which the role of fire at some point becomes enough, and with it the change to virtue. The formulation of 'enough' is opaque here, but the likelihood is that Cleanthes may have described the change to virtue as a change to fire only.[100]

This admittedly speculative interpretation of the change to wisdom as a physical change should not obscure the fact that the change to wisdom will have to be prepared for by a long strenuous process of improving one's rational faculty. The pivotal point here is that towards the end of that process the sage-to-be apparently undergoes a qualitative, physical change to fire. This interpretation can now be seen to serve the explanation of the change in the parts of ethics and indeed logic, too.[101] With regard to ethics we have already seen in Section

96 τοῦ γὰρ ὑπὸ πληγῆ ς φύσεως πάντ' ἔργα...

97 κἂν ἱκανὸς ἐν τῇ ψυχῇ γένηται πρὸς τὸ ἐπιτελεῖν τὰ ἐπιβάλλοντα.

98 ἰσχὺς καλεῖται καὶ κράτος.

99 ὅταν μὲν ἐπὶ τοῖς φανεῖσιν ἐμμενετέοις ἐγγένηται, ἐγκράτειά ἐστιν, ὅταν δ' ἐπὶ τοῖς ὑπομενετέοις, ἀνδρεία· περὶ τὰς ἀξίας δὲ δικαιοσύνη· περὶ δὲ τὰς αἱρέσεις καὶ ἐκκλίσεις σωφροσύνη.

100 In von Arnim's reading of the *Compendium of Greek Theology* 31 (*SVF* 1.514) by Cornutus, a first-century CE Stoic philosopher, a passage which von Arnim ascribed to Cleanthes, Heracles is allegorically interpreted as tension at its highest level and identified with strength and power. Rather than tension the manuscripts have λόγος, however, which Hays (1983) *ad loc.* simply retains.

101 The point made by Solmsen (1961) 20 that 'Stoic originality lies not in the creation of such [biological] concepts ...; where they did break new ground was in transferring them to physics, cosmology, and even theology' should hence be extended with 'and even ethics and logic'. Cf. Rist (1969) 89: 'All moral behaviour ... must be related to physical facts ... It is necessary to understand the physical structure

2.2.2a that the Stoics described virtue (also) as the state of the soul that does not allow a more or less, or as the state that in contrast to non-virtuous states cannot be intensified or relaxed any more. The change from the state of vice to the character of virtue is in physical terms, then, the change to the state of unmixed, pure fire. With regard to 'logic' (i.e. including above all epistemology) the Stoics define knowledge in the by now familiar fashion as a set of cognitions, but also as a secure and unshakeable grasp of reason, and as a disposition that is receptive of impressions and otherwise unshakeable by reason.[102] As Zeno, Cleanthes and their followers identified reason with fire, the specific physical basis of knowledge becomes even more apparent. The change from opinion to knowledge is then presumably yet again a change to the unmixed state of fire.

2.3 Unnoticed

The final characteristic of the change – that is, that the sage at first is unaware of his wisdom – remains to be discussed. Besides in *Progress* [ix], it occurs in four other extant pieces of evidence: two of these are yet again written by Plutarch, the other two can be found in Stobaeus and Philo of Alexandria, respectively. I will first briefly present these passages before offering an interpretation of this characteristic.

In line with the hostile character of *On Stoic Contradictions* 1042F–3A (*FDS* 1234), so clearly expressed in its title, Plutarch discusses the contradiction between Chrysippus' statement in the first book of his *On Ends* that the good is perceptible on the one hand and the doctrine of the sage not perceiving his own virtuous state on the other: 'If the good can be perceived and if a great difference exists between it and evil, how is it not most absurd that someone who was an inferior person and has become a sage does not know that, and does not perceive the

of man in order to grasp the nature of moral problems', Bénatouïl (2005), who also stressed the physical dimension of virtue and knowledge, Horn (2006) 354–6, Vogt (2008) esp. 134–48, Liu (2009) 262 n. 19.

[102] See Section 2.2.2b, and esp. Section 1.2.2c.

presence of virtue, but thinks that vice is residing in him?'[103] In the second Plutarchean passage, *On Common Notions* at 1062B (*FDS* 1235) Plutarch criticises the Stoics again, although this time, in line with the general character of this work, Plutarch argues that it goes against what people ordinarily believe ('the common notion') that the Stoics hold that the man who has acquired virtue and happiness 'often does not even perceive that he has acquired them, and fails to notice that he has now become prudent and blessed, when a little earlier he was most wretched and foolish'.[104] Stobaeus 2.113.12–16 (*SVF* 3.540, *FDS* 1231) runs thus: 'They believe that someone becomes a sage without having been aware of it at first, who neither strives nor wishes in any of the specific forms of wishing, because he does not think that he has what is needed.'[105] Here Stobaeus informs us that the sage does not think that he is already 'wishing' (*boulesthai*), which implies his contributing actively to the order of things, because he is not yet aware of the fact that he already has what is needed to be able to strive

[103] αἰσθητοῦ γὰρ ὄντος τἀγαθοῦ καὶ μεγάλην πρὸς τὸ κακὸν διαφορὰν ἔχοντος, τὸν ἐκ φαύλου γενόμενον σπουδαῖον ἀγνοεῖν τοῦτο καὶ τῆς ἀρετῆς μὴ αἰσθάνεσθαι παρούσης ἀλλ' οἴεσθαι τὴν κακίαν αὐτῷ παρεῖναι, πῶς οὐκ ἔστιν ἀτοπώτατον;

[104] πολλάκις οὐδ' αἰσθάνεσθαι τὸν κτησάμενον οἴονται διαλεληθέναι δὲ αὐτὸν ὅτι μικρῷ πρόσθεν ἀθλιώτατος ὢν καὶ ἀφρονέστατος νῦν ὁμοῦ φρόνιμος καὶ μακάριος γέγονεν. The 'often', absent in the other passages, appears to be an addition by Plutarch. See Casevitz and Babut (2002) 151, who speak of an approximation by which Plutarch may have involuntarily but 'fâcheusement' deformed the Stoic position.

[105] γίνεσθαι δὲ καὶ διαλεληθότα τινὰ σοφὸν νομίζουσι κατὰ τοὺς πρώτους χρόνους οὔτε ὀρεγόμενόν τινος οὔτε [νομίζειν] βουλόμενον ἔν τινι τῶν ἐν τῷ βούλεσθαι εἰδικῶν ὄντων, διὰ τὸ μὴ κρίνοντι αὐτῷ παρεῖναι ὧν χρή. The text has been considered problematic for two reasons. First, τινὰ can both be used in a substantive manner, as I have done in my translation, as well as in an adjective manner: 'some sage would at first not notice'. On this reading it could thus be connected with the 'often' in *On Common Notions* at 1062B: together they would thus represent 'a more sympathetic tradition' (Tieleman (1996) 182 n. 151), in which the sage would not always be unaware of his wisdom. Furthermore, the οὔτε νομίζειν βουλόμενον in the manuscripts was changed by von Arnim – rather 'audaciously' as he himself already called it *ad SVF* 3.540 – to οὐθ' ὅλως γινόμενον (followed by most modern commentators, such as Viano in Natali (1999), *FDS* and Pomeroy (1999)). On this reading the sage has not yet become completely wise, apparently assuming that, without awareness of his wisdom, the sage is not a sage yet. But rather than βουλόμενον the problem is νομίζειν, which seems a repetition from νομίζουσι in l. 13. If νομίζειν were simply deleted (as already suggested by Wyttenbach (1810) 555), the stress would exactly be where ll. 12–13 put it: that the sage is already a sage, but that he does not know it yet.

for what is good only.[106] In the last passage, Philo of Alexandria, *On Agriculture* 160–1 (*SVF* 3.541, *FDS* 1232), a discussion of the biblical image in *Deuteronomy* 20.5, yet again no trace of that 'tradition' can be found. The man who has built a new house, but not yet dedicated it, and thus – according to the biblical passage – can refrain from going to war, should according to Philo of Alexandria's interpretation be taken as a reference to a soul that is already perfect, but 'not yet thoroughly practised in virtue' (*oupō atribēs aretēs*), and should thus – again according to Philo – not yet wage a battle with the sophists:

[T5] Just as plaster needs to harden in a stable way and acquire firmness, so the souls of those who have become perfect need to be more solidly settled and held together by constant care and continuous exercise. [161] Those who have not had that are called among the philosophers sages without awareness of their wisdom. For they say that it is impossible that those people who have reached the highest wisdom and touched upon its borders for the first time, know their own perfection; for the two things do not happen at the same time, namely the arrival at the border and the cognition of arrival; in between the two there is ignorance of such a sort that is not far removed from knowledge, but close to it and on its doorstep.[107]

[106] According to the Stoics only rational beings can strive for the good, and striving can hence apply to rational beings only. Striving encompasses both 'desire' (ἐπιθυμία), i.e. 'striving for what appears to be good' (ὄρεξις οὖσα ὡς φαινομένου ἀγαθοῦ, see ps.-Andronicus, *On Emotions* 1.1 Glibert-Thirry, *SVF* 3.391, LS 65B or Aspasius (first half of the second century CE), *Commentary on Aristotle's Nicomachean Ethics* 45.20–1, *SVF* 3.386), and 'wishing', i.e. 'striving for what is good' (εὔλογος ὄρεξις, see Diogenes Laertius 7.116, *SVF* 3.431, LS 65F). Of rational beings, imperfect rational beings will always be in doubt as to whether what they are striving for is either the good or only the apparent good. Once a rational being has become perfect, however, he will not be in that position any more. He will strive for the good, i.e. he will wish only, or – as Stobaeus has it – wish in any of the variants of wishing. Although Stobaeus does not elaborate upon them, they are well known and include kindness, generosity, warmth and affection (see ps.-Andronicus, *On Emotions* 1.6 Glibert-Thirry, *SVF* 3.342, and (again) Diogenes Laertius 7.116, *SVF* 3.341, LS 65F). See further Inwood (1985) 236, Graver (2007) 51–9.

[107] δεῖ δ' ὥσπερ τὰ κονιάματα στηριχθῆναι βεβαίως καὶ λαβεῖν πῆξιν, οὕτως τὰς τῶν τελειωθέντων ψυχὰς κραταιωθείσας παγιώτερον ἱδρυθῆναι μελέτῃ συνεχεῖ καὶ γυμνάσμασιν ἐπαλλήλοις. οἱ δὲ μὴ τούτων τυγχάνοντες παρὰ τοῖς φιλοσόφοις διαλεληθότες εἶναι λέγονται σοφοί. τοὺς γὰρ ἄχρι σοφίας ἄκρας ἐληλακότας καὶ τῶν ὅρων αὐτῆς ἄρτι πρῶτον ἁψαμένους ἀμήχανον εἰδέναι φασὶ τὴν ἑαυτῶν τελείωσιν· μὴ γὰρ κατὰ τὸν αὐτὸν χρόνον ἄμφω συνίστασθαι, τήν τε πρὸς τὸ πέρας ἄφιξιν καὶ τὴν τῆς ἀφίξεως κατάληψιν, ἀλλ' εἶναι μεθόριον ἄγνοιαν, οὐ τὴν μακρὰν ἀπεληλαμένην ἐπιστήμης, ἀλλὰ τὴν ἐγγὺς καὶ ἀγχίθυρον αὐτῇ.

Although Philo of Alexandria ascribes the doctrine to 'the philosophers', from the fact that in the foregoing passages the doctrine is clearly ascribed to the Stoics it seems most likely that he refers to them.[108] Yet again we find that every sage necessarily ('it is impossible') is at first unaware of his wisdom.

In the modern literature two noteworthy attempts at an explanation have thus far been undertaken. First, Sedley, in a brief treatment of the feature, connected it with the dialectical argument known as the 'elusive argument' (*ho dialelēthōs logos*), mentioned at Diogenes Laertius 7.82 (*SVF* 2.274, LS 37D, *FDS* 1207) and in Chrysippus' book title *On the Elusive Argument, Addressed to Athenades*, that can be found in the catalogue of his writings in a section in which reference is made to other dialectical arguments (see Diogenes Laertius 7.198, SVF 2.15, LS 37B, *FDS* 194). The key difficulty with the 'elusive argument' is – how appropriate – that it is nowhere explained in the extant evidence. Sedley made the interesting suggestion that the argument could have been inherited by the Stoics from the Megarians, among whom Eubulides of Miletus (mid fourth century BCE) is reported to have introduced the argument (see Diogenes Laertius 2.108, fr. 64 Döring, fr. 13 Giannantoni). Eubulides could have confronted the Stoics with the problem that the sage whom

[108] An additional reason for identifying Philo's 'philosophers' with the Stoics is the contrast that he offers between 'the philosophers' in 161 and the sophists in 159–60. These sophists are depicted negatively as quarrelsome, disturbing the acquisition of truth, and to be avoided by those who strive for it, whereas no such negative connotations accompany the philosophers. In *On Flight and Finding* 209–10 a similar contrast is presented between the doctrines to be defended against the attacks by sophists, who this time are clearly presented as sceptics, 'with pretence of excessive open-mindedness, and love of arguing for arguing's sake' (σοφιστοῦ γὰρ βούλημα τοῦτο τὸ λίαν σκεπτικὸν ἐπιμορφάζοντος καὶ λόγοις χαίροντος ἐριστικοῖς). It is tempting to identify them here with (Academic?) sceptics, as Früchtel (1968) 139 already did. In *On Agriculture* the philosophers called in to support Philo's allegorical interpretation of *Deuteronomy* 20.5 are presented as dogmatic (cf. *On Flight and Finding* 210: the learned fight back defending – as they would defend their own offspring – 'the doctrines' to which 'their soul has given birth' (ἔτεκεν αὐτῶν ἡ ψυχὴ δογμάτων).). As the main professional rivals of the Sceptics were obviously the Stoics, it is thus even more likely that with 'the philosophers' the Stoics are meant.

nothing should have escaped would have had one thing escape him, namely that he has become a sage. The argument could thus point to the unattainability of wisdom, as upon the moment of becoming wise the single most important fact about himself would escape the sage, i.e. that he has now become wise. From their predecessors the Stoics would thus have inherited this dialectical problem, which would put in doubt the ideal of the sage as having this kind of self-knowledge, and which their adversaries were all too happy to exploit.[109] However, as I will discuss in a moment, against Sedley's suggestion it should be noted that it is rather doubtful that the Stoics understood this awareness as a necessary condition of wisdom. Second, Alesse, in her fuller treatment of the feature of the sage's initial unawareness, and following Sedley in connecting it to the dialectical argument, came up with the proposal that the characteristic would have been used by the Stoics to account for the possibility of moral progress. Alesse interpreted the 'ignorance of the sort not far removed from knowledge' in Philo of Alexandria, *On Agriculture* 161, as an intermediate state between vice and virtue, arguing that the possibility of progress would be lost if such an intermediate state were not to exist, and if the change were to be radical.[110] This interpretation is problematic, too. The assumption that the possibility of progress would be lost if the change were to be radical is already doubtful. Although someone's physiological state is still one of badness, he may well gain more and more insight (or have 'cognitions', *katalēpseis* in the Stoic terminology) into his place in the order of the world and hence make progress. Even more problematic in this interpretation is her denial that the change is abrupt.

[109] Prantl (1855) 490 n. 210, Döring (1972) 112 n. 5, Sedley (1977) 94.

[110] Alesse (1997) 75. Vimercati (2011) 591 also suggests an intermediate stage, describing this 'passagio di condizione' as a 'novità' (cf. n. 4) in comparison with the early Stoic doctrine of the radical change. He refers to the phrase ἕτοιμον εἶναι δεῖ πρὸς τὸ φιλοσοφεῖν ('he [i.e. the sage-to-be] needs to be ready for loving wisdom') in Stobaeus 2.104.15–16 (*SVF* 3.682). A simpler reading, in line with early Stoic doctrine, is that the reference is already to the sage rather than the sage-to-be, since the sage needs to be already in the disposition of wisdom before he can (start to) love wisdom.

For the Stoics, as we have seen throughout this chapter, the change to wisdom *is* radical.

I suggest another interpretation. As discussed in Chapter 1, and developed further in physiological terms in Section 2.2.3c, wisdom consists in the special disposition of character. As this disposition is the (only) condition for wisdom, the virtuous (or expert) disposition of the sage need not be accompanied by the awareness of the fact that it is a virtuous disposition. This is exactly how we found it expressed in Stobaeus 2.113.15–16: the awareness thereof is not 'needed'. The disposition of character is thus all that matters, on the basis of which the sage will always have a perfect grasp of the impressions. (Once again the dispositional meaning of wisdom thus turns out to be the primary meaning, with the cognitional meaning thus secondary only.)

This sequence, where the disposition comes first, only to be followed by the awareness of being in that condition, the Stoics compared with the initial unawareness of someone who becomes an expert in an ordinary craft. The continuation of the Stobaeus passage, at 2.113.16–17, makes this clear: 'Such distinctions [between being a sage and having the awareness of being a sage] will occur not only with regard to practical wisdom, but also with regard to the other types of expertise.'[111] The comparison makes perfect sense. If someone has mastered playing the flute, the awareness thereof will only follow after the mastery itself. The awareness that he has performed well will arise as a matter of course only after the actual performance itself, when the flute-player has directed his attention not to the demands of the activity itself (i.e. blowing into the flute with the proper force, placing his fingers correctly on the instrument, etc.), but rather realises how easy it has all become. In the same manner, only *after* having mastered his wisdom, while already doing well anything he does, can the sage come to the awareness that he has indeed lived by the perfection that comes with being a sage.

[111] οὐ μόνον δ' ἐπὶ τῆς φρονήσεως ἀλλὰ καὶ ἐπὶ τῶν ἄλλων τεχνῶν τὰς τοιαύτας ἔσεσθαι διαλήψεις.

This interpretation that it is the condition of mastery that counts, rather than the awareness thereof, finds confirmation, too, in the words used by Philo of Alexandria, *On Agriculture* 161. As with the ordinary expert, in the special case of wisdom where, as Philo put it, the sage is 'not yet thoroughly practised in virtue', but is apparently already virtuous, the sage will have the 'cognition of arrival', only once he has started to think about himself and his position in the world. Only then can and will he become aware of the fact that the life he lives is in complete harmony with the active principle in the world.

That it is the mastery that counts, not the awareness thereof, is in line with the earliest known usage of wisdom, as in Homer's *Iliad*, at 15.410–13: 'As the carpenter's rule makes a ship's timber straight in the hands of an experienced carpenter, whenever he knows all of his expertise [*sophia*] well by the instructions of Athena, so evenly was conducted their war and battle.'[112] 'Wisdom' is here used in the sense of a fully mastered expertise, such that a craftsman is able to do something well.[113] As in their understanding of philosophy the Stoics appeared to have a preference for its traditional meaning of 'dealing with',[114] so their understanding of wisdom as a mastered disposition is in line with the traditional meaning, too.

For the Stoics, then, the characterisation of the change as a radical opposition between the inferior person and the sage puts the emphasis on the exceptionality of the sage, whereas the characteristic that the change goes unnoticed rather points to what has been characterised as the 'ordinariness' of the sage.[115] On the one hand, as we have seen throughout in this chapter, the sage is very special in comparison to the inferior

[112] ἀλλ' ὥς τε στάθμη δόρυ νήϊον ἐξιθύνει / τέκτονος ἐν παλάμῃσι δαήμονος, ὅς ῥά τε πάσης / εὖ εἰδῇ σοφίης ὑποθημοσύνῃσιν Ἀθήνης, / ὣς μὲν τῶν ἐπὶ ἶσα μάχη τέτατο πτόλεμός τε.
[113] See e.g. Leisegang (1927) 1019, Gladigow (1965) 9–11, Maier (1970) 17, Kerferd (1976) 24, Hadot (1991) 9.
[114] See Section 1.3.1.
[115] I borrow the expression 'ordinariness' from Liu (2009). Cf. Annas (2008) 16: 'not rising above the everyday'.

person. The inferior person has to judge each impression and place it within its systematic context, which is an arduous, Herculean task, and which all too often goes wrong. By contrast, the sage, having acquired his special disposition of character, will not be faced with such difficulties. Out of this disposition the sage will be able to deal correctly with each impression without further ado. On the other hand, the sage is in a way ordinary, too, in the sense that he remains doing what he did before, that is judging each impression and placing it in the overall scheme of things. As it turns out, Stoic wisdom is very much a this-worldly affair: the person who becomes a sage, will continue to live life as he did before, dealing with judging impressions. However, the disposition out of which the sage is able to do this, this embedded disposition in the structure of the whole which cannot be lost, will make the sage at some point realise that something very special has happened to him.[116]

This 'ordinary' aspect of the change to wisdom comes out, too, in the comparison of the change with an initiation into one of the mystery cults. As we have already seen earlier (in Section 2.2.2c), the Stoics dealt with this comparison: Cleanthes described the sage as an initiate, 'filled with the divine', Chrysippus discussed the connection between perfection and initiation. The initiation into the mysteries, on the one hand, and the Stoic conception of the change to wisdom, on the other, differ in two important ways. First, with regard to the mysteries, it is the ritual that causes the change. However well the secret of the mysteries has been kept, this is how it is formulated in a reliable piece of evidence, Proclus, *Commentary on Plato's Republic* 2.108.17–30: 'The Eleusinian mysteries [. . .] cause sympathy of the souls with the ritual in a way that is unintelligible to us, and divine, so that some of the initiands are stricken with panic, being filled with divine awe; others assimilate themselves to the holy symbols, leave their own identity, become at home with the gods, and

[116] For a discussion of an example of the sage unaware of his wisdom see *infra* Section 4.5.

experience divine possession.'[117] By contrast, with regard to the change to wisdom, the cause of the change lies with oneself, that is with the development of one's reason.[118] The other difference between initiation into the mysteries and the change to wisdom lies in the awareness thereof. Whereas for the initiand in the mysteries it is the direct experience of the ritual that apparently brings about an immediate life-changing experience, for the Stoics the moment of achieving stability is not experienced immediately.

In this context, where the fresh sage learns more about his new disposition later on, the otherwise obscure account in which Chrysippus connected perfection and initiation makes good sense. It is preserved in the *Great Etymological Dictionary*, already referred to above (n. 43):

> Chrysippus says that the doctrines [*logoi*] on divine things are rightly called initiations: for these should be the last things to be taught, when the soul has found its stability and has become in control, and is capable of keeping silent [*amuētous*] towards the uninitiated. For it is a great reward to hear the correct things about the gods and to gain control.[119]

The phrase 'the soul [that] has found its stability' is a now obvious reference to the stable disposition just acquired by the person who is now a sage. After he has become a sage, however, he can still learn about his disposition. Just as he can become aware of the fact that he has become a sage, he can come to understand the 'correct things about the gods'. Chrysippus does not tell us in this account what these doctrines are,

[117] αἱ τελεταί ... συμπαθείας εἰσὶν αἴτιαι ταῖς ψυχαῖς περὶ τὰ δρώμενα τρόπον ἄγνωστον ἡμῖν καὶ θεῖον· ὡς τοὺς μὲν τῶν τελουμένων καταπλήττεσθαι δειμάτων θείων πλήρεις γιγνομένους, τοὺς δὲ συνδιατίθεσθαι τοῖς ἱεροῖς συμβόλοις καὶ ἑαυτῶν ἐκστάντας ὅλους ἐνιδρῦσθαι τοῖς θεοῖς καὶ ἐνθεάζειν. For the translation and the reliability of the evidence see Burkert (1987) 114.

[118] Cf. on the question of Stoic 'mysticism' see Wlosok (1960) 39: 'Von wirklicher Mystik ist keine Rede, die erlösende Kraft ist die Philosophie, eine, wenn auch göttliche, Errungenschaft des Menschen selbst, der Schauende[,] der rationale, selbsttätige Menschengeist ..., und der erkannte Gott ist die stoische Allnatur, die sich allzeit in ihren Werken preisgibt.'

[119] Χρύσιππος δέ φησι, τοὺς περὶ θείων λόγους εἰκότως καλεῖσθαι τελετάς· χρῆναι γὰρ τούτους τελευταίους καὶ ἐπὶ πᾶσι διδάσκεσθαι, τῆς ψυχῆς ἐχούσης ἕρμα καὶ κεκρατημένης καὶ πρὸς ἀμυήτους σιωπᾶν δυναμένης· μέγα γὰρ εἶναι τὸ ἆθλον ὑπὲρ θεῶν ἀκοῦσαί τε ὀρθὰ καὶ ἐγκρατεῖς γενέσθαι αὐτῶν.

but it does not seem a wild guess to assume that he refers to the doctrines we found ascribed to him by Philodemus, in *On Piety*, e.g. that the gods are a special part of nature, and that the sage himself has become such a special part of nature, too (see Section 2.2.2c). Here it might be objected: if the differences between the initiation and the change to wisdom are so substantial (i.e. that the change is brought about by oneself rather than a ritual, and that the change is not immediately experienced), what is the connection between the change and the initiation, to which Chrysippus wanted to draw attention? The answer has presumably to be found in the phrase 'keeping silent towards the uninitiated'. This aspect goes back to the origin of the notion of mysticism, although the etymological connection with *muō*, 'to keep silent' is uncertain.[120] Just as it is the duty of the initiates to guard what has been revealed to them, so Chrysippus apparently considered it prudent that the real truth about the nature of the gods should be kept secret, too. Chrysippus does not tell us why, but a suggestion is that bringing out truths that reduce the traditional gods to a force in nature did not go down well with the traditional supporters of Athenian civic religion, who on several occasions – with e.g. Anaxagoras, who was banished to Lampsacus, or Socrates – had made that clear.[121]

To sum up this section: whereas the change to wisdom is very exceptional indeed, with the sage becoming an active part of the one and only force pervading the cosmos, at the same time the change is ordinary, too, in the sense that the sage will continue to operate in the same manner as the inferior person he was just a moment before, without even noticing that he has become a sage. As a sage, however, he has found his stability in a specific physiological disposition, and will not make any of the mistakes of the inferior person any longer.

[120] On mystical silence and the etymology see the somewhat sceptical Burkert (1987) 7, and (1995) 82 n. 9: 'Die beliebte Ableitung von *muein* 'die Augen schliessen' – die das -*s*- des Stammes unerklärt läßt – hat nur den Wert einer Volksetymologie.'

[121] For a reassessment of the charge against Socrates in the modern literature, in which it is taken more seriously again as an impiety charge, and the 'underlying' political motives of the trial are downplayed, see Smith and Woodruff (2000).

If this explanation of the characteristic is indeed correct, the question can still be raised as to what may have motivated the Stoics to formulate this characteristic of the change. An answer to that question is best postponed here: I will return to it in Section 4.5.

2.4 Conclusion

Taking as our starting point the passage in the Plutarchean *Synopsis*, which turned out to be a reliable piece of evidence for our reconstruction of Stoic doctrine, we have seen that the Stoics described the change to wisdom as a radical change in the nature of a rational being. The immediate change from the one extreme state to the other could be explained as a qualitative change to the state of the soul that has been brought to perfection. As such, this state is characterised as virtue, as (perfect) reason, or even as divine fire. Out of this perfect condition, or character, the sage will live 'a good flow of life' (*euroia biou*),[122] doing what he can do, and leaving out what he cannot, while feeling joy when appropriate,[123] but at any rate not emotionally suffering from the mistakes that inferior persons make when judging their impressions.[124] In the exalted language that the Stoics used with regard to the description of their sage,[125] it can be said that the sage is both in *apathy*, in *eupathy* and in *sympathy*: in *apathy*, as the sage is freed from such incorrect judgements on his place in the course

[122] See e.g. Stobaeus 2.77.20–23 (*SVF* 1.184, 554, 3.16, LS 63A): τὴν δὲ εὐδαιμονίαν ὁ Ζήνων ὡρίσατο τὸν τρόπον τοῦτον· εὐδαιμονία δ' ἐστὶν εὔροια βίου. κέχρηται δὲ καὶ Κλεάνθης τῷ ὅρῳ τούτῳ ἐν τοῖς ἑαυτοῦ συγγράμμασι καὶ ὁ Χρύσιππος καὶ οἱ ἀπὸ τούτων πάντες.

[123] The technical term for 'doing what he or she can do, leaving out what he or she cannot, while feeling joy when appropriate' are the three 'good states' (εὐπάθειαι): βούλησις, εὐλάβεια and χαρά. See e.g. Diogenes Laertius 7.116 (*SVF* 3.341, LS 65F).

[124] The Stoic theory of '[bad] emotions' (πάθη) is based on the idea that such emotions are incorrect judgements (see e.g. Stobaeus 2.88.8–12, *SVF* 3.378, LS 65A), and once turned into dispositions will become diseases of the soul. The literature on the Stoic theory of emotions is vast. For a good recent survey, with stress on the dispositional, physiological character of the Stoic account of the inferior person's emotions, see e.g. Prost (2004) 193–319.

[125] See Pohlenz in the Introduction (p. 1), n. 4.

of things;[126] in *eupathy*, as the sage will do what is up to him, or accept what he cannot change, while being joyful when appropriate;[127] in *sympathy*, as the sage lives in accordance with and is part of the substantive reason that orders and guides the world.[128]

The Stoic interpretation of the change to wisdom can be interestingly contrasted with Plato's interpretation of the final moment of achieving wisdom, as for example in the *Phaedrus* or the *Republic*.[129] In the *Phaedrus* at 250B–C Plato 'himself' (*hēmeis*[130]) describes the ultimate moment as an exalted vision of the Form of beauty, placing it in an other-worldly, heavenly realm. In the *Republic* at 532C the philosopher-king reverts

126 For the sage as ἀπαθής see Diogenes Laertius 7.117 (*SVF* 3.448), Persaeus *ap.* Themistius, *Orations* 32.358B (*SVF* 1.449); for the connection between 'good flow of life' and 'apathy' see Epictetus, *Dissertations* 1.4.28–9 (*SVF* 3.144) ἵνα γνῷς, φησίν [sc. Chrysippus], ὅτι οὐ ψευδῆ ταῦτά ἐστιν, ἐξ ὧν ἡ εὔροιά ἐστι καὶ ἀπάθεια ἀπαντᾷ, λάβε μου τὰ βιβλία καὶ γνώσῃ ὡς <ἀκολουθά, Schenkl, cf. Dobbin (1998) 98> τε καὶ σύμφωνά ἐστι τῇ φύσει τὰ ἀπαθῆ με ποιοῦντα.

127 According to one of the notorious Stoic paradoxes the sage is even happy, when tortured, as e.g. roasted in the belly of the copper bull of the tyrant Phalaris (see Gregory of Nazianzus (329–89), *Letters* 32.7 (*SVF* 3.586): εἶναι τὸν σπουδαῖον μακάριον κἂν ὁ Φαλάριδος ταῦρος ἔχῃ καιόμενον, cf. Vegetti (1998) 277–81). The sage will be in a state of acceptance, and not in the accompanying state of joy.

128 On Stoic sympathy see further Brouwer (forthcoming). The sage is thus said to be a true citizen of the universe, friends with other sages (if there are any others around) and friends with gods as naturally perfect beings. On Stoic cosmopolitanism (and the sage's participation in law, with law as yet another name for the force pervading the cosmos) see e.g. Plutarch, *On the Fortune or Virtue of Alexander* 329A–B (*SVF* 1.262, LS 67A), about which e.g. Obbink (1999), Schofield (1999) 97–101, Brouwer (2006), (2011) and Vogt (2008) can be consulted. (Unfortunately, in most accounts of cosmopolitanism this materialist version is missing, see e.g. Kleingeld and Brown (2006), cf. Kleingeld (2012) 4, otherwise perhaps the best overview to date of different kinds of cosmopolitanism.) On friendship with other sages (if others exist, of course; if not, the sage retires into himself, for which see Seneca, *Letter* 9.16, *SVF* 2.1065, LS 40O), see the 'slightly adventurous account' (this understatement is by Diels (1917) 6), as in e.g. Plutarch, *On Common Notions* 1068F (*SVF* 3.627), of an invisible bond, 'with all other sages in the world benefitting, if one sage stretches out his finger prudently' (ἂν εἷς σοφὸς ὁπουδήποτε προτείνῃ τὸν δάκτυλον φρονίμως, οἱ κατὰ τὴν οἰκουμένην σοφοὶ πάντες ὠφελοῦνται). On friendship with the gods see e.g. ps.-Plutarch, *On Homer* 2.143, Clement of Alexandria, *Miscellanies* 1.168.4 (*SVF* 3.332), and in connection with the Stoic definition of wisdom Cicero, *On Proper Functions* 1.153: *illa autem sapientia, quam principem dixi, rerum est divinarum et humanarum scientia, in qua continetur deorum et hominum communitas et societas inter ipsos.* The theme of friendship is discussed in the literature on Stoic cosmopolitanism mentioned above, too.

129 Cf. also *Symposium* 210E–11A.

130 See Hackforth (1975) 93 n. 2.

towards a different, transcendent, world.[131] Whereas for Plato the change thus consists in a direct experience of a different reality (indeed often clad in mystery terminology[132]), for the Stoics the change rather consists in becoming an active part of this world,[133] that even at first goes unnoticed.[134] The difference in terminology, 'turn towards' (*metastrophē*) vs. 'change' (*metabolē*), respectively, is wholly explicable in this context.[135] In the Western tradition the transcendental approach has been very influential, if only because of Christianity. It may explain why Clement of Alexandria (see Section 2.1) connected the change with a turn towards the divine, and not of becoming divine. It may also explain why Bickel and Passmore (see again Section 2.1) incorrectly used Christian examples or formulated their interpretations in transcendent language.

131 ἡ ... λύσις τε ἀπὸ τῶν δεσμῶν καὶ μεταστροφὴ ἀπὸ τῶν σκιῶν ἐπὶ τὰ εἴδωλα καὶ τὸ φῶς καὶ ἐκ τοῦ καταγείου εἰς τὸν ἥλιον ἐπάνοδος.

132 See Riedweg (1987) 1–69.

133 The contrast between Plato and the Stoics is nicely captured by the Christian theologian Tatian (second century), *Address to the Greeks* 4 p. 5.2–3 Schwartz (presumably referred to by von Arnim at *SVF* 2.1035, reading p. 5 rather than p. 4): πνεῦμα ὁ θεός, οὐ διήκων διὰ τῆς ὕλης, πνευμάτων δὲ ὑλικῶν καὶ τῶν ἐν αὐτῇ σχημάτων κατασκευαστής ('God is breath, not going through matter, but the constructor of material breath and of the shapes in matter'), thus opposing the Stoic conception of god as breath going through matter and the Platonic conception of god as the 'constructor' thereof. This difference in physical terms can also be formulated in the ethical terms of the good life. For Plato, the good life consists in becoming like god so far as is possible for a human being (see e.g. Sedley (1999b), Lavecchia (2006)), for the Stoics the ideal is to become god in the sense of becoming part of the divine power that structures the world.

134 I will return to this contrast between Plato and the Stoics in Section 4.5.

135 Cf. White (1979) 178, who notes that in contrast with Plato's depreciation of the sensible world relative to another intelligible world the Stoics appreciated the sensible world as exhibiting perfect order, making it central to their ethical doctrine.

CHAPTER 3

SAGEHOOD

3.1 Introduction

Thus far we have discussed the Stoic definitions of wisdom, and how the change to wisdom comes about. The question that can be posed now is where the Stoics themselves stand with regard to wisdom. Did they profess themselves to be sages? In the literature, two main answers have been formulated, usually in the form of a simple assertion. The first answer is that they did not.[1] It was the second answer, formulated by Hirzel, which generated the only elaborate treatment of the question to date. Hirzel claimed that the earliest Stoics, such as Zeno and his immediate pupils Persaeus and Sphaerus, did consider themselves to be sages, but that Chrysippus came to the conclusion that neither Zeno nor his immediate followers could have lived up to the requirements needed to be a sage, and that from Chrysippus onwards the Stoics did not consider themselves sages any longer.[2]

The answer to this question has profound consequences for the status of Stoic theory. If either all or some Stoics did not claim wisdom for themselves and therefore did not claim their

[1] The thesis that Stoics did not consider themselves to be sages is asserted by: Lipsius (1604) bk 2 ch. 8 (repr. in Bouillet (1827) cxi–xciv), Fabricius (1718) 455 note U, Ravaisson (1877) 81, Adam (1911) 183, Tarn (1913) 32, Festugière (1932) 69, Pohlenz (1992) 157, Ganss (1952) 96, Luschnat (1958) 181 n. 1, Edelstein (1966) 12, Daraki (1989) 137, Bett (1997) 198, cf. (2009) 539, Korhonen (1997) 67, Vogt (2008) 82, Liu (2009) 249.

[2] See Hirzel (1882), 271–98, which is vol. 2, part 1 of Hirzel (1877–83), and which bears the subtitle *Die Entwicklung der stoischen Philosophie*. (It should perhaps be added here that the difficulty of handling the *Entwicklung* (566 pages in one, chapterless go, although vol. 3, 535–9, contains an analytical table of contents) is well outweighed by the range and depth of Hirzel's treatment of the evidence.) Authors also offering a developmental assessment, whether explicitly following Hirzel or not, include: Pearson (1891) 282, Pease (1955–8) 1176, Sandbach (1989) 44, Isnardi Parente (1993) 7, Nussbaum (1995) 38–9, Walsh (1997) 211, Schofield (1999).

theories to be expressions of wisdom, the question arises what status other than wisdom the Stoics did assign to their theories. Hirzel's answer will have to deal with issues such as: how did Zeno justify his claim, and what status did Chrysippus assign to Zeno's theories? It will also have to give a developmental account of Stoicism. It will have to explain the change in Chrysippus' position: did Chrysippus only say that he himself was not a sage, while still maintaining that Zeno and his immediate followers had been sages, or did his position also imply disagreement with Zeno and his colleagues, i.e. that they were wrong in considering themselves to be sages?

In this chapter an answer will be sought to the initial question based on an investigation of the available evidence. Taking the *status quaestionis* into account, I will focus upon the first generations of Stoics, although given the state of the evidence with regard to them, later Stoics will sometimes also be dealt with.

3.2 The argument of *Against the Professors* 7.432–5

I will take as a starting point a little-discussed passage in Sextus Empiricus, *Against the Professors*, at 7.432–5 (*SVF* 3.657, *FDS* 360A). The seventh book of *Against the Professors* is a carefully structured treatise, in which Sextus Empiricus discusses primarily the notion of what 'the dogmatic philosophers' call the 'logical criteria' as the means for the discovery of truth (33). The logical criterion, Sextus Empiricus explains in 35, is understood in three senses: the first sense is 'by which', i.e. man, as it is man who is able to distinguish between truth and falsehood; the other senses are secondly 'through which', i.e. perception or the intellect or both, as the faculties can discover what is true; and thirdly 'in virtue of which', that is the impression. After having set out the views of various philosophers on the criterion in 46–260 Sextus Empiricus concentrates his criticism on the 'by which' criterion for, as he says in 263: 'I think that when we have brought this already into perplexity, there will be no longer any need to go on to further discussion of the other criteria. For the other criteria are either parts or actions or affections of man.'[3] Nevertheless, Sextus Empiricus also fights with his adversaries on the other two criteria, although far more briefly. With regard to the third criterion, Sextus Empiricus provides arguments against the impression in general in 372–400, the 'cognitive impression' (*katalēptikē phantasia*) as brought forward by the Stoics in 401–35, and the 'probable impression' (*pithanē phantasia*) as brought forward by the Academics in 435–9.[4]

At the end of Sextus Empiricus' critical discussion of the Stoic cognitive impression a new argument is introduced in 432–5, beginning 'in another way' (*allōs*). It should be noted that the argument contained in it does not deal directly with the cognitive impression and seems to be an insertion. For it deals not so much with impressions, but with the related topic of cognition. I quote the passage here in full, while subdividing it, for ease of reference:

432 In another way, if, [i] according to them, every supposition of an inferior person is ignorance and only the sage speaks the truth and has stable knowledge of the true, and since [iiA] up till now the sage has not been found, [iiiA] it follows necessarily that the true has also not been found, and that because of this all things turn out to be incognitive, for if [iiB] we are all inferior persons, [iiiB] we have no stable cognition of existing things.

433 And this being so, [iv] it cannot be other than that the things that were brought forward by the Stoics against the Sceptics are said by the Sceptics against the Stoics.

For since, [v] according to the Stoics themselves, Zeno and Cleanthes and Chrysippus and the others from their school are reckoned among the inferior persons, and every inferior person is ruled by ignorance, [vi] Zeno was completely ignorant whether he was contained in the cosmos or he himself contained the cosmos, or whether he was a man or a woman, and [vii] Cleanthes did not know whether he was a human being or a more complex animal than Typhon. 434 Also [viii] Chrysippus either knew this dogma, being a Stoic one, I mean 'The inferior person is ignorant of all things', or he did not know this. And [viiiA] if he knew it, then it is false that the inferior person is ignorant of everything; for Chrysippus, being an inferior person,

[3] οἶμαι γὰρ ὡς τούτου προαπορηθέντος οὐδὲν ἔτι δεήσει περιττότερον περὶ τῶν ἄλλων κριτηρίων λέγειν· ταῦτα γὰρ ἢ μέρη ἐστὶν ἀνθρώπου ἢ ἐνεργήματα ἢ πάθη.

[4] For a more elaborate discussion of the structure of Sextus Empiricus' treatise on the criterion see esp. Long (1978a), Brunschwig (1988) and Bett (2005).

knew this very thing – that the inferior person is ignorant of all things. But [viiiB] if he did not know even this fact that he is ignorant of all things, why does he utter opinions about many things, laying down that there is one cosmos, and that it is ordered by providence, and that its being is entirely changeable, and many other things?

435 [ix] And it is possible, should anyone so desire, for the opponent to bring against them all other perplexities which they themselves are accustomed to bring forward against the Sceptics.[5]

The passage falls into two parts. The first part deals with the Stoics in general, the second part with individual Stoics. The first part, which is but one sentence, contains [i]–[iiiB], and is the thrust of the passage. The following sentence [iv] is apparently only an inference to be drawn from that first part. Sentences [v]–[viii] are presented as a substantiation of [iv]. It seems sensible therefore to start with the first part of the passage and to deal with the second part thereafter.

The first part starts with the premiss [i] that the Stoics distinguished between the sage and the inferior person: only the sage speaks the truth and has stable knowledge of it; the inferior person is ignorant. It is followed by [iiA], stating that the sage has not yet been found. From [i] and [iiA], [iiiA] necessarily follows: the true is also undiscovered and therefore all things turn out to be incognitive. The sentence, long as it already is, does not stop here, but continues with a sort of

[5] 432 ἄλλως τε, [i] εἰ πᾶσα φαύλου κατ᾽ αὐτοὺς ὑπόληψις ἄγνοιά ἐστι καὶ μόνος ὁ σοφὸς ἀληθεύει καὶ ἐπιστήμην ἔχει τἀληθοῦς βεβαίαν, ἀκολουθεῖ [iiA] μέχρι δεῦρο ἀνευρέτου καθεστῶτος τοῦ σοφοῦ [iiiA] κατ᾽ ἀνάγκην καὶ τἀληθὲς ἀνεύρετον εἶναι, διὰ δὲ τοῦτο καὶ πάντα ἀκατάληπτα τυγχάνειν, ἐπείπερ [iiB] φαῦλοι πάντες ὄντες [iiiB] οὐκ ἔχομεν βεβαίαν τῶν ὄντων κατάληψιν.
433 τούτο δὲ οὕτως ἔχοντος [iv] ἀπολείπεται τὰ ὑπὸ τῶν Στωικῶν πρὸς τοὺς ἀπὸ τῆς σκέψεως λεγόμενα παρὰ μέρος καὶ ὑπὸ τῶν σκεπτικῶν πρὸς ἐκείνους λέγεσθαι.
ἔπει γὰρ [v] φαύλοις κατ᾽ αὐτοὺς ἐγκαταριθμοῦνται Ζήνων τε καὶ Κλεάνθης καὶ Χρύσιππος καὶ οἱ λοιποὶ τῶν ἀπὸ τῆς αἱρέσεως, πᾶς δε φαῦλος ἀγνοίᾳ κρατεῖται, [vi] πάντως ἠγνόει Ζήνων πότερον ἐν κόσμῳ περιέχεται ἢ αὐτὸς τὸν κόσμον περιέσχηκεν καὶ πότερον ἀνήρ ἐστιν ἢ γυνή, καὶ [vii] οὐκ ἠπίστατο Κλεάνθης εἴτε ἄνθρωπός ἐστιν εἴτε τι θηρίον Τυφῶνος πολυπλοκώτερον. 434 καὶ [viiiA] μὴν ἢ ἐγίνωσκε τὸ δόγμα τοῦτο Χρύσιππος Στωικὸν ὄν (φημὶ δὲ τὸ ‘πάντα ἀγνοεῖ ὁ φαῦλος’), ἢ οὐδὲ αὐτὸ τοῦτο ἠπίστατο. καὶ εἰ μὲν ἠπίστατο, ψεῦδος τὸ πάντα ἀγνοεῖν τὸν φαῦλον· αὐτὸ γὰρ τοῦτο φαῦλος ὢν ἐγίνωσκεν ὁ Χρύσιππος, τὸ πάντα ἀγνοεῖν τὸν φαῦλον. [viiiB] εἰ δ᾽ οὐδ᾽ αὐτὸ τοῦτο ᾔδει τὸ ὅτι πάντα ἀγνοεῖ, πῶς περὶ πολλῶν δογματίζει, τιθεὶς τὸ ἕνα εἶναι κόσμον καὶ προνοίᾳ τοῦτον διοκεῖσθαι καὶ διόλου τρεπτὴν εἶναι τὴν οὐσίαν καὶ ἄλλα παμπληθῆ;
435 [ix] πάρεστι δέ, εἴ τινι φίλον ἐστί, καὶ τὰς ἄλλας ἀπορίας τὸν ἀντερωτῶντα, ὡς ἔθος ἔχουσιν αὐτοὶ τοῖς σκεπτικοῖς . . . προσάγειν.

appendix: '[F]or if we are all inferior persons, we have no stable cognition of the existing things.' The first part of the apposition [iiB] reads as the counterpart of [iiA]: 'we are all inferior persons'; and the second part [iiiB] as a reformulation of the conclusion [iiiA]: 'we have no stable cognitions of existing things.' I will therefore concentrate upon [i], [iiA] and [iiiA]. The question I will address here and which may help to decide the main question posed in the Introduction to this chapter is: does Sextus Empiricus distort the Stoic position, at least partially? To answer this question I will treat the parts separately.

3.2.1 *The distinction between the inferior person and the sage*

The doctrines expressed in [i], 'according to them, every supposition of an inferior person is ignorance and only the sage speaks the truth and has stable knowledge of the true', are introduced by Sextus Empiricus, as if they were held 'according to the Stoics themselves' (*kat' autous*). Were they?

The distinction between the inferior person and the sage, as we have seen in Section 2.2.2, is perfectly Stoic: it can in general terms already be found in Zeno's *Politeia*,[6] and is reported by Stobaeus,[7] as well as by Cicero.[8] The characterisation of the inferior person in terms of ignorance is perfectly Stoic, too, as the evidence quoted in Section 2.2.2b shows. The characterisation of the sage in terms of truth is in *Against the Professors* 7.42 (*SVF* 2.132, *FDS* 324): 'Who has truth, is a sage.'[9] Of Sextus Empiricus' phrase 'the sage has stable

[6] According to Cassius the Sceptic (first half of the first century BCE?, see Schofield (1999) 20–1) *ap.* Diogenes Laertius 7.32 (*SVF* 1.226, LS 67B): ἐχθροὺς καὶ πολεμίους καὶ δούλους καὶ ἀλλοτρίους λέγειν αὐτὸν ἀλλήλων εἶναι πάντας τοὺς μὴ σπουδαίους ('He says that all who are not virtuous are foes, enemies, slaves and aliens to one another').

[7] Stobaeus 2.99.3–5, already quoted in Section 2.2.3.

[8] *Tusculan Disputations* 4.54 (*SVF* 3.665): *Stoici, qui omnes insipientes insanos esse dicunt* ('The Stoics, who say that everyone who is not wise, is inferior'), *In Defence of Murena* 61 (*SVF* 1.227): *nos autem qui sapientes non sumus fugitivos, exsules, hostis, insanos denique esse dicunt* ('They say that we, who are not wise, are runaways, exiles, enemies and in fact mad').

[9] ὁ ἔχων ταύτην [sc. τὴν ἀλήθειαν] σοφός ἐστιν. Cf. Sextus Empiricus, *Outlines of Pyrrhonism* 2.83 (*FDS* 322): τὴν μὲν ἀλήθειαν ἐν μόνῳ σπουδαίῳ φασὶν εἶναι ('They say that the truth exists only in the sage').

knowledge of the true' the first part, 'the sage has stable knowledge', is by now familiar enough: in Chapter 1 we have seen that the Stoics described knowledge as a secure and stable cognition. The addition that it is knowledge of the true is in fact superfluous: according to standard Stoic doctrine knowledge is based on a cognition, which on its turn is based on a true impression, that is in its most basic formulation an impression 'arising from what is'.[10] So the doctrines Sextus Empiricus cites in [i] are indeed Stoic.

3.2.2 'Up till now the sage has not been found'

The question that will occupy us in this section is the status of [iiA], 'up till now the sage has not been found'. Does [iiA] contain a Stoic observation, or should it be considered a Sextan inference? It should be noted that because of the construction of the (Greek) sentence, 'according to them' in [i] does not rule [iiA] and thus that Sextus Empiricus does not explicitly present [iiA] as Stoic. I submit that the question can be resolved by looking at parallel texts. As we will see, quite a number of texts contain a similar expression. This section will be devoted to a discussion of these texts and the question whether they are to be taken as Stoic or as hostile inferences against the Stoics.[11] The fact that there are quite a few of these texts makes it useful, I think, to discuss the evidence under separate headings. In Section 3.2.2a I will consider more passages from Sextus Empiricus, in Section 3.2.2b non-Sextan evidence will be presented, and in Section 3.2.2c I will discuss the related expression that the sage 'is rarer than the phoenix'. It should also be noted that in these sections I shall restrict myself to the passages in which the observation

[10] See e.g. Chrysippus, *Physics* 2 *ap.* Diogenes Laertius 7.54 (*SVF* 2.105, *FDS* 255, LS 40A): κριτήριον δὲ τῆς ἀληθείας φασὶ τυγχάνειν τὴν καταληπτικὴν φαντασίαν, τουτέστι τὴν ἀπὸ ὑπάρχοντος, καθά φησι Χρύσιππος ἐν τῇ δευτέρᾳ τῶν Φυσικῶν. On the relation between truth and true see *infra* n. 65.

[11] Some of the passages are cited in Lipsius (1604) bk 2 ch. 8, and in *SVF* 3.657–70. Various scholars present more or less complete lists of them: Fabricius (1718) 435 n. U, Reid (1885) 339–40, Mayor (1880) 285, Pease (1920–3) 265–6, Zeller and Wellmann (1923) 276, Pease (1955–8) 1176, Sharples (1983) 162–3, Pohlenz (1990) 84.

is connected with the Stoics in general. A discussion of the passages related to the individual Stoics will follow in Section 3.2.4.

3.2.2a Parallels in Sextus Empiricus

Sextus Empiricus uses the expression in three other passages, at *Against the Professors* 2.43, *Outlines of Pyrrhonism* 1.91 and *Against the Professors* 9.133. At *Against the Professors* 2.43 the Academics are cited as saying that rhetoric is not an expertise, arguing against two groups of adversaries, both referred to as 'some', who defend rhetoric as an expertise. For our purposes we can leave the second group aside here.[12] The first group defends rhetoric by making a distinction: 'Some say there are two forms of rhetoric, the one wise and in use among the wise, the other intermediate and in use among human beings.'[13] They defend the wise kind of rhetoric as an expertise, and deny that the other or intermediate kind of rhetoric is an expertise. At 45 Sextus Empiricus gives a reply to the defence of rhetoric by these 'some' who argue against the Academics: 'But the first group fails to notice that against their will they have granted the non-existence of rhetoric. For since the wise man is never, or at least rarely, found, it must follow that the rhetoric in use among the wise is also either non-existent or

[12] Bury's Loeb translation is deceptive here. He translates subordinately 'some' (43) and 'some of them' (44), whereas Sextus Empiricus offers two parallel defences, which he later on in 45 and 46 respectively refers to as 'first [group]' and 'second [group]'.

[13] τινὲς μέν φασιν ὅτι διττῆς οὔσης ῥητορικῆς, τῆς μὲν ἀστείας καὶ ἐν σοφοῖς τῆς δὲ μέσης ἐν ἀνθρώποις. The manuscripts have τῆς δὲ ἐν μέσοις ἀνθρώποις, which is printed by Fabricius (1718) 297–8, Bekker (1842) 683, Mutschmann and Mau (1961) 92. Since 'intermediate' with regard to human beings is somewhat odd, Bekker suggested to change it into μοχθηροῖς ('wretched human beings'), as the two forms of rhetoric are immediately contrasted again as rhetoric that is refined and rhetoric of the μοχθηροί. Another possibility is to connect intermediate with expertise, as the connection is fairly common in Stoic texts, for which see e.g. Simplicius, *Commentary on Aristotle's Categories* 284.32–3 (*SVF* 2.393, *FDS* 863). This would also take away the further oddity that unlike the former kind of rhetoric the latter kind of expertise is not identified in the Greek of the manuscripts. My preferred reading, which may at least convey the author's intention, is τῆς δὲ μέσης ἐν ἀνθρώποις. Fortunately not much depends upon the precise formulation of the distinction. What is important is *that* the distinction is made.

rare.'[14] Who are these 'some', this 'first group'? The context offers some clues for identification. The exposition of *Against the Professors* 2.43–5 is presented as a criticism of the Academic position, which was set out in *Against the Professors* 2.20–42. As adversaries of the Academics the Stoics had already made their appearance in *Against the Professors* 2.6, with the mention of their definition of expertise as having stable cognitions and existing only in the sage. It is therefore likely that the first group in *Against the Professors* 2.43–5 should be identified with the Stoics and that it is their 'wise' rhetoric and their sage that are targeted by Sextus Empiricus.[15] But even if the Stoics are targeted here, it may still be questioned whether the minor premiss of Sextus Empiricus' argument (or, for that matter, the argument as a whole) would have been endorsed by the Stoics. Our discussion of this passage thus only provides us with a parallel to [iiA], but cannot help in deciding what its status is: simply a hostile inference, or actual Stoic doctrine.

In my second passage, *Outlines of Pyrrhonism* 1.91, Sextus Empiricus introduces his third sceptical mode of arguing against the dogmatists, which contains a very interesting snippet: 'Nonetheless, so as to arrive at suspension of judgement even when resting the argument on a single person, such as on their 'dreamed up' (*oneiropolomenou*) sage, we bring out the mode which is third in order.'[16] Although 'their' refers back to the 'self-satisfied dogmatists' (*philautoi dogmatikoi*) in *Outlines of Pyrrhonism* 1.90, it is likely that the Stoics are more specifically targeted here. For 'to dream up' occurs again in *Outlines of Pyrrhonism* 3.240, this time explicitly related to the Stoics and their 'celebrated' practical wisdom: 'Yet, even if they [the dogmatists who have different conceptions of the expertise of life] were all to agree by hypothesis that there is a single expertise of

[14] λέληθε δὲ τοὺς μὲν πρώτους ὅτι ἄκοντες δεδώκασι τὴν ἀνυπαρξίαν τῆς ῥητορικῆς· μηδενὸς γὰρ εὑρισκομένου σοφοῦ ἢ σπανίως γε εὑρισκομένου δεήσει καὶ τὴν ἐν αὐτοῖς ῥητορικὴν ἢ ἀνύπαρκτον ἢ σπάνιον εἶναι.

[15] Cf. Radermacher (1915) xv: 'Nach der Art, wie Sextus die Einwände vorführt, stellt sich das Ganze als ein geschlossener Angriff gegen die Stoa dar.'

[16] ὅμως δ' οὖν ἵνα καὶ ἐπὶ ἑνὸς ἀνθρώπου τὸν λόγον ἱστάντες, οἷον τοῦ παρ' αὐτοῖς ὀνειροπολουμένου σοφοῦ, ἐπὶ τὴν ἐποχὴν καταντῶμεν, τὸν τρίτον τῇ τάξει τρόπον προχειριζόμεθα.

life, such as, for example, the celebrated practical wisdom whereof the Stoics dream, and which seems to be more striking than everything else, even so equally absurd consequences will follow.'[17] *Outlines of Pyrrhonism* 1.91 offers another interesting clue that its target must be the Stoics. Sextus Empiricus argues for his sceptical position of suspension of judgement, 'even when resting the argument on a single person'.[18] This phrase Sextus may have taken from the conclusion of Zeno's argument that 'the second speaker must therefore not be heard', preserved in Plutarch, *On Stoic Contradictions* 1034E (*SVF* 1.78, *FDS* 40).[19] This argument can be reconstructed as follows: if the first speaker is a sage, the second speaker need not be heard. For if the sage proved his point or brought the searching to an end, there was a case; if he could not, there was none. So Sextus Empiricus in *Outlines of Pyrrhonism* 1.91 may not only have used a phrase that goes back to a Stoic argument, he also offers a clue about how to understand this argument.[20] However, even if Sextus Empiricus is indeed referring to the Stoics here, it is again not clear from either passage whether the expression that the sage is dreamed up or that they dream of (practical) wisdom was endorsed by the Stoics.

The third passage, *Against the Professors* 9.133 (*SVF* 1.152 (Zeno's argument only), *SVF* 3 Diogenes of Babylon, fr. 32, LS 54D), contains the following argument:

> Zeno propounded this argument also: 'One may reasonably honour the gods; but those who are non-existent one may not reasonably honour; therefore gods exist.'
>
> But some parallel (*paraballontes*) this argument saying: 'One may reasonably honour the sages; but those who are non-existent one may not reasonably honour; therefore sages exist.'

[17] εἰ μέντοι καὶ μίαν εἶναι πάντες λέγοιεν καθ' ὑπόθεσιν τὴν περὶ τὸν βίον τέχνην, οἷον τὴν ἀοίδιμον φρόνησιν, ἥτις ὀνειροπολεῖται μὲν παρὰ Στωικοῖς, μᾶλλον δὲ πληκτικωτέρα τῶν ἄλλων εἶναι δοκεῖ, καὶ οὕτως οὐδὲν ἧττον ἀτοπίαι παρακολουθήσουσιν.

[18] ἐπὶ ἑνὸς ἀνθρώπου τὸν λόγον ἱστάντες.

[19] οὐκ ἀκουστέον ἄρα τοῦ δευτέρου λέγοντος.

[20] Cf. Glucker (1988) 488, who considers the anecdote 'no piece of philosophical doctrine, taken out of one of Zeno's serious books, but an amusing χρεία', or Repici (1993) 257, who also does not consider the possibility that the argument may make sense from the perspective of the sage.

Which conclusion was not congenial to the Stoics, as up till now their sage has not been found.[21]

The passage consists of three parts: Zeno's argument, the parallel argument and an appendix. Zeno's argument is a proof for the existence of the gods. The parallel argument, a contemporary way of attacking Zeno's cosmological arguments,[22] is a proof for the existence of the sage. Why should this be an attack? Why should the conclusion be 'not congenial' to the Stoics? The answer surely must lie in what Sextus Empiricus tells us: '[U]p till now their sage has not been found.' Although the arguments on the existence of the gods and on the existence of the sage have a parallel structure, the Stoics only endorsed the conclusion of the argument on the gods. What Sextus Empiricus tells us must thus be a report of the Stoic position, rather than his inference. Therefore, the Stoics must have held that the sage had not yet been found.[23]

Confirmation that the Stoics did not like the conclusion of the parallel argument, and that they did not think that the sage had already been found, follows from Diogenes of Babylon's reinterpretation of 'existent' in Zeno's argument, which is offered in *Against the Professors* 9.134–6 (*SVF* 3 Diogenes of Babylon, fr. 32), in the immediate continuation of Zeno's and the parallel argument. Diogenes interprets 'existent' as 'of such a nature as to exist'.[24] A distinction between gods and sages results: gods are of such a nature that they necessarily exist,

[21] Ζήνων δὲ καὶ τοιοῦτον ἠρώτα λόγον· 'τοὺς θεοὺς εὐλόγως ἄν τις τιμῴη· <τοὺς δὲ μὴ ὄντας οὐκ ἄν τις εὐλόγως τιμῴη·> εἰσὶν ἄρα θεοί.'
ᾧ λόγῳ τινὲς παραβάλλοντές φασι· 'τοὺς σοφοὺς ἄν τις εὐλόγως τιμῴη· τοὺς δὲ μὴ ὄντας οὐκ ἄν τις εὐλόγως τιμῴη· εἰσὶν ἄρα σοφοί.'
ὅπερ οὐκ ἤρεσκε τοῖς ἀπὸ τῆς Στοᾶς, μέχρι τοῦ νῦν ἀνευρέτου ὄντος τοῦ κατ' αὐτους σοφοῦ.
οὐκ ἤρεσκε can also be rendered as 'is contrary to the doctrines' (cf. τὰ ἀρέσκοντα, *placita*), but as 'the sage has not yet been found' seems strictly speaking to be an empirical observation of fact, rather than a doctrine, I prefer 'was not congenial'.

[22] On Zeno's syllogism and the parallel argument see further Schofield (1983), and *infra* Section 3.2.4c.

[23] Cf. Fabricius (1718) 582 n. 1, Schofield (1982) 15: 'But (as Sextus notes) [1]35 [i.e. sages exist – RB] is a conclusion repugnant to the Stoics, who hold that nobody has yet . . . become a sage.'

[24] πεφυκότας εἶναι rather than the ὄντας of Zeno's original argument.

whereas sages are not of such nature. If Diogenes' interpretation is applied to Zeno's argument, then Zeno's argument still stands, as the gods are of a nature as to exist, but it makes the parallel argument harmless, as the sages are not of a nature as to exist necessarily, and so it does not lead to the conclusion that the sage exists.[25]

The intermediate answer to the question on the status of the expression 'up till now the sage has not been found' is that, where *Against the Professors* 2.45 and *Outlines of Pyrrhonism* 1.91 are unclear, *Against the Professors* 9.133 is our best evidence up till now that the Stoics held that the sage has not yet been found.

3.2.2b Other parallels

More parallels to [iiA] can be found in the writings of Cicero and Seneca. Cicero offers at least six passages in which our expression appears. In two cases it is mentioned only in passing, when Cicero or one of his dialogue characters criticises the Stoics. In *On Ends* 4.65 Cicero criticises the Stoics for their doctrine that there is no difference among the non-virtuous, and then exclaims: 'And yet there was no sage: for who is one? where? where from?'[26] And in *On Divination* 2.61 Cicero, in relation to a Chrysippean argument directed against the existence of portents, introduces the non-existence of the sage thus: 'It happens more often that a mule begets than that a sage comes into existence.'[27] In these cases the doctrine of the non-existence of the sage is never directly attacked, but is mentioned in passing in an attack against another Stoic doctrine. The suggestion is thus that the observation that the sage has yet to be found is again another weird doctrine held by the Stoics.

The third Ciceronian passage is *Tusculan Disputations* 2.51, which gives us a description of the sage: 'The man in whom there shall be perfect wisdom – whom until now we have not

[25] On this earliest ontological argument for the existence of the gods see Schofield (1982) and Brunschwig (1994).

[26] *nec tamen ille erat sapiens: quis enim hoc aut quando aut ubi aut unde?*

[27] *saepius enim mulam peperisse arbitror quam sapientem fuisse.*

seen, but what he will be like, if he will come into existence one day, has been described in the doctrines of the philosophers – this person then or such reason that will be perfect and absolute in him.'[28] Although Cicero does not attribute the passage explicitly to the Stoics, book 2 is generally considered to be influenced by Stoicism,[29] and furthermore, the description of the sage as 'absolute' reason is Stoic. As the passage says that the sage has not yet come into existence, but may come into existence one day, this is therefore most likely to be Stoic, too.

Two passages that contain expressions similar to 'that the sage has not yet come into existence' are *On Proper Functions* 3.14–16 and *On Friendship* 18. In *On Proper Functions* 3.14–16 Cicero explicitly attributes to the Stoics the distinction between second-rate proper functions, which he will speak about in book 3 and the perfect proper functions of the sage, which he will not deal with, as no one has yet proven to be wise 'as we want to understand wise'.[30] The sceptical reader may still object that this is an exposition of Stoic doctrine followed by Cicero's own inference about the non-existence of the sage. In *On Friendship* 18 Cicero makes it clear that he will discuss friendship from the perspective of everyday life and that he will pass over the real friendship that can be found with the wise only. (He repeats the distinction with regard to virtue in 21.) He will pass over the real friendship as 'wisdom is interpreted such that no human being has until now been able to attain it'.[31] People that were considered wise by our forefathers, Cicero explains, 'were not wise by their standards'.[32] Here Cicero's formulations are such that they cannot be dismissed as his own inferences about the unattainability of wisdom. But in *On Friendship* there is another problem: Cicero does not

[28] *in quo vero erit perfecta sapientia – quem adhuc nos quidem vidimus neminem; sed philosophorum sententiis, qualis hic futurus sit, si modo aliquando fuerit, exponitur –, is igitur sive ea ratio, quae erit in eo perfecta atque absoluta.*

[29] Cf. Dougan (1904) xxv. On the Stoic character of many arguments in book 2 of the *Tusculan Disputations* see e.g. Gawlick and Görler (1994) 1042.

[30] *ut sapientem volumus intellegi.*

[31] *eam sapientiam interpretantur, quam adhuc mortalis nemo est consecutus.*

[32] *numquam ego dicam C. Fabricium, M. Curium, Ti. Coruncanium, quos sapientes nostri maiores iudicabant, ad istorum normam fuisse sapientes.*

explicitly tell us who offers this interpretation of wisdom 'such that no human being until now has been able to attain it', or who are the 'they' that held these standards. However, as *On Proper Functions* 3.14–16 offers a similar distinction between 'everyday' and 'real', there clearly attributed to the Stoics, *On Friendship* 18 is likely to express a Stoic distinction, too, and thus the 'interpretation' or the 'they' is likely refer to the Stoics, or in other words: the expression that 'the sage has not yet been found' is likely to be Stoic, too.[33]

I will end my brief presentation of the Ciceronian passages with *On the Nature of the Gods* 3.79, in which the theme that the sage has not yet been found nicely illustrates the difference between the Stoic and the Academic position. Cicero's character Cotta, of Academic persuasion, presents the following syllogism which, like the syllogisms in Sextus Empiricus, *Against the Professors* 7.432 and *Against the Professors* 2.45, contains the minor premiss that no one has yet attained wisdom:

> For if by the general consent of all philosophers foolishness is a greater evil than all the evils of fortune and of the body when put together on the other side,
>
> and yet no one has attained wisdom,
>
> we, for whose welfare you say that the gods have cared most fully, are really in the depth of misfortune. For just as it makes no difference whether no one *is* in good health or no one *can be* in good health, so I do not understand what difference it makes whether no one *is* wise or no one *can be* wise.[34]

The Stoicism of the minor premiss is confirmed by the explanatory sentence, which contains the Academic criticism of a Stoic distinction. The Academic sees no difference, or rather does not want to see the difference, between the assertion that no one at this moment *is* healthy or wise and the assertion that no one *can be* healthy or wise. But this distinction must be crucial

[33] On the Stoic character of the *On Friendship* passage see e.g. Seyffert and Müller (1876) 107, Reid (1879) 83, Ganss (1952) 94, Steinmetz (1967) 9–10, Powell (1990) 86.

[34] *nam si stultitia consensu omnium philosophorum maius est malum quam si omnia mala et fortunae et corporis ex altera parte ponantur,*
sapientiam autem nemo adsequitur,
in summis malis omnes sumus, quibus vos optume consultum a dis inmortalibus dicitis. nam ut nihil interest utrum nemo valeat an nemo possit valere, sic non intellego quid intersit utrum nemo sit sapiens an nemo esse possit.

to the Stoics. For the Stoics could agree with the Academics that no one is wise, but held on to the possibility that someone might become wise.[35]

Next, Seneca, who is usually considered a follower of the core doctrines of the founders of the Stoic school,[36] also speaks of the non-existence of the sage. If you want to follow a living paradigm, you had better choose the least bad, Seneca says in *On Tranquillity* 7.4: 'Yet I would not prescribe that you are to follow, or attach to yourself, no one but a sage. For where do you find him, whom we sought for so many centuries? Choose as the best the least bad.'[37] Although sometimes Seneca tries to make a case for Marcus Porcius Cato Uticensis as a sage, as in *On Constancy* 7.1:

> There is no reason for you to say, Serenus, as your habit is, that this wise man of ours is nowhere to be found. He is not a fiction of us Stoics, a sort of phantom glory of human nature, nor is he a mere conception, the mighty semblance of a thing unreal, but we have shown him in the flesh just as we delineate him, and shall show him – though perchance not often, and after a long lapse of years only one. For greatness that transcends the limit of the ordinary and common type is produced but rarely. But this self-same Marcus Cato, the mention of whom started this discussion, I almost think surpasses even our exemplar.[38]

But Seneca's attempt to describe Cato (or rather his act of suicide[39]) as wise is of course no proof of the fact that the early Stoics had found a sage. Seneca's attempt, far from

[35] *Lucullus* 145 is sometimes cited in this context too (as e.g. by Reid (1885) *ad loc.*). See further Section 3.2.4c, n. 106.

[36] On Seneca as a follower of early Stoic doctrines see e.g. Rist (1989), Inwood (1993) 150–1/(2005) 24: '[Seneca] is prepared to propose changes in traditional Stoicism, but those changes never threaten the core of Stoic ideas', Grimal (1994) 107, Boys-Stones (2001) 18.

[37] *nec hoc praeceperim tibi, ut neminem nisi sapientem sequaris aut adtrahas. ubi enim istum invenies quem tot saeculis quaerimus? pro optimo sit minime malus.*

[38] *non est quod dicas, ita ut soles, hunc sapientem nostrum nusquam inveniri. non fingimus istud humani ingenii vanum decus nec ingentem imaginem falsae rei concipimus, sed qualem conformamus exhibuimus, exhibebimus, raro forsitan magnisque aetatium intervallis unum; neque enim magna et excedentia solitum ac vulgarem modum crebro gignuntur. ceterum hic ipse M. Cato, a cuius mentione haec disputatio processit, vereor ne supra nostrum exemplar sit.*

[39] Cf. Alexander (1946) 64: 'With Seneca a single historical event [i.e. Cato's suicide] becomes the consummation of a whole system of philosophic belief.' For Cato's suicide see esp. Plutarch, *Life of Cato the Younger* 66–71.

contradicting the view that the Hellenistic Stoics held that no sage has yet been found, tends to confirm it.[40]

As with the Sextan parallel passages in Section 3.2.2a we again find passages that leave us in doubt as to whether the expression that the sage has not been found was formulated by the Stoics or by the Stoics' adversaries. However, notably Cicero, *On Friendship* 18 and Seneca, *On Tranquillity* 7.4 make it clear that the Stoics themselves formulated or endorsed it.[41]

3.2.2c 'Rarer than the phoenix'

In two other reports related to the Stoics we do not read that the sage has yet to be found, but that the sage is 'rarer than the Ethiopians' phoenix', or 'as rare as the phoenix', and moreover that one or two sages have existed. We will have to decide whether this is Stoic, too and, if so, whether it contradicts the other formulation that 'the sage has not yet been found'.

The first report is by the Aristotelian Alexander of Aphrodisias in his *On Fate* 199.14–22 (*SVF* 3.658, LS 61N), written in the second century CE:

> If according to them virtue and vice are the only things that are good and bad, respectively, and none of the other living creatures [than human beings]

[40] Cf. Pohlenz (1992) 267: 'Und damit gab Cato der Stoa jedenfalls für Rom etwas, was ihr bisher gefehlt hatte: sie war nicht mehr auf das Phantasiebild des Weisen angewiesen, sondern hatte von nun an eine ideale historische Persönlichkeit, an der sie sich aufrichten konnte.'

[41] Two even more doubtful passages can be found in Plutarch and Quintilian. In Plutarch, *On Common Notions* 1076A–B ('They [the Stoics] say that a human being not being deficient in virtue has no lack of happiness, but that the unfortunate (τὸν ἀτυχῆ) is blessed equal to Zeus the Saviour, even when he commits suicide because of bodily disease and mutilation, if he be a sage. But this sage does not exist anywhere on earth, nor has he ever existed') the expression about the non-existence of the sage in the second sentence could be read as a report of Stoic doctrine, but as 'the unfortunate' in the first sentence should reflect Plutarch's usual depreciation of the Stoic sage in the position of bodily disease and mutilation, the status of the whole passage as evidence for Stoicism becomes unclear. In Quintilian, *Institutions* pr. 19 ('Most of the ancients . . . supposed that the sage had not yet been found') the reference of 'the ancients' is as broad (see e.g. *Institutions* 9.3.1: *omnes veteres et Cicero praecipue*) as it is obscure. However, Quintilian's negative stance towards his contemporaries (see e.g. von Schwabe (1909) 1860, Winterbottom (1964) 90–7), as well as his positive stance towards the Stoics (see e.g. Appel (1914) 13–5, 39–41, Lévy (2010) 120–2) may be good reasons to think that Quintilian (also) refers to the Stoics.

> are capable of receiving either of them; and if most men are bad, or rather, if there have been just one or two good men, as is fabulously related by them, like some absurd and unnatural creature rarer than the Ethiopians' phoenix, and if all bad man are as bad as each other, without any differentiation, and all who are not wise are alike mad,
>
> how could man not be the most miserable of all the creatures in having vice and madness innate in him and allotted?[42]

The first part of the passage, until Alexander's question, is in fact a long conditional, in which Alexander seems to offer a report of Stoic doctrines. After beginning with the Stoics' absolute distinction between virtue and vice and their contention that most people are vicious, he then adds a new element: 'It is related fabulously by them that one or two sages have come into existence.' Some modern scholars have interpreted this expression as that according to the Stoics the sage has indeed come into existence, and that he should be identified with Socrates, or the Cynic Diogenes of Sinope (*c.* 412/403–324/321).[43]

But there are two problems with this interpretation. In the first place, there is little evidence that suggests that the early Stoics acknowledged Socrates or Diogenes as a sage.[44] In fact only two passages are relevant here. The first passage is strictly speaking not evidence on the early Stoics, but rather on Posidonius. It is, however, often discussed in this context. It is unfortunately anything but clear. According to Diogenes

[42] εἰ γὰρ ἡ μὲν ἀρετή τε καὶ ἡ κακία μόναι κατ' αὐτοὺς ἡ μὲν ἀγαθόν, ἡ δὲ κακόν, καὶ οὐδὲν τῶν ἄλλων ζῴων οὐδετέρου τούτων ἐστὶν ἐπιδεκτικόν, τῶν δὲ ἀνθρώπων οἱ πλεῖστοι κακοί, μᾶλλον δὲ ἀγαθὸς μὲν εἷς ἢ δεύτερος ὑπ' αὐτῶν γεγονέναι μυθεύεται, ὥσπερ τι παράδοξον ζῷον καὶ παρὰ φύσιν σπανιώτερον τοῦ φοίνικος τοῦ παρ' Αἰθίοψιν, οἱ δὲ πάντες κακοὶ καὶ ἐπίσης ἀλλήλοις τοιοῦτοι, ὡς μηδὲν διαφέρειν ἄλλον ἄλλου, μαίνεσθαι δὲ ὁμοίως πάντας ὅσοι μὴ σοφοί,
πῶς οὐκ ἂν ἀθλιώτατον ζῷον ἁπάντων ὁ ἄνθρωπος εἴη, ἔχων τήν τε κακίαν καὶ τὸ μαίνεσθαι σύμφυτα αὑτῷ καὶ συγκεκληρωμένα;

[43] See e.g. Hirzel (1882) 281, Kerferd (1978) 127, LS vol. 2, 367. Interestingly, neither of them provides evidence for this identification.

[44] As for Socrates, also later Stoics, such as Epictetus in the extant works, are reluctant to refer to Socrates as a sage. Remarkably, in the long list of passages in Long (2002) 37, where Epictetus alludes to the Stoic sage in the early Stoic manner, Socrates is only once referred to as an example of the highly traditional καλὸς καὶ ἀγαθός person (4.5.1), which offers little support for Long's contention that 'for Epictetus, Socrates was not an approximation to wisdom but the paradigm of a genuinely wise person' (33). For an assessment of Diogenes among later Stoics, such as Epictetus, see Long (2002) 58.

Laertius 7.91 (fr. 29 Edelstein and Kidd, Diogenes fr. 512 Giannantoni, Antisthenes (around 400 BCE) fr. 137 Giannantoni): 'Posidonius in his first book *On Ethics* says that evidence for virtue existing is the fact that (those around?) Socrates, Diogenes and Antisthenes got to a state of progress.'[45] The ambiguity lies in the use of *hoi peri*, literally 'those around'. In principle it can be used to refer exclusively to (i) the followers of some persons, but in Hellenistic and later Greek texts it usually refers inclusively to (ii) the person and his followers, or even (iii) the person himself only.[46] If *hoi peri* is read exclusively, it can be inferred from this passage that the followers of Socrates etc. would have made progress, and that Socrates, etc. are perhaps sages.[47] ('Progress' (*prokopē*) is the technical term the Stoics used to designate someone who is on the right track to becoming a sage, but who is still an inferior person.[48]) If *hoi peri* is read inclusively, Socrates, etc. would also be on the right track. This inclusive 'Hellenistic and later Greek' usage applies to Diogenes Laertius, too: the expression is popular with Diogenes Laertius, especially in book 7.[49] Only in a few cases does the context suggest that the person himself is meant.[50]

[45] τεκμήριον δὲ τοῦ ὑπαρκτὴν εἶναι τὴν ἀρετήν φησιν ὁ Ποσειδώνιος ἐν τῷ α' τοῦ Ἠθικοῦ λόγου τὸ γενέσθαι ἐν προκοπῇ τοὺς περὶ Σωκράτη, Διογένη, Ἀντισθένη.

[46] For the general account see Kühner-Gerth (1898) no. 403d ('eine Person mit ihren Begleitern, Anhängern, Schülern ... Erst bei den griechischen Grammatikern ... eine Person allein'), Kidd (1988) 37 and Gorman (2001) 201–5, who modifies Radt (1980) 47 ('immer inklusiv'). For an exception see Alexander of Aphrodisias, *On Fate* 171.11–15 (I owe this reference to David Sedley), where Socrates is said to disagree with his associates: εἰπόντος γοῦν Ζωπύρου τοῦ φυσιογνώμονος περὶ Σωκράτους τοῦ φιλοσόφου ἄτοπά τινα καὶ πλεῖστον ἀφεστῶτα τῆς προαιρέσεως αὐτοῦ τῆς κατὰ τὸν βίον καὶ ἐπὶ τούτοις ὑπὸ τῶν περὶ τὸν Σωκράτη καταγελωμένου οὐδὲν εἶπεν ὁ Σωκράτης ἐψεῦσθαι τὸν Ζώπυρον.

[47] Bonhöffer (1894) 217 n. 1, unfortunately unaware of its different meanings and taking οἱ περί in its exclusive meaning only, remarks that the reference to the pupils is then in fact superfluous, and that it would have been sufficient to point to the wisdom of the masters.

[48] On 'progress' or 'the person who makes progress' (προκόπτων) see e.g. Bonhöffer (1894) 144–53, Luschnat (1958), Decleva Caizzi and Funghi (1988) 85–124, Hengelbrock (2000) 9–22 and Roskam (2005).

[49] It occurs in book 7 in 32, 68 (5 times), 76, 84 (7 times), 92 (4 times), 128, 144, and 146, and elsewhere in 1.12, 1.30, 2.24, 2.38, 2.43, 2.62, 2.77, 2.105, 2.134, 4.41, 9.42, 9.46, 9.62, 9.88, 9.107, 10.4, 10.8.

[50] The clearest example is in 2.77, where the reference is to Bion, 'who in his *Dissertations* says: ...', cf. 1.12, where Homer and Hesiod are likely to be referred to as sages, in 2.62, where Plato and Aristippus are 'held in high esteem'.

In the other cases (with the exception of 10.8, where Epicurus distinguishes between Plato and his associates) it is at least probable that the person himself is meant,[51] and that the person himself could be included. Applied to our passage, this means that *hoi peri* in Diogenes Laertius 7.91 most likely includes Socrates, Diogenes and Antisthenes, or even refers to them only.[52]

The second passage, not very well known, is anything but ambiguous. It is contained in the *Address to the Greeks* by the Christian theologian Tatian (second century). At 3.2 (not in von Arnim's *SVF*, although the passage links *SVF* 1.109 and 1.159) Tatian states that Zeno did consider Socrates a sage, or – in his Christian terminology with an allusion to the Day of Judgement – that 'Zeno in his account of the conflagration introduces more wicked than just persons – one Socrates and a Heracles, and a few more others'.[53] Of course, this puts *hoi peri* in Diogenes Laertius 7.91 in a different light, too: if we accept the Tatian passage (as von Arnim apparently did not), the Diogenes passage may well be an exception to the general Hellenistic usage, and thus understood exclusively.[54] I will return to the assessment of Socrates as a sage in more detail in Section 4.5.

A second problem with the identification of the one or two sages in the passage in Alexander of Aphrodisias' *On Fate* is that it does not explain why Alexander would report that 'it has been "related fabulously" (*mutheuetai*) by them' that there are one or two sages. Socrates and Diogenes are historical personalities; there appears to be no need to relate fabulously about them. A way out of these difficulties could of

[51] See Kidd (1988) 37: 'Diogenes Laertius appears to incline to this usage.'

[52] See Kidd (1988) 153 (cf. (1999) 85): 'Even the traditional great figures … are represented as merely progressors.'

[53] ὅστις [sc. Zeno] ἐν τῷ κατὰ τὴν ἐκπύρωσιν λόγῳ πλείονας τοὺς μοχθηροὺς τῶν δικαίων εἰσηγεῖται, Σωκράτους ἑνὸς καὶ Ἡρακλέους καί τινων ἄλλων τοιούτων, γεγονότων ὀλίγων καὶ οὐ πολλῶν.

[54] As Sedley (2007) 233 n. 67 does, connecting it with a psychological argument: 'Socrates, Diogenes, and Antisthenes must have possessed virtue or they would not have been so succesful at promoting moral progress in their pupils.' On this psychological argument see *infra* n. 92.

course be to dismiss the expression 'to relate fabulously' as Alexander's own hostile expression. But for one thing this goes against the nature of the first part of the passage as an exposition of Stoic doctrine. Thus far in the passage no un-Stoic elements have yet been encountered (and this will remain so: for the phoenix see my discussion immediately below, and the doctrine that all vices are equal is perfectly Stoic, too). Moreover, if we were to take Alexander to report that one or two sages have indeed come into existence, this would contradict the reports we saw earlier that the sage has yet to be found. A simple solution for all these problems is to take 'to relate fabulously' literally. The Stoics maintained that in a mythological past one or two sages have come into existence. The passage would thus remain completely Stoic, and it would not contradict the earlier reports (with the exception of the Tatian passage, of course) that in historical times the sage has not yet been found. This literal reading is furthermore strengthened by the mention of the mythological creature the phoenix that, as myth has it, is a rare bird that comes into existence every five hundred years and which in one version after a long life is burned by fire, but rises from the ashes and gets a new life.[55] The reference to the phoenix can definitely not be dismissed as Alexander's own way of speaking, for it also occurs in the earlier, first-century CE account, in Seneca's *Letter* 42.1:

Do you know what kind of man I now mean when I speak of a 'good man'? I mean one of the second grade, like your friend. For one of the first class perhaps springs into existence, like the phoenix, only once in five hundred years. And it is not surprising, either, that greatness develops only at long intervals; fortune often brings into being commonplace powers, which are born to please the mob; but she holds for our approval that which is extraordinary by the very fact that she makes it rare.[56]

[55] I have followed the formulation by Türk in Roscher (1884–1937) vol. 3, 3450–66.

[56] *iam tibi iste persuasit virum se bonum esse? atqui vir bonus tam cito nec fieri potest nec intellegi. Scis quem nunc virum bonum dicam? hunc secundae notae; nam ille alter fortasse tamquam phoenix semel anno quingentesimo nascitur. nec est mirum ex intervallo magna generari: mediocria et in turbam nascentia saepe fortuna producit, eximia vero ipsa raritate commendat.*

I leave aside the distinction between first- and second-class sages, as only first-class sages are real sages, and second-class 'sages' are in fact not sages at all, but those ordinarily thought of as sages.[57] The reference to the phoenix thus seems to be Stoic. We can go even a step further by identifying these one or two (first-class) sages with mythological figures. There is evidence that the Stoics identified these 'one or two sages' with Odysseus and Heracles. This comes out clearly in Seneca's *On Constancy* 2.1, in his attempt to present a case for Cato's wisdom: 'The immortal gods had given us in Cato a more assured example of the wise man than Odysseus and Hercules in earlier centuries. For we Stoics have proclaimed that these were wise men, not being conquered by effort, despising pleasure, and victorious over the whole world.'[58] Further evidence for Odysseus as a Stoic sage is to be found especially in ps.-Plutarch, *On Homer* 2.136, who reports that the Stoics found Odysseus described as a sage in two passages in the *Odyssey*, 4.242–6 (Odysseus bravely entering Troy in rags) and 9.29–33 (Odysseus resisting both Calypso and Circe), and that the Stoics compared him favourably to Achilles.[59] Further evidence for Heracles as a Stoic sage is preserved by the presumably first-century CE allegorist Heraclitus, *Homeric Problems* 33.1, who describes Heracles as 'an intelligent man and an initiate [*mustēs*] in heavenly wisdom ..., as also the most famous of the Stoics agree'.[60] The portrayal of Heracles in Seneca's (?) tragedy *Hercules on*

[57] Similar to the distinction offered in Cicero, *On Proper Functions* 3.14–16 and *On Friendship* 18, mentioned in Section 2.2.2.

[58] *Catonem autem certius exemplar sapientis viri nobis deos inmortalis dedisse quam Ulixem et Herculem prioribus saeculis. hos enim Stoici nostri sapientes pronuntiaverunt, invictos laboribus et contemptores voluptatis et victores omnium terrarum.* With Pfister (1937) 44 I see no need to change the *terrarum* of the *consensus codicum* into the un-Stoic *terrorum* (un-Stoic, as for the sage there are no terrors) as suggested by Lipsius and followed by modern editors such as Reynolds (1977) and Costa (1994).

[59] See Buffière (1956) 374–7, Hillgruber (1994–9) 304. Further late Stoic evidence can be found in Epictetus, *Dissertations* 1.12.3, 3.24.13, 3.24.18–20, 3.26.33–4, fr. 11, Heraclitus, *Homeric Problems* 70, discussed by Stanford (1963) 121–7.

[60] ἀνὴρ ἔμφρων καὶ σοφίας οὐρανίου μύστης ..., καθάπερ ὁμολογοῦσι καὶ Στωικῶν οἱ δοκιμώτατοι.

Mount Oeta,[61] and as 'reason in the whole, under which aspect nature is strong and powerful'[62] by Cleanthes (?) *ap*. Cornutus (first century CE), *Compendium of Greek Theology* 31 (*SVF* 1.514) can be mentioned in this context, too.[63]

So Alexander of Aphrodisias' report with the expressions 'rarer than the Ethiopians' phoenix' and 'that there have been just one or two good men' turns out to contain a correct report on the rarity of the sage according to early Stoics, in line with the expression in [iiA] that (with the possible exception of the intriguing case of Socrates, to which I will come back in Section 4.5) 'up till now the sage has not been found'.

3.2.3 *The inference in Sextus Empiricus*

[iiiA] contains the claim that 'it follows necessarily that the true has also not been found, and that because of this all things turn out to be incognitive'. Can this inference be endorsed by a Stoic? A Stoic would point to two distinctions: between true and truth, and between cognitions and secure cognitions.

The first distinction has been preserved by Sextus Empiricus. In *Against the Professors* 7.38–45 (*SVF* 2.132, *FDS* 324), immediately before starting his discussion of the criterion, Sextus Empiricus sets out the Stoic distinction between the truth and the true, stating at 38: 'Some, especially the Stoics, think that truth differs from the true in three ways: in being, in composition and in power.'[64] It is not necessary to deal with all three

[61] On Heracles and the Stoics see Edert (1909) 47–59. For the Cynic background to Heracles as a sage see Höistad (1948) 22–72. On the tragedy see Edert (1909) 29 ff., Ackermann (1912) 426: 'H[ercules] O[etaus] eine Verherrlichung des stoischen Weisen', Pfister (1937) 44. Cf. Ackermann (1907) 412: *Herculem ... qui deus in caelum receptus sit, lectoribus Herculem exemplum ad imitandum proponat* [sc. Seneca].

[62] ὁ ἐν τοῖς ὅλοις λόγος καθ' ὃν ἡ φύσις ἰσχυρὰ καὶ κραταιά ἐστιν.

[63] See also Plutarch, *Isis and Osiris* 367C (*SVF* 2.1093): 'The Stoics say that the breath ... that is powerful and problem solving is Heracles' (ἐκεῖνοι τὸ μὲν γόνιμον πνεῦμα καὶ τρόφιμον Διόνυσον εἶναι λέγουσι, τὸ πληκτικὸν δὲ καὶ διαιρετικὸν Ἡρακλέα). 'Powerful' (πληκτικὸν) reminds one of the πληγὴ πυρὸς in Cleanthes' *Physical Treatises* (*ap*. Plutarch, *On Stoic Contradictions* 1034D) and the πληγή of Zeus's thunderbolt in the *Hymn to Zeus* l. 11, both discussed in Section 2.2.3c.

[64] τὴν δὲ ἀλήθειαν οἴονταί τινες, καὶ μάλιστα οἱ ἀπὸ τῆς Στοᾶς, διαφέρειν τἀληθοῦς κατὰ τρεῖς τρόπους, οὐσίᾳ τε καὶ συστάσει καὶ δυνάμει.

distinctions here, just the last one, 'in power'.[65] The Stoics said that truth belonged to the sage exclusively, whereas the true can belong to the sage and the inferior person alike. For, at 42 we find: 'The true is not at all dependent upon knowledge . . . , but the truth is considered according to knowledge.'[66] Truth is therefore possessed by the sage only, which the true is not: 'For in fact the inferior person and the infant and the madman at times say something true, but they do not possess knowledge of the true.'[67]

A parallel passage can be found in *Outlines of Pyrrhonism* 2.83 (*FDS* 322), although this time it is not explicitly ascribed to the Stoics: 'Therefore they say that truth exists only in the sage, but the true also in the inferior person; for it is possible for the inferior person to utter something true.'[68] The true is not dependent upon knowledge. The inferior person, the infant and the madman, who have no knowledge, may at times say something true.

A similar distinction was made with regard to cognitions. As we have seen in Section 2.2.2b, the Stoics distinguished sharply between cognitions, on the one hand, and stable cognitions or knowledge, on the other. Just as an inferior person can at times say something true, he can at times have a cognition. Just as an inferior person has no truth, he has no stable cognitions. And just as truth exists only in the sage, only the sage has stable cognitions.[69]

Thus the Stoics did not endorse the claim that the true cannot be discovered, nor that no cognitions are possible. Against the background of these distinctions [iiiA] is not an

[65] The first way, 'being', is that the truth is corporeal, whereas the true is not. The second way, 'composition', is that the truth is composite and the true is simple. The distinctions are discussed by Bridoux (1966) 90–1, Goldschmidt (1979) 165–6 and esp. Long (1978a) 297–315. Annas and Barnes (2000) 87–8 unfortunately translate the distinction between ἀλήθεια and ἀληθές with 'truth' and 'truths', respectively.

[66] τὸ μὲν ἀληθὲς οὐ πάντως ἐπιστήμης εἴχετο . . ., ἡ δὲ ἀλήθεια κατ' ἐπιστήμην θεωρεῖται.

[67] καὶ γὰρ ὁ φαῦλος καὶ ὁ νήπιος καὶ ὁ μεμηνὼς λέγει μέν ποτέ τι ἀληθές, οὐκ ἔχει δὲ ἐπιστήμην ἀληθοῦς.

[68] διόπερ τὴν μὲν ἀλήθειαν ἐν μόνῳ σπουδαίῳ φασὶν εἶναι, τὸ δὲ ἀληθὲς καὶ ἐν φαύλῳ· ἐνδέχεται γὰρ τὸν φαῦλον ἀληθές τι εἰπεῖν.

[69] In a similar manner the Stoics distinguished between a 'proper function' (καθῆκον) and a 'perfect proper function' or 'right action' (κατόρθωμα).

account that a Stoic could endorse. In *Against the Professors* 7.432 Sextus Empiricus seems to have blurred the distinctions, which he had himself carefully discussed earlier. But, of course, Sextus Empiricus' primary interest is to fight the Stoics' dogmatic doctrines rather than to be a faithful presenter of Stoic doctrine. So [iiiA] is definitely a Sextan inference.

I close my discussion of [i]–[iv] in *Against the Professors* 7.432–3 with a brief mention of [iiB], [iiiB] and [iv]. [iiB], which reads 'we are all inferior persons', and the inference [iiiB], 'we have no stable cognition of existing things', could also be endorsed by a Stoic. However, the Stoic would point out that it does not mean that the inferior person can have no cognitions at all. [iv], at the beginning of *Against the Professors* 7.433, 'it cannot be other than that the things that were brought forward by the Stoics against the Sceptics are said by the Sceptics against the Stoics' is thus correct, too, although only as far as concerns the fact that up till now the truth and stable cognitions have not been found. My interim conclusion is thus that [i]–[iv] in *Against the Professors* 7.432–3, were endorsed by the Stoics, with the exception of [iiiA] only.

3.2.4 The Stoics

Sextus Empiricus states in [v]: '[A]ccording to the Stoics themselves, Zeno and Cleanthes and Chrysippus and the others from their school are reckoned among the inferior persons.' It is a perfectly valid inference from [iiA] interpreted as a Stoic thesis: since according to the Stoics themselves the sage has not been found, the Stoics could not have declared themselves sages. We find the account that the Stoics themselves did not consider themselves sages also in two other Sextan passages, in *Against the Professors* 11.181: 'If the expertise of life, consisting in practical wisdom, is virtue, and only the sage has virtue; the Stoics not being sages will not possess practical wisdom, nor some expertise of life',[70] and more briefly in the parallel of

[70] εἰ γὰρ ἡ μὲν περὶ τὸν βίον τέχνη φρόνησις οὖσα ἔστιν ἀρετή, τὴν δὲ ἀρετὴν μόνος εἶχεν ὁ σοφός, οἱ Στωικοὶ μὴ ὄντες σοφοὶ οὐχ ἕξουσι φρόνησιν οὐδὲ τέχνην τινὰ περὶ τὸν βίον.

Outlines of Pyrrhonism 3.240: 'For if practical wisdom is a virtue, and only the sage has virtue, the Stoics not being sages have no expertise of life.'[71] 'The Stoics not being sages' is again inserted as a subsidiary premiss and although the expressions as such or their immediate contexts do not make clear whether the Stoics endorsed these expressions themselves, after our discussion in Section 3.2.3 there seems to be no serious objection to assuming that they did.[72]

But an objection can nevertheless be formulated based on the following passage. Quintilian, *Institutions* 12.1.18–19 (*SVF* 1.44, *FDS* 127), asked whether Cicero and Demosthenes can be considered to be perfect orators, replies 'in the manner in which the Stoics would reply':

> But even if these men lacked the perfection of virtue, I will respond to those who ask if they were orators, in the manner in which the Stoics would reply, if asked whether Zeno, Cleanthes and Chrysippus themselves were sages. I shall say that these men were important and worthy of our veneration, but that they did not achieve what is the highest in the nature of man. For did not Pythagoras desire that he should not be called a wise man, like the sages who preceded him, but rather a lover of wisdom (*studiosum sapientiae*)?[73]

At first sight this passage seems to confirm that the Stoics did not consider themselves to be sages. But theoretically an objection is possible here: for Quintilian's Stoics, who were asked whether Zeno, Cleanthes and Chrysippus were sages, could be later Stoics. These later Stoics would have come to the conclusion that, contrary to what these early Stoics thought themselves, Zeno and his immediate followers were no sages. If this were true, it would put the passages discussed in Section 3.2.2 in an altogether different perspective. For if in these passages

[71] ἐπεὶ γὰρ φρόνησίς ἐστιν ἀρετή, τὴν δὲ ἀρετὴν μόνος εἶχεν ὁ σοφός, οἱ Στωικοὶ μὴ ὄντες σοφοὶ οὐχ ἕξουσι τὴν περὶ τὸν βίον τέχνην.

[72] As such it was understood by the invaluable Fabricius (1718) *ad locc.* and Bett (1997) 198.

[73] *quod si defuit his viris summa virtus, sic quaerentibus an oratores fuerint respondebo quo modo Stoici, si interrogentur an sapiens Zenon, an Cleanthes, an Chrysippus ipse, respondeant, magnos quidem illos ac venerabiles, non tamen id quod natura hominis summum habet consecutos. nam et Pythagoras non sapientem se, ut qui ante eum fuerunt, sed studiosum sapientiae vocari voluit.*

reference is made to the Stoics, we should consider the possibility that only later Stoics are referred to.

To give this objection at least some *prima facie* plausibility, one should ask the question as to what the motivation of these later Stoics could have been to distort the position of the early Stoics. Hirzel's suggestion was that under the influence of their Cynic teachers, Zeno and the other early scholarchs would have considered themselves sages. Only with later Stoics would Cynic arrogance have disappeared.[74] Perhaps this suggestion should be connected with the depreciation of the Cynic doctrines of the founders of the school. In order to make Stoicism respectable to the very conservative Roman elite, later Stoics, such as Panaetius (*c.* 185–109), did try to hide provocative doctrines, such as the allowance of incest or cannibalism, held by the founders of their school.[75] As for the abandonment of these Cynic doctrines within Stoicism, the same late Stoics were perhaps also responsible for not considering the early Stoics sages any more.

The best way to assess this objection and, if true, to find a more proper interpretation of the motives of these later Stoics, is to consider the evidence with regard to individual early Stoics. The remainder of this chapter will therefore be devoted to a discussion of the little evidence there is with regard to the positions of the founders of the Stoic school. I will present them in chronological order, as Sextus Empiricus also does by dealing with Zeno, Cleanthes and Chrysippus in [vi], [vii] and [viii]. However, as Hirzel gives attention to some anecdotes with regard to two of Zeno's immediate followers, Sphaerus

[74] Hirzel (1882) 274, 276. See also Section 3.2.4c.

[75] The embarrassment about these has been identified as Panaetius' on the basis of Cicero, *On Proper Functions* 1.99 (fr. 107 Van Straaten, fr. 72 Alesse; in Cicero's discussion of Panaetius' notion of *decorum*) and 1.128 (fr. 73 Alesse). The embarrassment can also be found in Philodemus, *On the Stoics* col. 14.1–16 Dorandi, in Cicero, *On Ends* 3.68 (*SVF* 3.645), in Epictetus, *Dissertations* 3.22, and in Diogenes Laertius 7.34, in which it is ascribed to Stoics whose opinion was followed by the Pergamene librarian Athenodorus the Stoic, who expunged passages from Zeno's *Politeia* (for the vandalism see further Schofield (1999) 7). Cf. Mansfeld (1986) 347–9. The provocative *Cynica* are conveniently assembled in *SVF* 1.250–7 and 3.743–56.

and Persaeus, who are not mentioned by Sextus Empiricus, I will start by dealing with them.

3.2.4a Sphaerus

Anecdotes may, of course, not be worth much. But Hirzel (1882, 274–6) uses them to include Sphaerus and Persaeus among the Stoics who considered themselves wise. My aim here is to show that this conclusion does not necessarily follow from these anecdotes. The (one) anecdote on Sphaerus is reported both by Diogenes Laertius and Athenaeus (around 200 CE), the author of the *Learned Banqueters*, the tale of an extravagant dinner and drinking party.[76] I shall quote the version in Diogenes Laertius 7.177 (*SVF* 1.625, LS 40F, *FDS* 381). The setting is the Ptolemaic court in Alexandria:

> One day a conversation took place on whether the wise man would hold opinions, and Sphaerus said that he would not. Wishing to refute him, the king ordered wax pomegranates to be placed before him. Sphaerus was deceived and the king cried out that he had given his assent to a false impression. Sphaerus gave him a shrewd answer, saying that his assent was not [to the impression] that they were pomegranates but [to the impression] that it was reasonable that they were pomegranates. He pointed out that the cognitive impression is different from the reasonable one.[77]

According to Hirzel, if Sphaerus had not considered himself to be a sage, he should simply have declined the honour of answering the challenge. As he did not, it proves that he considered himself to be a sage.[78] So initially Sphaerus may have thought he was a sage, but was proven to be no such thing. To save his face he gave a clever answer.

But on closer inspection it turns out that the refutation of Sphaerus' alleged wisdom is not the thrust of the anecdote, for two reasons. In the first place the interpretation in which

[76] Modern discussions include Brennan (1996) 318–34 and Striker (1997) 257–76.

[77] λόγου δέ ποτε γενομένου περὶ τοῦ δοξάσειν τὸν σοφὸν καὶ τοῦ Σφαίρου εἰπόντος ὡς οὐ δοξάσει, βουλόμενος ὁ βασιλεὺς ἐλέγξαι αὐτόν, κηρίνας ῥόας ἐκέλευσε παρατεθῆναι· τοῦ δὲ Σφαίρου ἀπατηθέντος ἀνεβόησεν ὁ βασιλεὺς ψευδεῖ συγκατατεθεῖσθαι αὐτὸν φαντασίᾳ. πρὸς ὃν ὁ Σφαῖρος εὐστόχως ἀπεκρίνατο, εἰπὼν οὕτως συγκατατεθεῖσθαι, οὐχ ὅτι ῥόαι εἰσίν, ἀλλ' ὅτι εὔλογόν ἐστι ῥόας αὐτὰς εἶναι· διαφέρειν δὲ τὴν καταληπτικὴν φαντασίαν τοῦ εὐλόγου.

[78] Hirzel (1882) 275–6.

it is assumed that Sphaerus was *not* a self-proclaimed sage seems rather more persuasive. The anecdote should then be taken as an example of the fact that Sphaerus as an inferior person speculated on the tenets of the Stoic sage, i.e. that the sage would not hold opinions. Of course, Sphaerus would do everything to be as sage-like as possible. He therefore did not decline the honour of being put to the test by the king. Nor did he show signs of embarrassment because he was refuted. As an ignorant inferior person there would have been no need to be embarrassed about that. What is more, he showed himself not to be an average inferior person. He made his retort to the king's practical joke by giving a shrewd answer. He showed that he had made progress on the road to wisdom. In the second place, this interpretation is the one endorsed by Diogenes Laertius (or his underlying source). For this is how the anecdote is introduced: 'Of him [Cleanthes], as we said before [at 7.37], Sphaerus of the Bosporus became also a pupil after [the death of] Zeno, who having made considerable progress in reasoning departed for Alexandria, to Ptolemy Philopater.'[79] 'Progress', as I mentioned above (Section 3.2.2c), is a technical term in Stoicism, referring to the progress that someone makes towards wisdom, while still being in a state of inferiority. The introductory comment thus makes clear that in the anecdote Sphaerus, as an inferior person, not a sage, shows indeed that he has made considerable progress in his attempt to achieve wisdom. Sphaerus is thus someone who has cognitions, but still no stable cognitions or knowledge or, in the words of Zeno's simile in Cicero's *Lucullus* 145 (*SVF* 1.66, LS 41A, *FDS* 369), no 'hand over fist', in which the fist stands for a cognition and the hand over fist for a stable cognition. That is not to say that others, like Diogenes Laertius, might not put their hands together.

[79] τούτου, καθάπερ προειρήκαμεν, ἤκουσε μετὰ Ζήνωνα καὶ Σφαῖρος ὁ Βοσποριανός, ὅς προκοπὴν ἱκανὴν περιποιησάμενος λόγῳ εἰς Ἀλεξάνδρειαν ἀπῆρε πρὸς Πτολεμαῖον τὸν Φιλοπάτορα. This introductory sentence is omitted by von Arnim (*SVF* 1.625), by Long and Sedley (LS 40F in vol. 1, but vol. 2 has it in small print), and by Brennan (1996), but is included by Hülser (*FDS* 381, and also 146, in a different section on 'Zenons Schüler').

To applaud, that is to say, out of admiration for Sphaerus' progress and his clever answer.

3.2.4b Persaeus

Persaeus is more than once connected with the (Stoic) sage, as the evidence in Themistius (fourth century CE) and Athenaeus shows.[80] But did he consider himself to be a sage? The evidence on Persaeus again consists mainly of anecdotes. Two anecdotes deal with Persaeus alone, each one in two different sources. A third anecdote relates an encounter between Persaeus and Aristo.

The first anecdote as discussed by Hirzel (1882, 276) is in Plutarch, *Life of Aratus* 23.5–6 (*SVF* 1.443). It is related to the historical events of 243 BCE: on behalf of Antigonus Gonatas, king of Macedonia, Persaeus unsuccesfully defended the acropolis of Corinth against Aratus of Sicyon, general of the Achaean League.[81] This is how according to Plutarch the events developed:

> As for Persaeus, on the capture of the acropolis, he made his escape to Cenchreae. And at a later time, we are told, when he was leading a life of leisure, and someone remarked that in his opinion only the wise man could be a good general, he said: 'By the gods, there was a time when I particularly liked Zeno's doctrines; but now, since the lesson I got from the young man of Sicyon, I am of another mind.'[82]

According to Hirzel this anecdote makes clear that as a general in Corinth Persaeus had the pretension to be a sage, but that in defending the citadel he discovered that he was a bad general, much less a sage.

There are good reasons to dismiss Plutarch's account altogether as anti-Stoic polemic. Firstly, earlier, at *Life of Aratus* 18.1 (also in *SVF* 1.443), Plutarch referred to

[80] See e.g. Themistius, *Orations* 32.358B–D (*SVF* 1.449), Athenaeus 4.162B (*SVF* 1.452), 13.607A (*SVF* 1.451).

[81] For the historical setting see e.g. Walbank (1984) 251, Green (1990) 151.

[82] Περσαῖος δὲ τῆς ἄκρας ἁλισκομένης εἰς Κεγχρεὰς διεξέπεσεν. ὕστερον δὲ λέγεται σχολάζων πρὸς τὸν εἰπόντα μόνον αὐτῷ δοκεῖν στρατηγὸν εἶναι τὸν σοφόν 'ἀλλὰ νὴ θεούς' φάναι 'τοῦτο μάλιστα κἀμοί ποτε τῶν Ζήνωνος ἤρεσκε δογμάτων· νῦν δὲ μεταβάλλομαι, νουθετηθεὶς ὑπὸ τοῦ Σικυωνίου νεανίου'.

Persaeus as 'governor' (*archōn*), and not as a general.[83] Secondly, it is peculiar that Persaeus is said to have abandoned one of Zeno's doctrines, whereas Persaeus is otherwise presented as one of Zeno's most faithful students.[84] Thirdly, in a variant of the anecdote ascribed to the Peripatetic biographer Hermippus of Smyrna (third century BCE) *ap.* Athenaeus 4.162D (*SVF* 1.452, fr. 40a Bollansée) Persaeus is depicted even more disgracefully, not only as betraying the citadel (and his Stoic persuasion), but also as being drunk during his expulsion from it. Fourthly, and most importantly, a completely different and simpler version of the events is extant. According to Pausanias (around 150 CE), the author of the travel guide to Greece, and the Epicurean Philodemus, in Aratus' conquest of the citadel Persaeus lost his life.[85] Of course, it cannot surprise us that Plutarch, as an adversary of the Stoics, would have preferred the 'hostile' version.[86]

A second anecdote (not discussed by Hirzel), preserved by Themistius, *Orations* 32.358B–D (*SVF* 1.449) and Diogenes Laertius 7.36 (*SVF* 1.435), relates how Persaeus showed himself, unlike a sage, to be upset when he was falsely told by Antigonus that his family had suffered some severe blows. This anecdote shows either that Persaeus considered himself to be a sage, but discovered that he was not, *or* that he

[83] Cf. Tarn (1913) 374 n. 15, who furthermore remarks that the atticised ἄρχων should presumably be understood as the Hellenistic ἐπιστάτης, or an agent of the king within a subject city.

[84] See Diogenes Laertius 7.36 (*SVF* 1.435), Philodemus, *Index of the Stoics* 12.3–6 (*SVF* 1.437).

[85] See Pausanias, *Description of Greece* 2.8.4, 7.8.3 (both in *SVF* 1.442) and Philodemus, *Index of the Stoics* 15 (*SVF* 1.445). Philodemus' text is badly preserved, but seems to have contained both versions. Von Wilamowitz-Moellendorff (1881) 108 n. 10, Deichgräber (1937) 927, Pohlenz (1990) 15 and Isnardi Parente (1994) 270 n. 7 (cf. 265) all accept the version in which Persaeus dies. Tarn (1913) 398 n. 9 is critical, suggesting that the version in which Persaeus dies 'may have been a tradition by the later Stoics,' but even he describes the second and last sentence of Plutarch's anecdote as 'malicious gossip of a later day' (397).

[86] Plutarch's 'hostile' version may well have originated with the often sensationalist Hermippus, as Hermippus is not only explicitly mentioned by Athenaeus, but also – with the book title *On Those Who Pass from Philosophy to Power* – in the immediate context of the story by Philodemus, *Index of the Stoics* 16 (cf. Dorandi (1994) 13).

realised that he was still not a sage, however much he would have liked to be one.

In a third anecdote in Diogenes Laertius 7.162 (*SVF* 1.347, 461, *FDS* 139) Persaeus also appears:

> The Stoic doctrine to which he [Aristo] attached most importance was that the sage holds no opinions. In opposition to this Persaeus made one of a pair of twin brothers deposit a certain sum with Aristo, and then made the other reclaim it. And so being in perplexity, he was refuted.[87]

Perhaps the anecdote should not be taken too seriously.[88] But if we do try to take it seriously, why would Persaeus have wanted to refute Aristo, by making him confused about the identity of the person he was supposed to return the money to?

Let me first note that the anecdote states that the doctrine that the sage holds no opinions is Stoic, confirmed in other sources.[89] Furthermore, Aristo is said to hold the doctrine. Why could this be significant? Perhaps the immediate context of the anecdote provides the answer. In the preceding sentence (*SVF* 1.333, *FDS* 139) Aristo is depicted as an unorthodox Stoic, disagreeing with Zeno, even as the founder of his own 'Aristonean' school (see Diogenes Laertius 7.161, SVF 1.333, *FDS* 139). As Persaeus was a faithful pupil of Zeno,[90] he must have held on to the Stoic doctrine, too.[91] His attack could thus not be directed against the doctrine itself, but rather against Aristo holding the doctrine. If so, this may imply that Aristo *did* consider himself a sage.[92] For Aristo should either have attached much importance to the doctrine that the sage does not hold opinions and not have claimed wisdom for himself, or have claimed to be a sage and (like a Cynic?) have attached not much importance to the doctrine. But both attaching

[87] μάλιστα δὲ προσεῖχε Στωικῷ δόγματι τῷ τὸν σοφὸν ἀδόξαστον εἶναι. πρὸς ὃ Περσαῖος ἐναντιούμενος διδύμων ἀδελφῶν τὸν ἕτερον ἐποίησεν αὐτῷ παρακαταθήκην δοῦναι, ἔπειτα τὸν ἕτερον ἀπολαβεῖν· καὶ οὕτως ἀπορούμενον διήλεγξεν.

[88] Ioppolo (1977) 121–2 referring to Diogenes Laertius 7.162: 'Anche i rapporti con Perseo furono amichevoli perché la polemica dottrinale intercorsa tra loro ha toni piuttosto scherzosi.'

[89] See Section 2.2.2b.

[90] See above n. 82.

[91] *Pace* the translations by Hicks in his Loeb edition of Diogenes Laertius, *ad loc.*, and by Goulet in Goulet-Cazé (1999) *ad loc.*

[92] Cf. Hirzel (1882) 275, Ioppolo (1986) 83, followed by Striker (1997) 268–9.

importance to doctrine and claiming wisdom for himself made him vulnerable to a refutation like Persaeus'. Moreover, it should be noted that our anecdote is the only piece of evidence that may imply that Aristo considered himself a sage,[93] and furthermore that Aristo, as a deviant 'Stoic' (if he can be called even that), cannot be held to represent the Stoa.

As for Persaeus, on the basis of this interpretation of the anecdote, it can still not be ruled out that he claimed wisdom for himself (by knowing how to distinguish between identical twins), but it seems rather more likely that he wanted to make clear that he did not share Aristo's pretensions.

As already suggested above, the anecdotes do indeed not contain much that will decide the matter. In any case, and that was my principal aim here, they cannot be unequivocally used, as Hirzel did, to establish that Sphaerus and Persaeus, unlike perhaps the deviant Aristo, considered themselves to be sages.

3.2.4c Zeno

Hirzel resorts to a psychological and a historical argument to show that Zeno considered himself a sage. His psychological argument is that Zeno would not have been able to find many followers if he had presented the ideal sage as if it were only 'a noble dream'.[94] Why should people study philosophy when they would gain nothing and would stay inferior? Hirzel's historical argument is that the Cynics considered themselves to be sages and that Zeno, under their influence,[95] would have considered himself to be a sage as well.

Hirzel's psychological argument proves nothing, of course. Socrates without ever claiming that his life of searching and refuting led to his being wise (however much he wanted to) attracted generations of philosophers. Hirzel's historical argument should be put in doubt, too. The Cynic influence on Zeno's philosophical activities is indeed well attested: Zeno

[93] Cf. Ioppolo (1980) 117 n. 59: 'Ne sarebbe una conferma che il fatto che egli stesso si riteneva saggio, da quanto si desume da DL, VII, 162.'
[94] Hirzel (1882) 272: 'Ein schöner Traum.'
[95] Hirzel (1882) 276 speaks of the influence 'des kynischen Hochmuthsteufels'.

had Crates the Cynic (*c.* 360–*c.* 280) as a teacher and even wrote his famous *Politeia* 'on the dog's tail',[96] as Diogenes Laertius 7.4 has it, an obvious reference to the cynical or 'doggish' persuasion to be found in it. But Hirzel's evidence that the Cynics considered themselves to be sages is unconvincing.[97] Moreover, even if the Cynics had considered themselves sages, it does not follow that Zeno would have agreed with them on this particular point. In fact, Zeno's initial motivation to study with the Cynics at all seems to have been that the Cynics were presented to him as followers of Socrates, and that Socrates did not consider himself a sage. I will return to these topics in Chapter 4.

Apart from these general considerations raised by Hirzel, which on their own leave the question on Zeno's position unresolved, an investigation into the sources may bring some clarity. I will first return to Sextus Empiricus, *Against the Professors* 9.133 (already discussed in Section 3.2.2a). For if we can establish that the parallel argument was formulated during Zeno's lifetime, he should presumably be included among the Stoics who did not hold the conclusion of the parallel argument that the sage exists. Hirzel maintained that these opponents should probably not be considered Zeno's contemporaries.[98] He argued that Zeno's doctrines were often only written down by later Stoics, and then criticised by their opponents. Thus this passage, at least in Hirzel's opinion, can

[96] τινὲς ἔλεγον παίζοντες ἐπὶ τῆς τοῦ κυνὸς οὐρᾶς αὐτὴν γεγραφέναι.

[97] Already admitting that his sources if taken separately are unconvincing, Hirzel (1882) 274 n. 2 points to the following texts, to be considered 'im Ganzen': Epictetus 3.24.67 (Diogenes fr. 290 Giannantoni): 'He [Diogenes] said: "From the time that Antisthenes set me free, I was no longer a slave any more"', Diogenes Laertius 6.10–13 (Antisthenes fr. 134 Giannantoni): 'He kept to the following doctrines. He showed that virtue could be taught', etc., Diogenes Laertius 6.105 (Antisthenes fr. 99 Giannantoni): 'They [the Cynics] hold further that virtue can be taught, as Antisthenes says in his *Heracles*, and once acquired cannot be lost: that the wise man is worthy of love', Stobaeus 2.157.8–9 (Diogenes fr. 148 Giannantoni): 'Diogenes said that he believed to see Fortune approaching him and saying [quoting *Iliad* 8.299]: "This enraged dog, I cannot smite him."' However, these texts do not mention the sage explicitly, with the exception of Diogenes Laertius 6.105, a passage that counts as Stoicised (see Goulet-Cazé (1982) 233 ff., Goulet-Cazé (1986) 33, 220, Mansfeld (1986) 340).

[98] Hirzel (1882) 281–2, in a long footnote.

only serve as evidence that Stoics later than Zeno held that the sage did not exist. However, Schofield (1982, 34–7) argued that the parallel argument might have been derived from a contemporary source. He shows that besides *Against the Professors* 9.133 three arguments of similar parallel form and directed against Zeno's syllogisms have been handed down to us.[99] Two of these are anonymous,[100] but the third one, in *Against the Professors* 9.108 (fr. 94 Döring; Zeno's argument is in *Against the Professors* 9.104, *SVF* 1.111), is ascribed to Alexinus. Alexinus, nicknamed *Elenxinos* ('the Elenctic'), was a pupil of the dialectician Eubulides and a contemporary of Zeno, and an opponent of dogmatic philosophers.[101] One of Alexinus' opponents must have been Aristo, since from Diogenes Laertius 7.163 (*SVF* 1.333, Alexinus fr. 87 Döring) we know that Aristo wrote a book entitled *Against Alexinus' Counterwritings* (it is unclear whether 'counterwritings' was the title of a book by Alexinus, or just a general characterisation of his writings). But according to Diogenes Laertius 2.109–10 (fr. 92–3 Döring) Alexinus' special target was Zeno.[102] As Zeno's syllogisms survived *verbatim*, whereas almost all other Zenonian material is lost, Schofield (1983, 37) suggested that these parallel arguments might have been collected in a single book by Alexinus, such as the *Counterwritings*. So if the parallel argument in *Against the Professors* 9.133 can indeed be ascribed to Alexinus, Zeno himself would already have been confronted with it and not be pleased with its conclusion, as he did not think that the sage had already been found.[103]

[99] Schofield (1983) 38–9 suggested a fourth one: Zeno's argument in Calcidius (fourth century CE), *Commentary on the Timaeus* 220 (*SVF* 1.138) is paralleled by an argument in Sextus Empiricus, *Against the Professors* 8.306.

[100] One is preserved by Seneca, *Letters* 82.9–10 (*SVF* 1.196 contains only Zeno's argument), the other is not only preserved by Seneca, *Letters* 83.9 (*SVF* 1.229 has again only Zeno's argument), but also by Philo of Alexandria, *On Noah's Work as a Planter* 176–7 (*SVF* 1.229, only Zeno's argument).

[101] See further Muller (1989).

[102] Diogenes Laertius 2.109: διεφέρετο δὲ μάλιστα πρὸς Ζήνωνα, Diogenes Laertius 2.110: γέγραφε δ' οὐ μόνον πρὸς Ζήνωνα.

[103] Another passage already discussed in Section 3.2.2a, n. 18, *Outlines of Pyrrhonism* 1.91, can perhaps also be used as indirect evidence, again in relation to Plutarch,

I turn next to the biographical evidence on Zeno. Decleva Caizzi in her discussion of the material concluded that 'Zeno did nothing to present himself as a wise man' (1993, 322). However, she considers Diogenes Laertius 7.28, 'where he is described as "happy"', as an exception to this conclusion (321): 'Indeed in self-control, dignity and blessedness he surpassed all.'[104] But not even this text need be taken as evidence that Zeno's biographer considered him to be blessed, happy, or wise. Apart from the fact that the text apparently assumes degrees of blessedness, which is surely (in a technical manner) un-Stoic, in this text Zeno is not said to *be* blessed or happy, but only to have *surpassed* all others in blessedness. Here the Socratic perspective can be brought to the fore. While Socrates was considered the most excellent, the most wise and most just among all human beings of his time, according to Plato, *Apology* 23B, Socrates himself, interpreting the oracle who declared him the wisest among human beings, came to the following insight as to what that amounted to: 'That man is wisest who realises that in truth he is worth nothing in respect of wisdom.' Like Socrates, Zeno may have surpassed all others of his time in self-control, etc., but this was worth nothing in respect to true self-control, dignity and blessedness, too.[105]

There is another piece of evidence that is usually evinced to corroborate Zeno's stance as a sage. According to the

On Stoic Contradictions 1034E. I have used the Plutarch passage to establish that in *Outlines of Pyrrhonism* 1.91 the Stoics were specifically targeted. Here the inconsistency Plutarch formulates with regard to Zeno's argument 'that the second speaker need not be heard' is interesting. Plutarch wonders how Zeno could formulate this argument and at the same time argue against second speakers such as Plato, 'against whose *Politeia* Zeno himself continued to write'. In our discussion above (p. 100) in relation to *Outlines of Pyrrhonism* 1.91 we have already seen that Zeno's argument may have concerned the sage. Plutarch's alleged inconsistency is thus easily resolved if we simply assume that Zeno did not consider himself to be a sage, and thus had not brought his searching about the ideal *Politeia* to an end and must have considered his argument not to be applicable to himself.

104 τῷ γὰρ ὄντι πάντας ὑπερβάλλετο τῷ τε εἴδει τούτῳ [εἶναι ἐγκρατέστερος] καὶ τῇ σεμνότητι καὶ δὴ νὴ Δία τῇ μακαριότητι. Marcovich (1999), *ad loc.* emends μακαριότητι, which is in all manuscripts, into μακροβιότητι (thereby following Heine (1869) 614) and Madvig (1871) 715), but this is unnecessary.

105 On this usage of the superlative see further Section 4.3 and esp. Section 4.4.

Epicurean Philodemus, *On the Stoics* col. 14.19–22, the Stoics described 'him [Zeno] as great, as the founder of their school, but not wise'.[106] Zeno was great for having discovered the formulation of the moral end, but made mistakes especially with regard to the Cynic doctrines. Philodemus presents this information as if later Stoics, because of Zeno's embarrassing Cynic views, came to the insight that he had made mistakes, and had thus to admit that he was not a sage, just a great man, the founder of their school. But I submit that this is merely what Philodemus wants to make us believe. It is surely true, as I already mentioned at the beginning of Section 3.2.4, that later Stoics tried to hide embarrassing Cynic doctrines held by Zeno (or Chrysippus, for that matter). But this embarrassment need not have anything to do with their 'admission' that Zeno was only great and not a sage, if Zeno never considered himself one and they had been well aware of it. So Philodemus may present what the Stoics, including Zeno himself, held anyway, in the context of a very real difference of opinion within the Stoic school about what to do with the Cynic doctrines held by the founders of their school. Of course, for Philodemus, a member of the Epicurean school, whose founder considered himself to be a sage,[107] it no doubt added to the polemic to point out that Zeno was not a sage.

I shall close this section on Zeno by dealing with [vi]. Sextus Empiricus mentions that Zeno did not know whether he was in the cosmos or whether the cosmos was in him, or whether he was a man or a woman. The sceptically inclined Cicero makes a similar point at *Lucullus* 144–5 (*FDS* 369), illustrating it by examples, which like Sextus Empiricus' examples go against common sense. Cicero, making it clear that he follows Zeno and Antiochus of Ascalon in this, denies that his Stoic interlocutors have knowledge. He then presents Zeno's hand simile, in which the various stages or conditions for knowledge are set out, and continues with the ambiguous sentence that 'who is a

[106] μέγαν [δ' οὖν] αὐτọ́ν̣, εἰ καὶ μὴ σοφόν, ὁμο[λογοῦ]σιν γεγονέναι καὶ τῆς ἀγωγῆς ἀρχηγέτην.

[107] See further Section 4.5.

sage or ever has been, even they themselves are not in the habit of saying'.[108] He thereupon directs his words at his interlocutors Catulus and Hortensius saying that 'thus you, Catulus, do not know that it is day, or you, Hortensius, that we are in your house'.[109] However, even if [vi] (or *Lucullus* 144–5) contains a sceptical attack on Zeno, the attack fails. For as we have seen, although on the basis of indirect evidence only, such as *Against the Professors* 9.133 and, as we shall see in Section 4.6, there are good reasons to think that Zeno would not have disagreed with Sextus Empiricus' remark that he was 'completely ignorant', or for that matter that he had no knowledge, or that he did not consider himself a sage.

3.2.4d Cleanthes

Hirzel presents Cleanthes as an intermediate figure between Zeno, who did claim wisdom for himself, and Chrysippus. Although Cleanthes may not have presented himself as a sage any longer, according to Hirzel (1882) 275, Cleanthes 'had not yet lost his belief in the attainability of the ideal'.[110] According to Hirzel, this belief occurs elsewhere in Sextus Empiricus, at *Against the Professors* 9.90 (*SVF* 1.529). In the context of his proof of the existence of the gods, Cleanthes states: 'Yet man cannot be absolutely the best living being because, for instance, he walks in wickedness all his life or, if not, at least for the greater part of it (for if he ever were to attain virtue, he attains it late and at the sunset of life).'[111] This can surely be no proof that Cleanthes considered himself a sage.

108 *sed qui sapiens sit aut fuerit, ne ipsi quidem solent dicere*. The sentence is problematic in two ways. Firstly, the expression 'not in the habit of saying' leaves it undetermined whether they are not even able to tell who is a sage, or merely do not want to. In the second place: who are 'they themselves'? Options include Zeno and Antiochus, the Stoics in general, and later Stoics. The sentence can therefore not simply serve as yet another Ciceronian parallel to [iiA] (see Section 2.2.2).

109 *ita tu nunc Catule lucere nescis, nec tu Hortensi in tua villa nos esse.*

110 'Kleanthes war der Glaube an die Verwirklichung des Ideals noch nicht erloschen.'

111 καίτοι οὐ πάνυ τι ὁ ἄνθρωπος κράτιστον εἶναι δύναται ζῷον, οἷον εὐθέως ὅτι διὰ κακίας πορεύεται τὸν πάντα χρόνον, εἰ δὲ μή γε, τὸν πλεῖστον (καὶ γὰρ εἴ ποτε περιγένοιτο ἀρετῆς, ὀψὲ καὶ πρὸς ταῖς τοῦ βίου δυσμαῖς περιγίνεται).

As far as I am aware there is no other evidence that Cleanthes did consider himself a sage. If we take a closer look at [vii], the opposite is rather more likely. According to our passage, Cleanthes did not know whether he was a human being or a more complex animal than Typhon. Segment [vii] is a powerful reminder of what Sextus Empiricus wrote at *Against the Professors* 7.264, right at the beginning of his critical discussion of the criterion 'man'. He starts it off almost immediately by introducing Socrates:

> Socrates was in perplexity, remaining in doubt and declaring himself ignorant both of what he himself is and in what relation he stands to the universe – 'for I do not know', he says, 'whether I am a human being or some other kind of beast more complex than Typhon'.[112]

This passage is paralleled less explicitly by Sextus Empiricus at *Outlines of Pyrrhonism* 2.22, again right at the beginning of the discussion of the criterion 'man', with the extra information that it can be found in Plato: 'Thus in Plato we hear Socrates expressly agreeing that he does not know whether he is a man or something else.'[113] Rather than *Theaetetus* 174B,[114] the Plato text that these passages, [vii] at *Against the Professors* 7.433, 7.264, and *Outlines of Pyrrhonism* 2.22 refer to is near the beginning of Plato's *Phaedrus*, at 230A, as most editors of Sextus Empiricus acknowledge.[115] This is what Socrates states:

[112] Σωκράτης μὲν ἠπόρησε μείνας ἐν τῇ σκέψει καὶ εἰπὼν αὑτὸν ἀγνοεῖν τί τ' ἔστι καὶ πῶς ἔχει πρὸς τὸ σύμπαν· 'ἐγὼ γὰρ οὐκ οἶδα', φησίν, 'εἴτε ἄνθρωπός εἰμι εἴτε καὶ ἄλλο τι θηρίον Τυφῶνος πολυπλοκώτερον.'

[113] ἀκούομεν γοῦν τοῦ παρὰ Πλάτωνι Σωκράτους διαρρήδην ὁμολογοῦντος μὴ εἰδέναι, πότερον ἄνθρωπός ἐστιν ἢ ἕτερόν τι.

[114] *Theaetetus* 174B reads in translation: 'It really is true that the philosopher fails to see his next-door neighbour; he not only does not notice what he is doing; he scarcely knows whether he is a man or some other kind of breed. The question he asks is "What is man? What actions and passions properly belong to human nature and distinguish it from all other beings?" This is what he searches for and wants to find out.' The question 'whether he is a man or some other kind of breed' here is less directly put and therefore a less likely candidate as Sextus Empiricus' Platonic source: Socrates in the *Theaetetus* is speaking about man in general, rather than himself.

[115] See e.g. Fabricius (1718), Bury (1933–49), Bett (2005), who all *ad loc.* refer to *Phaedrus* 230A, although via the cross-reference of *Against the Professors* 7.264. Mutschmann (1914), not referring to either passage, is the exception here.

'I inquire . . . into myself, to see whether I am actually a beast more complex and more violent than Typhon or a more cultivated and simpler creature, sharing some divine and "un-typhonic" portion by nature.'[116]

At first sight the alternatives at *Phaedrus* 230A, on the one hand, and the alternatives at *Outlines of Pyrrhonism* 2.22, *Against the Professors* 7.264 and [vii] at *Against the Professors* 7.433, on the other, seem to be somewhat dissimilar. Plato's Socrates offers himself two alternatives. He could either be 'a beast more complex and more violent than Typhon', or he could be 'a more cultivated and simpler creature, sharing some divine and "un-typhonic" portion by nature'. The alternatives at *Outlines of Pyrrhonism* 2.22 are 'man' or 'something else'. The alternatives at *Against the Professors* 7.264 as at 7.433 are 'man' or 'a beast more complex than Typhon'. But a closer inspection can show the similarities. 'A beast more complex than Typhon' is in all passages, with the exception of *Outlines of Pyrrhonism* 2.22. '[M]an' is in all passages, with the exception of *Phaedrus* 230A. Two simple identifications turn all the alternatives into one similar alternative. 'Something else' at *Outlines of Pyrrhonism* 2.22 can be identified with 'a beast more complex and more violent than Typhon'. (The rationale behind the change at *Outlines of Pyrrhonism* 2.22 in comparison with *Against the Professors* 7.264 and 7.433 could well be that in the abbreviated account of *Outlines of Pyrrhonism* 2.22 'man' is essential to the section on the criterion 'man', whereas the irrelevant expression 'a beast more complex than Typhon' can without distortion of the point be left out.) The other identification is between 'man' in the passages in Sextus Empiricus and 'a more cultivated and simpler creature, sharing some divine and "un-typhonic" portion by nature' at *Phaedrus* 230A.

So in [vii] Sextus Empiricus attributes to Cleanthes what he elsewhere attributes to Socrates. Is this attribution then a 'wilful misreading' on Sextus' part, to use Annas and Barnes'

[116] 'σκοπῶ ... ἐμαυτόν, εἴτε τι θηρίον τυγχάνω Τυφῶνος πολυπλοκώτερον καὶ μᾶλλον ἐπιτεθυμμένον, εἴτε ἡμερώτερόν τε καὶ ἁπλούστερον ζῷον, θείας τινὸς καὶ ἀτύφου μοίρας φύσει μετέχον.'

expression?[117] Or does [vii] ultimately go back to a Stoic interest in this part of the *Phaedrus*, such that Cleanthes would have come up with the characterisation himself? As I will show in Chapter 4, the Stoics were indeed interested in this depiction of Socrates. Unfortunately, as we will see, the extant evidence does not allow a more specific inference with regard to Cleanthes' characterisation of himself.

At any rate, as with the Stoics discussed before, the little evidence we have on Cleanthes does not show that he considered himself to be a sage.

3.2.4e Chrysippus

In two reports Chrysippus speaks explicitly about himself in relation to wisdom. The first brief passage is Plutarch, *On Stoic Contradictions* 1048E (*SVF* 3.662, 668):

> What is more, Chrysippus does not proclaim himself or any of his own acquaintances or teachers a sage. What then, do they think of the rest of mankind? Or do they think just what they say, that all are madmen and fools, impious and lawless, at the extremity of misfortune and utter unhappiness? And yet that our state, thus wretched as it is, is ordered by the providence of the gods?[118]

Here Plutarch informs us that Chrysippus did not proclaim himself (or his colleagues or teachers) a sage, from which it might be inferred that he did not consider himself (or any of his colleagues or teachers) a sage, either. Confirmation of this inference can be found in a second, longer account by Diogenianus *ap.* Eusebius of Caesarea, *Preparation for the Gospel* 6.8.8–24 (Diogenianus fr. 11 Gercke, *SVF* contains bits and pieces in various sections). Eusebius devotes several chapters to the refutation of the Chrysippean doctrine of fate, for which he quotes three Greek philosophers *verbatim*.[119] One of these

117 Annas and Barnes (2000) 73 n. 34.

118 καὶ μὴν οὔθ' αὑτὸν ὁ Χρύσιππος ἀποφαίνει σπουδαῖον οὔτε τινὰ τῶν αὑτοῦ γνωρίμων ἢ καθηγεμόνων. τί οὖν περὶ τῶν ἄλλων φρονοῦσιν; ἢ ταῦτα ἅπερ λέγουσι; μαίνεσθαι πάντας, ἀφραίνειν, ἀνοσίους εἶναι, παρανόμους, ἐπ' ἄκρον ἥκειν δυστυχίας, κακοδαιμονίας ἁπάσης· εἶτα προνοίᾳ θεῶν διοικεῖσθαι τὰ καθ' ἡμᾶς οὕτως ἀθλίως πράττοντας;

119 Alexander of Aphrodisias, *On Fate* 3–5 is quoted *verbatim*, thus we can trust Eusebius when he tells us that the other two authors are also quoted *verbatim*.

authors is Diogenianus, about whom we know nothing, apart from what we have in Eusebius. It is even a matter of debate whether he should be considered a Peripatetic or Epicurean, but what is most important for my present purposes is that he is in any case a hostile witness against Chrysippus.[120] Of the three long Diogenianus passages quoted by Eusebius in Chapter 8, the second (8–24) is our concern here. In it, Diogenianus criticises Chrysippus' view that the different names that have been given to it would support his doctrine of fate.[121] After presenting some Chrysippean examples, Diogenianus starts his argument thus, at 11: 'For let us suppose that people were using these notions, as explained in his own etymologies, when they assigned things their current names ... Why then, Chrysippus, do you follow all the opinions of people and does it appear to you that none of these opinions is mistaken, but that everybody is a perceiver of the truth?'[122] In the next sentences, at 13–14 (partly in *SVF* as 3.668 and 3.324), Diogenianus makes it clear why Chrysippus contradicts himself in following the opinions of the people in the names they have given to fate:

> But why then do you say that except for the sage there is no human being who does not seem to you to be as mad as Orestes and Alcmaeon, and say that there have been only one or two sages, but that the rest in their folly are just as mad as the above-mentioned? Why do you reject their opinions as wrong, such as the ones with regard to wealth and reputation and tyranny and pleasure in general, which most people regard as goods? And why do you say that all established laws and constitutions are wrong?[123]

120 In Eusebius' chapter heading Diogenianus is described as a Peripatetic, but his modern editor Gercke (1885) 701–2 considers him an Epicurean, for three reasons (cf. Isnardi Parente (1990) 2425 n. 4), as do von Arnim (1903) 777–8, Dorandi (1994) 833–4 and Bobzien (1998) 4. Amand (1945) 120 n. 4, Schröder (1969) 550–1 and Gottschalk (1987) 1142 n. 305 are critical.

121 See further Section 4.4.

122 ἔστω γὰρ ταύταις ταῖς ἐννοίαις κεχρημένους τοὺς ἀνθρώπους, καθὼς αὐτὸς ἐτυμολογεῖ, τὰ ὀνόματα τεθεῖσθαι τὰ ἐκκείμενα. . . τί οὖν ἀκολουθεῖς, ὦ Χρύσιππε, πάσαις ταῖς τῶν ἀνθρώπων δόξαις καὶ οὐδεμία σοι περὶ οὐδενὸς φαίνεται διεψευσμένη, ἀλλὰ πάντες τῆς ἀληθείας εἰσὶ θεωρητικοί;

123 πῶς οὖν οὐδένα φῂς ἄνθρωπον, ὃς οὐχὶ μαίνεσθαί σοι δοκεῖ κατ᾽ ἴσον Ὀρέστῃ τε καὶ Ἀλκμέωνι, πλὴν τοῦ σοφοῦ; ἕνα δὲ ἢ δύο μόνους φῂς σοφοὺς γεγονέναι, τοὺς δὲ ἄλλους ἐξ ἀφροσύνης ἐπ᾽ ἴσης μεμηνέναι τοῖς προειρημένοις; πῶς δὲ ἀνασκευάζεις αὐτῶν τὰς δόξας ἐκείνας ὡς διημαρτημένας, οἷον τὰς περὶ πλούτου καὶ δόξης καὶ τυραννίδος καθόλου τε

Diogenianus argues that Chrysippus cannot simultaneously both follow and reject the opinions of mankind. For Chrysippus also holds that human beings are mad. The exception to the overall madness is that one or two sages have come into existence (see the discussion in Section 3.2.2). But otherwise he considers every human being as mad as the mythological figures Orestes and Alcmaeon, who after murdering their mothers were both chased by the Erinyes.[124] Diogenianus illustrates this by Chrysippus' conviction that the various doctrines human beings hold on wealth, honour, tyranny and pleasure are wrong, just as the laws and constitutions they have made are. And furthermore, and importantly for our purpose, that Chrysippus does not exclude himself from mad mankind, at 15–16 (partly in *SVF* 3.668):

> Or why did you write so many books, if there is nothing about which men held mistaken opinions? For we shall not say that if they have the same opinions as you, they think rightly, and that if they have different opinions, they are mad. For, first, even you do not say of yourself that you are wise (and much less do we!), so as to make agreement with your opinion the criterion which identifies the occasions on which they are thinking correctly.[125]

The crucial sentence (the one printed in *SVF* 3.668) here is: '[E]ven you do not say of yourself that you are wise.'

Furthermore, at 16–17 Diogenianus makes it clear once again that Chrysippus' distinction between wisdom and madness is absolute, and that opinion should clearly be placed within the realm of madness:

> Furthermore, if this [agreement with you as the criterion] *were* true, why would you have to say that all are equally mad and why should you not praise them in so far as they appeared to have the same opinions as you, as

ἡδονῆς, ἅπερ ἀγαθὰ νενομίκασιν οἱ πλεῖστοι; πῶς δὲ τοὺς κειμένους νόμους ἡμαρτῆσθαι φῂς ἅπαντας καὶ τὰς πολιτείας;

[124] Orestes is a common example in Hellenistic epistemological debate: see e.g. Sextus Empiricus, *Against the Professors* 7.244, 249, 8.67 (Stoics), 7.170 (Academics), 8.63 (Epicurus).

[125] ἢ διὰ τί πλῆθος τοσούτων βιβλίων συνέγραψας, εἰ περὶ μηδενὸς εἶχον οἱ ἄνθρωποι δόξας διημαρτημένας; οὐ γαρ ὅταν μὲν ταὐτὰ σοὶ δοξάζωσιν, ὀρθῶς φρονεῖν αὐτοὺς φήσομεν, ὅταν δὲ διάφορα, μαίνεσθαι. πρῶτον μὲν γὰρ οὐδὲ σὺ φῂς σοφὸν εἶναι σεαυτόν, μή τι γε ἡμεῖς, ἵνα κριτήριον ποιώμεθα τοῦ καλῶς ποτε ἐκείνους φρονεῖν τὸ τῇ σῇ δόξῃ συνδραμεῖν.

having understood something correctly, and take them to be wrong when they disagreed with you? However, even so, we should not consider the opinions they hold sufficient evidence of the truth, for everyone would agree – even if not that they are mad, as you think – at least that they are far removed from wisdom.[126]

Diogenianus concludes his argument by repeating his point that Chrysippus cannot reject as well as accept the opinion of mankind, when it gave names for phenomena related to fate, at 18: 'It will be ridiculous therefore for you to use these men as witnesses because of their assignment of names, when you would say that they are no better than yourself in understanding,' Diogenianus sees only one way out for Chrysippus, but immediately adds that he considers it a dead end: 'unless it happens that those who originally assigned these names were sages – a thing which will be impossible for you to show.'[127]

Whatever the merits of Diogenianus' argument or Chrysippus' possible answer, the passage states clearly that Chrysippus did not consider himself a sage. (It also strongly implies that Chrysippus did not as a matter of fact maintain that the original name-givers were sages.)

That brings me to [viii]. Like the cases of Zeno in [vi] and Cleanthes in [vii], [viii] is not a clear report of Chrysippus' own assessment as to whether he considered himself a sage. Sextus Empiricus just takes Chrysippus' position to be one of considering himself ignorant and uses it in the following dilemma: either Chrysippus knows that he is ignorant, but then he is no longer ignorant, or he does not know that he is ignorant and is thus really ignorant, but then he could not lay down opinions about many things, which he obviously does. Of course, if Sextus Empiricus had used the Stoics' distinction between true

[126] ἔπειτ', εἰ καὶ τοῦτο ἦν ἀληθές, τί λέγειν ἐχρῆν μαίνεσθαι πάντας ἐπ' ἴσης καὶ οὐχὶ καθὸ μὲν ἐφαίνοντο ταὐτὰ σοὶ δοξάζοντες κατὰ τοῦτο αὐτοὺς ἐπαινεῖν, ὡς ὀρθοῦ τινος ἐπειλημμένους, καθὸ δὲ διεφώνουν ἁμαρτάνειν αὐτοὺς ὑπολαμβάνειν; μαρτύριον μέντοι τῆς ἀληθείας ἱκανὸν ἡγεῖσθαι τὸ δοκοῦν ἐκείνοις οὐδὲ οὕτως ἐχρῆν, οὓς εἰ καὶ μὴ μαίνεσθαι καθάπερ σὺ οἴει, ἀλλὰ πολύ γε ἀφεστηκέναι σοφίας πᾶς ἂν τις ὁμολογήσειε.

[127] εἰ μὴ ἄρα τοὺς ἐξ ἀρχῆς θεμένους ταῦτα τὰ ὀνόματα σοφοὺς εἶναι συμβέβηκεν, ὅπερ οὐδαμῶς δεῖξαι δυνήσῃ.

and truth, or between cognitions and stable cognitions (or knowledge), he could not have presented the dilemma: for Chrysippus would say that he does not have a stable cognition of his being ignorant, but that, if anything, he has a bare cognition thereof, just as he has of his doctrines that there is one cosmos, that it is ordered by providence and that its substance is wholly changeable.

3.3 Conclusion

In Section 3.2.3 I offered the interim conclusion that the evidence on the Stoics in general showed that they did not consider themselves to be sages. By now this interim conclusion has been well confirmed by the discussion of the material on the Stoics taken individually. Strong doubts were formulated with regard to Sphaerus, Persaeus, Zeno and Cleanthes. I tried to show that the anecdotes on Sphaerus and Persaeus do not necessarily suggest that they considered themselves to be sages, and indeed that the Sphaerus anecdote in Diogenes Laertius 7.177 makes more sense if based on the assumption that he did not consider himself a sage. As we have seen, one piece of anecdotal evidence in Diogenes Laertius 7.162 sets the unorthodox 'Stoic' Aristo apart from an orthodox Stoic like Persaeus in considering himself a sage. But even if one were to accept this anecdote as evidence for Aristo having declared himself a sage, Aristo could still fit into the general picture. Even if he did consider himself as the embodiment of the sage, he did not turn out to be one, 'refuted and brought to perplexity' by Persaeus. The characterisation of Zeno in [vi] that he did not consider himself to be a sage is indirectly confirmed by Sextus Empiricus, *Against the Professors* 9.133 and, as we will see in Section 4.6, by Cicero, *On Ends* 2.7. Cleanthes' position was more difficult to assess. The little evidence we have did not suggest that he considered himself a sage. The material on Chrysippus in Plutarch, *On Stoic Contradictions* 1048E and especially Diogenianus *ap.* Eusebius of Caesarea, *Preparation for the Gospel* 6.8.8–24 clearly showed that Chrysippus did not consider himself to be a sage.

3.3 Conclusion

The question whether Sextus Empiricus' account in *Against the Professors* 7.432–5 informs us correctly about the Stoics, can thus be answered in the affirmative, with the exception of [iiiA] and [viii] in particular. Given that material, my initial question is best answered by stating that the Stoics, Zeno included, were not self-declared sages.

CHAPTER 4

SOCRATES

4.1 Introduction

Why did the Stoics develop an ideal that is so difficult, if not almost impossible, to achieve? In this chapter I will give an answer to this question by looking at the influence Socrates exerted on the Stoics. Against the background of the oracle's pronouncement that no one was wiser than Socrates, Socrates searched for wisdom, becoming ever more aware that he could not claim sagehood for himself. It is my claim that the Stoics as 'followers of Socrates' took very seriously indeed both Socrates' search for wisdom and his denial of sagehood. If already Socrates as 'the wisest of all human beings' did not consider himself to be a sage, who else could claim to be one?

In this chapter I will first discuss the evidence in which Socrates is noted as an important source of inspiration for the Stoics (in Section 4.2). Here a remark about chronology is appropriate. When Zeno arrived in Athens, in 312 BCE, Socrates had been dead for almost ninety years. (By comparison, even Aristotle, often considered to be a reliable source on Socrates, was born some fifteen years after Socrates' death in prison.) In order for Zeno to appreciate Socrates, who did not write anything, he was dependent on what others wrote on Socrates, as we are today. (Perhaps like Aristotle, Zeno could also still rely on an oral tradition on Socrates.) An important difference between Zeno and us, of course, is that for us many of these writings on Socrates are lost, as Giannantoni's collection of Socratic fragments lamentably attests.[1] The Socrates that we will encounter

[1] Giannantoni (1990).

in these pages is thus not the 'historical' Socrates,[2] but rather the 'notional' Socrates as he can be encountered in the (extant) sources.[3] I will present two portraits of this 'notional' Socrates, in which Socrates presents his way of life as being in a state of ignorance.[4] The first portrait, in Plato's *Apology*, is best known and has exerted influence over the image of Socrates ever since, both in antiquity and thereafter. It will be discussed in Section 4.3. In the second portrait, in Plato's *Phaedrus*, Socrates stresses his being in a state of ignorance, too. This passage is important for another reason, since we possess evidence that the Stoics read and used the passage, and are thus likely to have picked up and endorsed Socrates' portrait. I will discuss the Stoics' use of the *Phaedrus* portrait in Section 4.4. In Section 4.5 I will round off my discussion of Socrates' philosophical personality, discussing whether the Stoics considered him a sage after all. The Stoics' almost hagiographical treatment of the portrait stands in stark contrast with the Epicurean rejection of it as an insincere account. In Section 4.6 I will reconstruct the traces of what must have been a fierce debate on the *Phaedrus* passage. This debate confirms the importance of this characterisation of Socrates for the development of the new Hellenistic schools of thought, either as an anathema as for the Epicureans, or as a source of inspiration, as surely for the Stoics. Thereafter, in Section 4.7, I will return to the main Stoic definition of wisdom with which I began in Chapter 1. Here, too, Socratic inspiration can be found, with the Stoics making explicit what they must have considered to lie at the core of Socrates' thoughts.

4.2 Socratic inspiration

The Socratic inspiration behind Stoicism is a common theme in the sources. It already plays an important role in the accounts

[2] That is to say: if such a reconstruction was ever a possibility. See on the problem of the historical Socrates Dorion (2011), who tranforms it into 'an exceptional occasion for enriching our understanding of Socratism' (19).

[3] I owe the expression to Cooper (2012) 29. Cooper restricts himself to the Platonic Socrates; the Stoics, as we will see, were not so picky.

[4] The portraits are more often discussed together: see e.g. Wilkins (1917) 41 and, more recently, Rowe (2007) 122–42, (2011).

on how Zeno became a philosopher, but it can also be inferred from Zeno's educational career, from his willingness to be called a Socratic, and – most importantly – from his interest in Socrates' thought.

According to the anecdotal evidence at the beginning of Diogenes Laertius' account of Stoicism, at 7.3, Zeno of Citium, on his arrival in Athens, heard a bookseller reading aloud from the second book of the *Memorabilia* by Xenophon (*c.* 430–354), one of Socrates' pupils. He was so impressed that he asked where such people could be found.[5] 'It so happened that Crates [the Cynic] passed by. The bookseller pointed at him, saying: "Follow that man." Thereupon Zeno became Crates' pupil.'[6] A prosaic version of the anecdote is given by the compilator Demetrius of Magnesia (first century BCE), also preserved in Diogenes Laertius, at 7.31 (Demetrius fr. 22 Mejer, *FDS* 100), in which Zeno's father by bringing 'Socratic books' home made his son familiar with Socrates. According to a late source (fourth century CE), Themistius, *Oration* 23.295A (*SVF* 1.9, *FDS* 101), it was rather Plato's *Apology of Socrates*, that drew Zeno from Phoenicia to the Painted Stoa.[7] It is noteworthy that each version stresses

[5] Hunter (2012) 129–30 suggests that what might have appealed to Zeno here is the choice between the easy road to pleasure and the difficult road to virtue, which is put to the dialogue partners, Aristippus and Socrates, at the beginning of book 2, and of course to Heracles in the Prodicus myth itself, as 'remembered' by Socrates, at 2.1.21–34. In further support of Hunter's suggestion, it should be recalled that Heracles is one of the few sages the Stoics explicitly acknowledged (see above Section 3.2.2c, and *infra* Section 4.5), and that Xenophon's version reappears in the Stoicised (Panaetian?) context of Cicero's *On Proper Functions* 1.118: *Herculi, 'Iovis satu edito'* [from an unknown tragedy according to Winterbottom *ad loc.*], *potuit fortasse contingere*. For a comparison between the passages in Xenophon and Cicero see esp. Alpers (1912) 31–2, on the myth and its afterlife see further Harbach (2010).

[6] εὐκαίρως δὲ παριόντος Κράτητος, ὁ βιβλιοπώλης δείξας αὐτόν φησι, 'τούτῳ παρακολούθησον.' ἐντεῦθεν ἤκουσε τοῦ Κράτητος.

[7] τὰ δὲ ἀμφὶ Ζήνωνος ἀρίδηλά τέ ἐστι καὶ ᾀδόμενα ὑπὸ πολλῶν, ὅτι αὐτὸν ἡ Σωκράτους Ἀπολογία ἐκ Φοινίκης ἤγαγεν εἰς τὴν Ποικίλην. Themistius most likely refers to Plato's (rather than e.g. Xenophon's) *Apology*: not only does Themistius in this *Oration* constantly echo Plato's *Apology* (see Smeal (1989) 84), he also shortly earlier mentions Plato's *Gorgias* and presumably the *Republic* (ἃ Πλάτωνι πεποίηται ὑπὲρ πολιτείας) (see Penella (2000) 123 and esp. Hunter (2012) 124 n. 43).

the 'bookish character' of Zeno's encounter with philosophy, or with Socrates.[8]

A further connection with Socrates is Zeno's oracle story, a connection to which already Epictetus, at *Dissertations* 3.21.19 (part in *SVF* 1.29), drew attention.[9] According to Diogenes Laertius 7.2, with reference to Hecato (fr. 5 Gomoll), a pupil of the Stoic Panaetius, and Apollonius of Tyre (first century BCE, see the geographer Strabo (64 BC– after 21 CE) 16.2.24, *SVF* 1.37), a historian of Zeno and his school (see Diogenes Laertius 7.6 and again Strabo), Zeno had consulted an oracle in order to know what he should do to attain the best in life. The god answered him that 'he should consort with the dead', which Zeno understood as that he should study the ancients.[10] With regard to Socrates, according to Plato, *Apology* 21A, Chaerephon, an old friend of Socrates, went to Delphi,[11] and ventured to ask the oracle whether any man was wiser than Socrates, which elicited the oracle's reply that 'no one was wiser'.[12] A similar report can be found in Xenophon's *Apology*, at 14, with the oracle declaring that 'no human being was more free, more just or more moderate than I'.[13] The parallel between the accounts on Zeno and Socrates, if not outright modelling of Zeno's story after Socrates' story, lies in the motif: becoming a philosopher is presented in the form of an unexpected, almost sacred moment in which life takes a

[8] See Brunschwig (2002) 16–17, followed by Hunter (2012) 127–8.

[9] According to Epictetus what is needed for care of young people is 'above all that the god counsels that one should hold this position' (πρὸ πάντων τὸν θεὸν συμβουλεύειν ταύτην τὴν χώραν κατασχεῖν), followed by god's specified counsels to Socrates, Diogenes of Sinope and Zeno.

[10] Ἑκάτων δέ φησι καὶ Ἀπολλώνιος ὁ Τύριος ἐν πρώτῳ Περὶ Ζήνωνος, χρηστηριασαμένου αὐτοῦ τί πράττων ἄριστα βιώσεται, ἀποκρίνασθαι τὸν θεόν, εἰ συγχρωτίζοιτο τοῖς νεκροῖς· ὅθεν ξυνέντα τὰ τῶν ἀρχαίων ἀναγινώσκειν. For the shameless (Cynical?) overtones of συγχρωτίζεσθαι in the sense of 'having intercourse' with the dead see Hunter (2012) 125–7.

[11] It had to be someone else: Socrates never wanted to leave his beloved Athens, he only left as he had to, 'for military service' (*Crito* 46B), as at 'Potidaea, Amphipolis and Delion, ... where those you had elected to command ordered me' (*Apology* 28E).

[12] μηδένα σοφώτερον εἶναι.

[13] μηδένα εἶναι ἀνθρώπων ἐμοῦ μήτε ἐλευθεριώτερον μήτε δικαιότερον μήτε σωφρονέστερον.

decisive turn.[14] In Socrates' oracle story the unexpectedness consists in the fact that the son of a craftsman was the wisest of all, which incited Socrates to become an even more intrepid enquirer after truth, thereby unmasking the pretensions of some of his fellow citizens. With Zeno, the unexpectedness lies in the fact that it is a foreigner, a Phoenician, who will become the founder of one of the most important schools in what was until then an essentially Greek undertaking. It is surely remarkable how much attention Diogenes Laertius (or his underlying sources, for that matter) gives to Zeno's foreign background.[15] In the first place there is the name of Zeno's father, 'Mnaseas or Demeas', both Phoenician (Diogenes Laertius 7.1). There is also the description of Zeno's physiognomy – swarthy, according to Apollonius of Tyre, which as Chrysippus stated in the first book of his *Proverbs* (Diogenes Laertius 7.1) led some to refer to him as an 'Egyptian vine-branch'. His teachers Crates and later Polemo (314/13–270/69), the head of the Academy, taunted him with his alien background: Crates called him 'my little Phoenician' (Diogenes Laertius 7.3), and Polemo is reported to have complained about Zeno stealing his doctrines and giving them a Phoenician appearance (Diogenes Laertius 7.25, *FDS* 107). Timon of Phlius (*c.* 320–230), the leading disciple of Pyrrho and a contemporary of Zeno, described him in his *Lampoons*, in a passage to which I will return later on (p. 154), as 'a Phoenician old woman' (Diogenes Laertius 7.15, *SVF* 1.22, fr. 812, Lloyd-Jones and Parsons (1983), LS 3F, *FDS* 108, fr. 38 Di Marco). Zeno's alien character is further stressed by his 'barbarian' niggardliness (Diogenes Laertius 7.16).[16] Zeno himself, far from denying his Phoenician background, insisted on it. According to his biographer Antigonus of Carystus (third century BCE), quoted in Diogenes Laertius 7.12 (fr. 32 Dorandi, presumably from Antigonus' biography *On Zeno*,

[14] Gigon (1946) 5: 'Der letzte Sinn des Motives ist der, daß gerade nicht derjenige der Glücklichste, Reichste oder Weiseste ist, der sich dafür hält oder der die Welt dafür hält, sondern vielmehr irgendein anderer, an den kein Mensch gedacht hätte.'

[15] For this background see esp. Pohlenz (1926), Brunschwig (2002).

[16] Hicks (1925) in his Loeb translation glosses βαρβαρικός as 'unworthy of a Greek'.

referred to by Diogenes Laertius, at 3.66, fr. 39 Dorandi), Zeno never denied he was born in Citium. On the contrary: Zeno even declined Athenian citizenship, 'in order not to seem unfaithful to his native city',[17] and wished his foreign background to be well known. In return for acting as a patron to the restoration of the baths, he was not satisfied with having 'Zeno the philosopher' inscribed on one of its pillars, and asked that 'of Citium' be added. Furthermore, Zeno wrote a book *On Greek Education*, referred to in the list of his works provided by Diogenes Laertius, at 7.4. The explicit stress on the Greekness of the education is of course remarkable.[18]

Also Zeno's educational career with Crates, Stilpo, Diodorus and Polemo can be understood as the expression of his search for a worthy successor to Socrates. As we have already seen in Diogenes Laertius' longer version of how Zeno became a philosopher, Crates is presented as a follower of Socrates. In Demetrius of Magnesia's prosaic version (also mentioned above) it was simply Zeno's reading of the 'Socratic books' that made him go to Crates and become his pupil. Zeno's next teacher, Stilpo (d. early third century BCE), head of the Megarian school, should principally be understood as a Socratic philosopher, too.[19] Apollonius of Tyre *ap.* Diogenes Laertius 7.24 (*SVF* 1.278, fr. 169 Döring, fr. 4 Giannantoni, *FDS* 107) presents Stilpo as a worthier substitute for Crates.[20] Zeno studied together with Diodorus Cronus, with whom he worked hard at the Socratic topic 'dialectic',[21] and who can perhaps also be understood from his perspective of finding

[17] Antipater of Tarsus, *On the Differences Between Cleanthes and Chrysippus ap.* Plutarch, *On Stoic Contradictions* 1034A (*SVF* 3 Antipater of Tarsus fr. 66): μὴ δόξωσι [i.e. Zeno and Cleanthes] τὰς αὑτῶν πατρίδας ἀδικεῖν.

[18] Cf. Pohlenz (1926) 258: 'Hätte ein echter Grieche des 4. Jahrhundert den Titel gewählt, der den Vergleich mit außergriechischer Bildung voraussetzt?'

[19] See von Fritz (1931) 707–18 and Döring (1972) 82–7, who both argue against the view that in the Megarian school Socratic and Eleatic elements have equal weight.

[20] For Stilpo as Zeno's teacher see also Diogenes Laertius 7.2 (fr. 168 Döring, fr. 4 Giannantoni, *FDS* 99), Diogenes Laertius 2.114 (not in *SVF*, fr. 165 Döring, fr. 35 Giannantoni, not in *FDS*), cf. Numenius (second century CE) *ap.* Eusebius of Caesarea, *Preparation for the Gospel* 14.5.11 (*SVF* 1.11, fr. 25 des Places, *FDS* 110).

[21] See Hippobotus *ap.* Diogenes Laertius 7.25 (fr. 10 Gigante). Cf. Diogenes Laertius 7.16 (fr. 104 Döring, fr. 3 Giannantoni, *FDS* 108).

someone like Socrates.[22] At any rate Diodorus Cronus was a contemporary of Stilpo, and was educated by Apollonius Cronus, who himself received his education in the school of Euclides of Megara, a pupil of Socrates.[23] Finally, Zeno studied with Polemo, by then the head of Plato's Academy. Zeno, as the historian of philosophy Hippobotus (around 200 BCE) put it, had such a 'lack of self-conceit' (*atuphia*), that even 'when he was already making progress', he still wanted to study with Polemo.[24] The reference to the lack of self-conceit is remarkable. On the origin of the term more will be said below, here it is surely used to express Zeno's ambivalent relationship with the Academy, or Plato's texts, for that matter. On the one hand, as we have seen, Zeno shared Plato's admiration for Socrates. On the other, Zeno disagreed with Plato, too. According to Plutarch, *On Stoic Contradictions* 1034E (*SVF* 1.260) Zeno criticised notably Plato's *Republic*, 'against which he continued to write'.[25] How should we interpret Zeno's criticism of Plato here? In modern scholarship three basic views on the relation between Socrates and Plato have been developed. According to the standard view Plato, at least from the *Republic* onwards, starts to use Socrates as the mouthpiece of his own thought.[26] According to another, 'unitarian', view Plato had already used Socrates for his own purposes from the very beginning of his career as a writer, and in the *Republic* moves into another, more advanced pedagogical register.[27] According to a third, yet again unitarian

[22] The evidence is particularly sparse here, see Alesse (2000) 66.

[23] See Diogenes Laertius 2.111 (fr. 96, 99 Döring, fr. 1 Giannantoni). On Diodorus Cronus and his position within the Socratic schools see Sedley (1977), (1999a) 360–1, Muller (1994), 780–1.

[24] See Diogenes Laertius 7.25, fr. 10 Gigante. On what Zeno might have learned from Polemo see Sedley (1999c).

[25] ἀντέγραφε μὲν πρὸς τὴν Πλάτωνος Πολιτείαν.

[26] In the standard developmental view, as set out in Hermann (1839) (e.g. 388: 'kein organischer Guss') and more recently Vlastos (1991) 45–80, Plato moves away from Socrates, under whose influence he wrote his early dialogues, and develops his own doctrines in the so-called 'middle dialogues'.

[27] In this unitarian view Kahn (1996) esp. 39–42 (following Schleiermacher's lectures on Socrates and Plato held between 1819 and 1823, (1839) 28, reprinted (1996) 8–9), argues for the unity of Plato's thought, with the 'early' dialogues intended as a first introduction into Platonism.

view, Plato considered himself a faithful follower of Socrates throughout.[28] The second view, that Plato in his writings was always his own man, can be left aside here: since Zeno distinguished between Socrates, on the one hand, and Plato, on the other, it is unlikely that Zeno adhered to it. The two other views can best be assessed against the background of what we do know about Zeno's critique of Plato's *Republic*. Two points of criticism are clearly attested in the sources. In the first place Zeno criticised Plato's stratified ideal society, against which Zeno argued in his own *Republic*, and in the second he rejected Plato's theory of the independent existence of Forms.[29] In the developmental view these doctrines are straightforwardly Platonic, and adhering to this view Zeno could thus have rightly taken Plato in his *Republic* as departing from his earlier Socratic approach. But even if he had accepted the third view, that Plato was a Socratic throughout, the *Republic* is 'Socratic' in a manner that shows substantial departures from what Plato wrote before. Zeno's criticism is thus directed either against the doctrines Plato develops himself in his *Republic*, but for which he still uses Socrates as his mouthpiece, or against the incorrect interpretation of the Socratic project, which Plato offers in his *Republic* and beyond.

The Socratic inspiration was apparently so strong that according to Philodemus, *On the Stoics*, at col. 13.3, Zeno and his followers were 'willing to be called Socratics'.[30] The 'willing' implies that the Stoics did not actively call themselves Socratics, but apparently did not object to being referred to as followers of Socrates. It is easy to see why the Stoics would not actively have advocated this name given to them. Obviously the Stoics were far from the only ones to lay a claim on Socrates as their intellectual ancestor, and 'Socratics' would thus surely not have been very distinctive. However, their

[28] Rowe (2007).

[29] On Zeno's city of sages see e.g. Plutarch, *On the Fortune or Virtue of Alexander* 329A–B (*SVF* 1.262, LS 67A), cf. Brouwer (2006). On Zeno's rejection of Plato's theory of Forms see Stobaeus 1.136.21–7.6 (*SVF* 1.65, LS 30A): according to Zeno Forms, 'as the ancients called them', are but figments of the soul.

[30] καὶ Σωκρατικοὶ καλεῖσθαι θέ[λ]ουσιν.

willingness to be referred to in this manner yet again makes clear that the Stoics did see themselves as followers of Socrates, one of the most inspiring figures who had emerged in Greek thought.[31]

Finally, next to Zeno's Socratic beginnings, his 'Socratic' education, and his willingness to be called a Socratic, there is ample evidence for Zeno's interest in the questions Socrates was occupied with as well as the answers that Socrates formulated. These Socratic questions and answers can be categorised under the headings of dialectic, ethics and theology.[32] An example in the realm of ethics is the Socratic thesis that the virtues are forms of knowledge, as set out in Plato's *Meno*, at 87C–9A.[33] An example in the realm of theology is provided by Sextus Empiricus, *Against the Professors* 9.101, where Zeno appropriates Socrates' argument on the existence of the gods, as presented by Xenophon's *Memorabilia*, at 1.4.2–8, and on the gods' benevolence towards human beings.[34] In the present chapter I will – not very suprisingly in this study – focus on the theme of wisdom. In relation to wisdom, I will claim here, Socrates is especially important in three ways. First, like the Stoics, Socrates puts great weight on the notion of wisdom. Second, like the Stoics, Socrates does not present himself as a sage or, rather, explicitly denies that he possesses true wisdom. With regard to the importance of wisdom and the denial of sagehood two characterisations of Socrates in Plato's texts are worth considering in closer detail: the positive characterisation in the *Apology* (in 4.3), and the 'self-portrait' in the *Phaedrus* (in 4.4). Third, and finally, going

[31] See Long (1988), repr. (1996), (2011), both with additions, Sedley (2007) 206. *Pace* Bees (2010) 48, who suggests a false opposition between 'sokratisches Philosophieren' and the Stoic conception of divine nature, or Bees (2011) 15–26, 31–6, where he proposes that the Stoic admiration for Socrates would have been invented by ancient historians of philosophy (19), apparently including Philodemus among them. Long's main argument, based on Philodemus' phrase 'willing to be called Socratics', would thus be a 'Fehlinterpretation' (34), 'bedenkenlos' (33) copied since.

[32] See further Long (1988), Alesse (2000) 265–343 (who deals with dialectic and ethics only).

[33] See Schofield (2013).

[34] See Sedley (2007) 212–25, Powers (2009).

back to where we began, I will discuss the Socratic roots of the Stoics' main definition of wisdom (Section 4.7).

4.3 The portrait in the *Apology*

In Plato's *Apology* Socrates describes both his main pursuit, searching for wisdom, and the epistemic condition that accompanies this search. Let us take a closer look at how he describes his activities and the disposition in turn.

Socrates describes his main 'pursuit' (*epitēdeuma*, 28B), in a passage (28A–34B) that is traditionally referred to as a digression. It is better characterised as the part in which he gives a more positive account of himself.[35] This positive part follows on a negative part in which he had set out what he is not, dealing both with the popular caricature that existed of him in Athens and with the charges brought against him. In this more positive account of himself, at 28D, Socrates explains that 'wherever a man posts himself, thinking it is the best place for him to be, or wherever he is posted by his commander', he must stick to that position. For Socrates himself that means sticking to the position on which the god stationed him, explaining this position by reference to the order of the god 'to live life searching for wisdom and examining myself and others' (28E).[36] For Socrates, this command has far-reaching implications. A first implication is that dangers should be faced, even at the risk of death. Another is related to the hypothetical situation in which the court might release him, under the condition that he no longer philosophise, as he states at 29D:

> If, as I say, you were to acquit me on those terms, I would say to you, men of Athens, I salute you and I am your friend, but I will obey the god rather than you, and as long as I breathe and am able I will not stop searching for wisdom.[37]

[35] Reeve (1989) 3–4.

[36] φιλοσοφοῦντά με δεῖν ζῆν καὶ ἐξετάζοντα ἐμαυτὸν καὶ τοὺς ἄλλους.

[37] εἰ οὖν με, ὅπερ εἶπον, ἐπὶ τούτοις ἀφίοιτε, εἴποιμ' ἂν ὑμῖν ὅτι Ἐγὼ ὑμᾶς, ὦ ἄνδρες Ἀθηναῖοι, ἀσπάζομαι μὲν καὶ φιλῶ, πείσομαι δὲ μᾶλλον τῷ θεῷ ἢ ὑμῖν, καὶ ἕωσπερ ἂν ἐμπνέω καὶ οἷός τε ὦ, οὐ μὴ παύσωμαι φιλοσοφῶν.

If the court were to offer Socrates a release under the condition that he would no longer strive for wisdom, he would disobey this (hypothetical) court order. Out of obedience to the order the god has given him, Socrates draws the conclusion that he will even go as far as to disobey the court. So Socrates makes it clear that his pursuit consists in striving for wisdom, and that nothing will make him abandon that.

His search for wisdom, however, is not very successful. Socrates makes this particularly clear, when he describes how his search gained a new impetus from trying to find wisdom in others. Confronted with the saying of the Delphic oracle, which proclaimed that 'no one is wiser' (21A),[38] while 'conscious of the fact that I am not wise at all' (21B),[39] he tries to find out what the god meant. In trying 'to refute the oracle' (*elenxōn to manteion*, 21C) Socrates investigates three groups of Athenian citizens with a reputation for wisdom: the politicians, the poets and the craftsmen. The text is carefully structured here, and works towards a climax. Athens' politicians (21B–22a) are the low point. Without mentioning names, Socrates starts off with one public figure (21C), then another one (21D), and thereafter continues his investigations 'in a systematic manner' (*ephexēs*, 21E). He makes the 'painful and alarming' discovery that the higher someone's reputation for wisdom is, the 'more deficient' (*endeeis*, 22A) the person is. For Socrates the reverse is rather true: the lower the reputation, the 'more reasonable' (*epieikesteroi*, 22A) the person. Here Socrates probably refers to the craftsmen,[40] of whom, as we will see shortly, he holds a much higher opinion. With the second group, the poets, he finds that at least some of them say many fine things. However, like seers and prophets, according to Socrates, these poets compose their poems without any understanding of what they say (22C). Finally, with regard to the 'handicraftsmen' (*cheirotechnas*, 22C) Socrates finds that the 'good craftsmen' (*agathoi dēmiourgoi*, 22D) among them

[38] The Greek is in n. 12 above.

[39] ἐγὼ γὰρ δὴ οὔτε μέγα οὔτε σμικρὸν σύνοιδα ἐμαυτῷ σοφὸς ὤν.

[40] Cf. de Strycker and Slings (1994) 278.

indeed have knowledge, and that they have knowledge of many fine things, too. However, these many fine things relate to their types of expertise, and not to 'the other, most important, matters' (*talla ta megista*).[41] Here the climactic build-up comes to an abrupt end: the otherwise good craftsmen make the erroneous inference that they also have knowledge of these more important matters. This 'false note' (*plēmmeleia*, Socrates uses a musical metaphor here), makes the wisdom they do have 'disappear from sight' (*apokruptein*). In short: in examining the oracle's claim Socrates met those with a reputation for wisdom, and discovered that they did not live up to their reputations, and did not possess the wisdom they claimed to possess. By contrast, Socrates at least is aware that he does not know and that therefore the oracle said that no one was wiser. From this Socrates infers:

> in fact it seems likely . . . that the god is really wise and in this oracle says this, that human wisdom is of little or no value; and it appears that he says this of Socrates, but has used my name, making me an example, as if he were to say: 'This one of you, human beings, is the wisest, who like Socrates has come to understand that in truth he is worth nothing in respect of wisdom.' (23A–B)[42]

In his search for wisdom Socrates comes to the conclusion that it is the god who is really wise, and that his own exemplary wisdom consists in his awareness of the fact that he does not possess knowledge of these most important matters.

Throughout the *Apology* Socrates makes it very clear what he means by these 'most important matters'. At e.g. 20B he refers to it as 'excellence of both the human and social kind',[43] at 30B as 'the best possible state of the soul'.[44] In persuading

41 22D: διὰ τὸ τὴν τέχνην καλῶς ἐξεργάζεσθαι ἕκαστος ἠξίου καὶ τἆλλα τὰ μέγιστα σοφώτατος εἶναι.

42 τὸ δὲ κινδυνεύει, . . . τῷ ὄντι ὁ θεὸς σοφὸς εἶναι, καὶ ἐν τῷ χρησμῷ τούτῳ τοῦτο λέγειν, ὅτι ἡ ἀνθρωπίνη σοφία ὀλίγου τινὸς ἀξία ἐστὶν καὶ οὐδενός. καὶ φαίνεται τοῦτον λέγειν τὸν Σωκράτη, προσκεχρῆσθαι δὲ τῷ ἐμῷ ὀνόματι, ἐμὲ παράδειγμα ποιούμενος, ὥσπερ ἂν <εἰ> εἴποι ὅτι 'οὗτος ὑμῶν, ὦ ἄνθρωποι, σοφώτατός ἐστιν, ὅστις ὥσπερ Σωκράτης ἔγνωκεν ὅτι οὐδενὸς ἄξιός ἐστι τῇ ἀληθείᾳ πρὸς σοφίαν.'

43 ἀρετῆς, τῆς ἀνθρωπίνης τε καὶ πολιτικῆς.

44 μήτε σωμάτων ἐπιμελεῖσθαι μήτε χρημάτων πρότερον μηδὲ οὕτω σφόδρα ὡς τῆς ψυχῆς ὅπως ὡς ἀρίστη ἔσται.

others of the importance of these things, he describes himself as 'the god's gift to you [the Athenians]' (30E).[45] Socrates' denial of wisdom does thus not imply that he is not able to have any understanding at all.[46] A distinction between two kinds of epistemic state can be made here: the state of knowledge that goes with true or divine wisdom, and the state in which one understands a few things, such as that he is not a sage, and that it is important to care for the best possible state of the soul.

This human epistemic condition, with Socrates as the prime 'example' thus has two sides. The positive side is that humans can understand a few things, such as the fact that they are far removed from divine wisdom, and that they have a duty to care for wisdom and goodness. The negative side is that their achievements in this respect are worth little or nothing in respect to divine wisdom. The point can also be put in terms of two types of self-knowledge: self-knowledge as the awareness of how ignorant and far from the divine one is, as opposed to self-knowledge as a perfect state that is well-nigh impossible to achieve for human beings.[47]

The Stoics followed Socrates in both attaching importance to the pursuit of striving for wisdom (see Chapters 1 and 2), and in denying for themselves perfect, divine, wisdom (see Chapter 3). The two different epistemic states that can be distinguished in relation to Socrates' denial of wisdom appear to have been taken over by the Stoics, too. At any rate, the Stoic distinction between, on the one hand, a cognition and, on the other, knowledge as a firm and secure cognition can serve to explain these different epistemic conditions. As the Stoics would formulate it, Socrates has cognitions. What he lacks (and what everyone else lacks, although unlike Socrates most

[45] τὴν τοῦ θεοῦ δόσιν ὑμῖν.

[46] The scope of Socrates' 'disavowal of knowledge' is obviously one of the big questions in Socratic scholarship. For a recent account see Bett (2011), who interprets disavowal of knowledge as a denial of possessing systematic understanding.

[47] See Wilkins (1917), Courcelle (1974–5), McPherran (1996) 292, Denyer (2001) 191 ('the maxim [to know oneself] enjoins us to know our limits'), Tsouna (2001).

seem to be unaware of this), is that these cognitions are not firm and secure, that is embedded in the disposition that would make him an active and divine part of the active force that pervades all.

4.4 The portrait in the *Phaedrus*

As we have already seen in Section 3.2.4d, Sextus Empiricus' inference at *Against the Professors* 7.433 (as well as his other two passages) ultimately refers back to the beginning of the *Phaedrus*, at 229E–230A, which contains what has been called a self-portrait of Socrates.[48] As in the *Apology*, in the *Phaedrus* Socrates presents himself both as searching for (self-) knowledge and claiming that he does not possess it. However, as will be remembered, it is unclear whether Sextus' implicit reference to the *Phaedrus* can be traced back to the Stoics. In his two other passages, at *Against the Professors* 7.264 and *Outlines of Pyrrhonism* 2.22, Sextus Empiricus ascribes variations of this confession of ignorance to Socrates rather than Cleanthes, whom Sextus otherwise obviously presents as one of his dogmatic adversaries. As I will show here, there are good reasons for Sextus Empiricus to refer to a Stoic here or, rather, even better reasons for a Stoic to have mentioned this reference himself. I will first discuss Socrates' portrait and its immediate context in the *Phaedrus*, and then move on to the question whether and, if so how, the Stoics made use of it.

At the beginning of the *Phaedrus*, Socrates and Phaedrus, taking a stroll outside Athens, arrive in the area where Oreithyia, daughter of Erechtheus, one of the first kings of Athens, was allegedly seized by Boreas, the North wind. Here Phaedrus asks Socrates whether he is convinced that this 'mythological account' (*muthologēma*, 229C) is true. Socrates answers that he rather accepts these accounts or – as he puts it at 230A – 'believes what is commonly said about them'. He admits that it would be normal not to be convinced by this

[48] That is of the historical Socrates, as suggested by Rowe (1988) 140, who describes Plato as 'extending a genuinely Socratic idea' here.

mythological account, just as the 'sages' (*sophoi*), as he calls them (only partly in jest, as we will see), are not convinced, either. He could, as he explains at 229C, like these sages, 'play the sophist' (*sophizomenos*), and explain instead that the wind blew the girl off the hill.[49] But, Socrates continues at 229D, this constitutes a heavy task for 'an excessively clever and industrious man who is not altogether fortunate',[50] for he can go on and on, having to give interpretations of the shape of the centaurs, of the chimaera, etc. This would imply, as he states at 229E, that:

> [i] if someone who is unconvinced by these [sc. mythological accounts], and tries to reduce each to what is likely, with some rustic [*agroikos*] wisdom, he will need a great deal of leisure.[51]

Usually *agroikos* is here interpreted as 'rude', 'boorish', opposed to 'civilised', 'urbane',[52] mostly combined with the interpretation that Socrates rejects the sages' wisdom altogether.[53] I propose that it can just as well be taken in its first meaning of 'rustic' (opposed to 'urban' (*asteios*), already mentioned in 227D), as a characterisation of the wisdom that concerns the countryside – a meaning towards which the setting of the dialogue in the immediate countryside that surrounds the city of Athens should already have made us sensitive. Rustic wisdom is thus knowledge of local geography, including the use of the method of interpreting mythological accounts to ascertain what is likely. This wisdom, Socrates explains at 229E–30A, concerns things that are 'alien' to him:

> [ii] But I have no leisure for these [mythological accounts] at all; and the reason for it, my friend, is this: I am not yet capable of, in accordance with the

[49] On revealing hidden meanings as an activity of (at least some of) the sophists see Richardson (1975), Morgan (2000) 66 and Yunis (2011) 92.

[50] λίαν δὲ δεινοῦ καὶ ἐπιπόνου καὶ οὐ πάνυ εὐτυχοῦς ἀνδρός.

[51] αἷς εἴ τις ἀπιστῶν προσβιβᾷ κατὰ τὸ εἰκὸς ἕκαστον, ἅτε ἀγροίκῳ τινὶ σοφίᾳ χρώμενος, πολλῆς αὐτῷ σχολῆς δεήσει.

[52] See the monograph on ἄγροικος by Ribbeck (1888) 39–40, where he deals with ἄγροικος in relation to Socrates, although *Phaedrus* 229E is missing.

[53] Cf. e.g. Hackforth (1952) 24, Verdenius (1955) 268.

Delphic inscription, knowing myself; it therefore seems ridiculous to me, while I am still ignorant of this subject, that I inquire into things that are alien.[54]

Some commentators have interpreted the rejection of rustic wisdom as an outright rejection of the method of 'reducing to what is likely', that is the method of rationally interpreting myth. I see no reason here to think of an all-out attack on the 'rationalists'[55] or, better but still inaccurately, of Socrates accepting these mythological accounts in so far as they are 'inoffensive'.[56] Rather, Socrates rejects these reductions or interpretations of mythological accounts, if they do not concern him, that is because they do not contribute to his quest for self-knowledge.[57] The reductive method can thus be useful in as far as it contributes to self-knowledge. Socrates already hinted at that at 229D by making clear that the sages' sayings are very 'attractive ... in other respects', and suggests that it ought to be applied to the mythological account of Typhon, at 230A:

[iii] So then saying goodbye to these things, and believing what is commonly thought about them, I inquire, as I was saying just now, not into these things, but into myself, to see whether I am actually a beast more complex and more violent than Typhon or a more cultivated and simpler living being, sharing some divine and *atuphos* portion by nature.[58]

Unlike the other savage monsters Typhon apparently can be connected with self-knowledge. As for the Greeks Typhon is a (source of) wind, the point can also be formulated in these mythological terms: whereas Socrates was dismissive of the mythological account on the death of Oreithyia explained as caused by Boreas the North wind, the mythological account of Typhon apparently contributes to self-knowledge.[59]

54 ἐμοὶ δὲ πρὸς αὐτὰ οὐδαμῶς ἐστι σχολή· τὸ δὲ αἴτιον, ὦ φίλε, τούτου τόδε. οὐ δύναμαί πω κατὰ τὸ Δελφικὸν γράμμα γνῶναι ἐμαυτόν· γελοῖον δή μοι φαίνεται τοῦτο ἔτι ἀγνοοῦντα τὰ ἀλλότρια σκοπεῖν.

55 De Vries (1969) 51, Rowe (1988) 139.

56 Hackforth (1952) 26.

57 Cf. Griswold (1986) 38–9, Bonazzi (2011) 17 n. 21.

58 ὅθεν δή, χαίρειν ἐάσας ταῦτα, πειθόμενος δὲ τῷ νομιζομένῳ περὶ αὐτῶν, ὃ νῦν δὴ ἔλεγον, σκοπῶ οὐ ταῦτα ἀλλ' ἐμαυτόν, εἴτε τι θηρίον τυγχάνω Τυφῶνος πολυπλοκώτερον καὶ μᾶλλον ἐπιτεθυμμένον, εἴτε ἡμερώτερόν τε καὶ ἁπλούστερον ζῷον, θείας τινὸς καὶ ἀτύφου μοίρας φύσει μετέχον.

59 On Typhon as a source of destructive winds see in particular Hesiod, *Theogony* 869–80, esp. 69–72.

As [iii] shows, Socrates' view as explored in his inquiry contains two alternatives, in which 'complex' (*poluplokos*) is contrasted with 'simple' (*haplous*), 'violent' (*epitethummenos*) with 'cultivated' (*hēmeros*). Two further noticeable features are the wordplay upon the root '*tuph-*' and 'divine portion' (*theia moira*). 'Violent' (*epitethummenos*) is derived from 'to puff up' (*epituphō*).[60] *Tuphos* (or *atuphos*, 'lacking *tuphos*') is impossible to translate, where *tuphos* can mean vanity or pride, but also delusion, or craziness.[61] In this context of playing with words a relation with Typhon is most likely: just as 'puffed up' can be associated with Typhon as a source of wind, so *atuphos*, especially in connection with 'divine' in 'divine portion' (on which more below), can be associated with Typhon as the many-headed monster, who challenged the rule of Zeus: having been chased by Typhon, Zeus finally managed to conquer the monster with the help of his fiery thunderbolts, thus establishing his world order, proving himself worthy of it.[62] The meanings of *atuphos* therefore include 'free from vanity', 'free from delusion' and – from a 'reductive' point of view – 'divine'. The other feature, 'divine portion', has been explained by Plato commentators in various ways.[63] Some take it as something outside human nature, that is divine

[60] The term is hence clearly difficult to translate. Apart from my simple, and admittedly rather bland 'violent', in which I followed Rowe (1988), translations include 'burning with pride or passion' in Thompson (1868), 'furious' in Fowler (1914) and Yunis (2011), 'puffed up with pride' in Hackforth (1952), Griswold (1986) and Ferrari (1987), 'fierce' in de Vries (1969), 'savage' in Nehamas and Woodruff (1997), 'fumant d'orgeuil' in Brisson (1989), (2008) and Moreschini (1985), (1998), 'pervasa di brame' in Reale (1998), 'fumante d'orgoglio' in Bonazzi (2011), 'aufgebläht' in Ritter (1922), 'aufgeblasen' in Heitsch (1993).

[61] See e.g. LSJ s.v., De Vries (1969) 52, Rowe (1988) 140–1 (cf. Rowe (2011) 202: 'un-Typhonic').

[62] Early accounts are in e.g. Hesiod, *Theogony* 853–8, Aeschylus, *Prometheus Bound* 358–61. The monster is also referred to as Typhoeus: Typhon at *Theogony* 306 and *Prometheus Bound* 354, and Typhoeus at *Theogony* 820–80 and *Prometheus Bound* 370 (cf. *Hymn to Apollo*: Typhon at 306 and 352, Typhoeus at 367). The variations on his name are of no significance, see West (1966) 252. For the interpretation of Zeus beating Typhon all by himself (unlike the previous battle against the Titans, which the gods won together), and thereby proving himself worthy of his rule, see Most (2006) xxxiii.

[63] See the literature mentioned in nn. 64–66 and also des Places (1949) 149–62, Canto (1993) 315 n. 338.

assistance or grace,[64] others as something inside human nature, where a distinction can be made between those who distinguish the divine part from human nature,[65] and those who identify the two.[66] I will return to the issue at the end of this section.

Just as in the *Apology*, then, so in the *Phaedrus* passage Socrates presents himself,[67] or is at least said to present himself, as searching for self-knowledge. He does not claim to possess it, but tries to find it by means of interpreting mythological accounts, which can be reduced to what is likely: by comparing himself to Typhon, he asks himself whether he is more complex, more violent, more vain, or more deluded than this beast, or whether he is more simple and cultivated, possessing something divine or sharing in the divine.

Let us now move on to the question whether, and if so how, the early Stoics used this portrait. Unfortunately, no explicit reference to the *Phaedrus* in relation to these Stoics has survived.[68] However, a variety of the most remarkable terms in the *Phaedrus* passage reappear in the extant sources, making the conclusion inescapable that the Stoics exploited the passage.

I will start with the occurrences of (variations on) *atuphos* in the extant Stoic corpus. A Stoic definition of *atuphos* can be found at Diogenes Laertius 7.117 (*SVF* 3.646): the sage is *atuphos*, as he has the same attitude towards fame (or a good reputation) as towards the absence of it.[69] Cleanthes *ap*. Clement of Alexandria, *Protrepticus* 6.72.2 (*SVF* 1.557) included *atuphos* in his long list of synonyms of good. In both cases

64 Festugière (1932) 102 n. 3: 'assistance divine', Shorey (1933) 199: 'grace of God', followed by Bluck (1961) 435–6: 'a divine allocation or dispensation'. Hackforth (1952) 24 suggests as much by translating 'whom heaven has blessed'.

65 Souilhé (1930) 25: 'Elle est l'expression d'une sorte de surnature qui se greffe sur la nature humaine.'

66 Berry (1940) 51: 'The sense of *moira* is perhaps best taken here as "part" or "share"', Greene (1944) 420: 'Θεία μοῖρα is associated or identified with φύσις.'

67 See Rowe's judgement quoted above in n. 48. Compare also *Symposium* 216D, *Theaetetus* 150C, Aristotle, *Sophistical Refutations* 183b6–8 (fr. 20 Giannantoni).

68 An explicit reference is first attested for Posidonius. See e.g. Hermias of Alexandria (fifth century CE), *Commentary on Plato's Phaedrus* 102.10–15 (fr. 290 Edelstein and Kidd).

69 ἄτυφόν τε εἶναι τὸν σοφόν· ἴσως γὰρ ἔχειν πρός τε τὸ ἔνδοξον καὶ τὸ ἄδοξον.

atuphos is obviously used in an ethical sense. Furthermore, with regard to Zeno *(a-)tuphos* is used twice. First, Zeno's eagerness for learning is described in terms of *tuphos*. As already referred to above,[70] his learning with Polemo, when already making progress, is a sign of his being *atuphos*, which in this context, where Zeno is said to have made already considerable progress in developing his own doctrines, surely means 'free from vanity'.[71] Secondly, at Diogenes Laertius 7.15 (already referred to on p. 140), a satirical characterisation has been preserved, composed by Timon of Phlius, in which Zeno is described in terms of *tuphos*:

> And I saw a greedy old Phoenician woman in her shadowy *tuphos*, desiring everything, but her basket was gone, small as it was, and she gained no more insight than the plunking of the four strings.[72]

The interpretation of the passage is notoriously difficult. It has been taken to show Zeno's 'vain attempts ... to catch philosophical fish in a net of fine mesh, a satirical representation of Stoic dialectic'.[73] However, like we saw in relation to the Polemo passage, Zeno is not usually presented as being particularly interested in (dialectically) fighting other philosophers (if anything other philosophers fought him), he is rather presented as wanting to learn from them.[74] Diogenes Laertius' introduction to Timon's three lines on Zeno as 'searching and precisely reasoning about everything'[75] fits in well here. Moreover, both expressions have Socratic connotations: 'searching' is a familiar way for Socrates to describe himself (see for

70 See n. 25.

71 See the parallel with Zeno's contemporary and rival Arcesilaus, declared 'free from [professional] vanity' by Diogenes Laertius at 4.42, in immediate opposition with Timon of Phlius' 'Why do you like a fool talk big (πλατύνεαι) of yourself?' (fr. 808 Lloyd-Jones and Parsons, LS 3E, fr. 34 Di Marco).

72 καὶ Φοίνισσαν ἴδον λιχνόγραυν σκιερῷ ἐνὶ τύφῳ / πάντων ἱμείρουσαν· ὁ δ' ἔρρει γυργαθὸς αὐτῆς / μικρὸς ἐών· νοῦν δ' εἶχεν ἐλάσσονα κινδαψοῖο.

73 E.g. by Long (1978b) 80, cf. LS 2, 15. Long followed Diels (1901) 194, whose argument is also quoted by Lloyd-Jones and Parsons (1983) 381; cf. Wachsmuth (1885) 104–6.

74 Cf. Pianko (1948–9) 122, Billerbeck (1987) 132, Di Marco (1989) 195. In the revised version of his (1978) Long (2006b) 92 took these criticisms into account.

75 ζητητικὸς καὶ περὶ πάντων ἀκριβολογούμενος.

example Plato, *Apology* 23B: 'I search and investigate in accordance with the [oracle of the] god'[76]); 'precise reasoning' is a quality that Timon elsewhere uses with respect to Socrates, in another one of his characterisations again preserved by Diogenes Laertius, at 2.19 (fr. 799 Lloyd-Jones and Parsons, fr. 25 Di Marco), in which he describes Socrates as 'having presented precise arguments'.[77] Timon's lines are therefore more appropriately interpreted as if Zeno desired to know about 'everything' (*ta panta*), but that his searching had little result: starting out from his 'shadowy confusion' (*skieros tuphos*), his shopping, perhaps even begging,[78] did not bring much: not only did the basket go missing in the process,[79] it also did not bring 'insight' (*nous*). Interestingly, as already mentioned in Section 2.2.3c, *nous* is just another Stoic way of describing the state of wisdom.[80] If his searching brought Zeno anything, Timon continues, then it is no more insight than a *(s)kindapsos*. The Stoics are attested to have used the word for a sound without significance,[81] but it was also used as the name of an instrument with four strings.[82] These two meanings probably go back to the onomatopoeic rendering of the sound of the instrument, and thus presumably also with regard to the Stoics both meanings should be taken into account.[83] Both

[76] ζητῶ καὶ ἐρευνῶ κατὰ τὸν θεόν.

[77] ἀκριβολόγους ἀποφήνας. Only two commentators discuss Diogenes Laertius' introductory words, although in a disappointing manner: as qualities that will be illustrated in Timon's persiflage (Billerbeck (1987) 132–3) or as insufficient to interpret them (Gannon (1987) 603).

[78] See Clayman (2009) 112.

[79] Di Marco (1989) 198 *ad* fr. 38 suggested reading ἔρρει as imperfect tense of ῥέω, 'to flow over', rather than the present tense of ἔρρω, 'to perish'. However, Trapp (1991) 470 rightly pointed out that 'to flow *over*' is an unlikely meaning of ῥέω.

[80] See e.g. Stobaeus 2.102.20 (*SVF* 3.563): πάντα τε εὖ ποιεῖ ὁ νοῦν ἔχων, Stobaeus 2.66.9 (*SVF* 3.717), Plutarch, *On Common Notions* 1068D (*SVF* 3.672), Plutarch, *On Stoic Contradictions* 1053E (*SVF* 3.701). Cf. Gannon (1987) 611.

[81] See esp. Galen, *On the Different Pulses* 8.662 Kühn (*SVF* 2.149, *FDS* 510): ἀλλὰ καὶ τὸ βλίτυρι, φασί, καὶ τὸ σκινδαψὸς ἄσημα παντελῶς ἐστι. Further (late and also non-Stoic) examples are mentioned by Hülser in *FDS* 509 (to which can be added Hermias of Alexandria, *Commentary on Plato's Phaedrus* 218.3, translated as 'XY' by Bernard (1997) 372).

[82] The instrument is described by Athenaeus 4.183A–B, in fact our only source (see Barker (1984) 269 n. 41), in which Athenaeus quotes the three comic poets Matron, Theopompus of Colophon and Anaxilas.

[83] See Gannon (1987) 611, Hülser *ad FDS* 509.

expressions 'to have insight' and 'the plunking of the . . . strings' are related to order: the former can be related to the 'order of things' (*kosmos*; cf. *ta panta*),[84] and the latter to an order of a musical kind. Thus when Timon ascribes to the Phoenician old woman not so much insight, but rather the sound of the plunking of strings, he could well be taken to say that she did not get insight into the order of things, but only produced some meaningless harmony (if even that) by the plunking of strings. If this is a correct interpretation of Timon's characterisation of Zeno, Timon's usage of *tuphos*, although presented in a satirical manner, could even have found approval of some kind from Zeno, who did not consider himself a sage, and therefore must have considered himself to be in a state of ignorance. With regard to *(a-)tuphos* the conclusion can thus be that it was used by the Stoics in the ethical sense as an aspect of the good, that it was used with regard to Zeno to declare him 'free from [professional] vanity', and that 'shadowy confusion' was used in relation to his state of ignorance.

However, it might be objected that these four occurrences of *tuphos* in the Stoic corpus, rather than pointing us to the *Phaedrus* passage, go back to the Stoics' more immediate predecessors, such as Stilpo and the Cynics. Stilpo was the subject of one of the parodies upon lines in Homer (sc. *Iliad* 11.582 and *Odyssey* 2.783) by Crates the Cynic (preserved at Diogenes Laertius 2.118, fr. 67 Giannantoni): 'And I saw Stilpo, suffering great pains in Megara, where they say the beds of Typhoeus are.'[85] As there is no mythological connection between Typhon/Typhoeus and Megara, whereas Stilpo was from Megara, an allusion to *tuphos* is likely.[86] Furthermore, there is something to be said for Stilpo himself, as having referred to Socrates' dilemma at *Phaedrus* 230A, if the

84 See e.g. Stobaeus 1.35.9 (*SVF* 1.157): Ζήνων ὁ Στωικὸς νοῦν κόσμου πύρινον [sc. θεὸν ἀπεφήνατο], Diogenes Laertius 7.138 (*SVF* 2.634, LS 47O): τὸν δὴ κόσμον οἰκεῖσθαι κατὰ νοῦν καὶ πρόνοιαν, καθά φησι Χρύσιππος ἐν τῷ πέμπτῳ Περὶ προνοίας.

85 καὶ μὴν Στίλπων' εἰσεῖδον χαλέπ' ἄλγε' ἔχοντα / ἐν Μεγάροις, ὅθι φασὶ Τυφωέος ἔμμεναι εὐνάς.

86 See e.g. Dudley (1983) 57, Marcovich (1999) *ad loc.*

anecdote preserved at Diogenes Laertius 2.119 (fr. 11 Giannantoni) is given any weight: Stilpo, drawing the masses, is said to have responded to the remark 'Stilpo, they stare at you as if you are a beast' with the phrase 'Not at all, ... rather as if I am a genuine human being'.[87] With regard to the Cynics and their predecessor Antisthenes, there is quite a bit of evidence that shows that they made *tuphos* into a *topos*.[88] For Antisthenes the goal in life is *atuphia* (Clement of Alexandria, *Miscellanies* 2.21.130, fr. 111 Giannantoni), where *tuphos* is guiding the masses (Stobaeus 3.593.15, fr. 289 Giannantoni). Furthermore, in the anecdotes preserved by Diogenes Laertius at 6.7 (fr. 27 Giannantoni) Antisthenes declared Plato to be 'puffed up' (*tetuphōmenon*), calling him a 'showy horse' (*hippos lampruntēs*), and expressed surprise at the fact that Plato, when ill, simply vomited bile rather than *tuphos*. With regard to Diogenes of Sinope an anecdote concerning an exchange with Plato survived in two versions (Diogenes Laertius 6.26, fr. 55 Giannantoni): in one version Plato responds to Diogenes who, trampling upon Plato's carpets, says 'I trample upon Plato's vainglory', with 'How much *tuphos* do you show, by appearing not to be puffed up',[89] in the other version Diogenes says: 'I trample upon Plato's *tuphos*', which drew Plato's response thus: 'With another kind of *tuphos*, Diogenes.'[90] With Crates the Cynic, besides the parody on Stilpo already mentioned on p. 156, there is even a second and third piece of direct evidence that he used *tuphos*: in the so-called Pera fragment (which survived in Diogenes Laertius 6.85, fr. 70 Giannantoni) he described Pera, his ideal community, as surrounded by *tuphos*; in another composition Crates declared that wealth may lead to *tuphos* (Diogenes Laertius 6.86, fr. 74 Giannantoni). Finally, Monimus of Syracuse, a pupil of Diogenes of Sinope and a companion of Crates, said according to Sextus

[87] 'Στίλπων, θαυμάζουσί σε ὡς θηρίον' ... 'οὐ μὲν οὖν, ... ἀλλ' ὡς ἄνθρωπον ἀληθινόν.'

[88] See further Norden (1892) 311–2, Dudley (1983) 56 ('almost a technical term'), Goulet-Cazé (1986) 17 n. 2 and esp. Decleva Caizzi (1980).

[89] πρὸς ὃν ὁ Πλάτων, 'ὅσον, ὦ Διόγενες, τοῦ τύφου διαφαίνεις, δοκῶν μὴ τετυφῶσθαι.'

[90] οἱ δέ φασι τὸν Διογένην εἰπεῖν, 'πατῶ τὸν Πλάτωνος τῦφον'· τὸν δὲ φάναι, 'ἑτέρῳ γε τύφῳ, Διόγενες.'

Empiricus, *Against the Professors* 8.5 (fr. 2 Giannantoni) that '"everything is *tuphos*", which is thinking of things that are not, as if they are',[91] and according to Menander in his play *The Groom ap*. Diogenes Laertius 6.83 (fr. 1 Giannantoni, fr. 193 Kassel and Austin) that 'all that is being undertaken is *tuphos*',[92] where it is used to emphasise that Monimus 'by Zeus, did not speak a word to match the saying "know thyself"'.[93] What we see here, thus, is a clear interest in *tuphos*, combined with some hints that may point in the direction of the *Phaedrus*: Socrates' dilemma in the anecdote on Stilpo, Diogenes using the word play 'puffed up' and Monimus being linked (however pejoratively) with the Delphic saying.

On the basis of this evidence it can be argued that the Stoics' interest in *tuphos* was simply taken over from their immediate teachers. However, there is evidence that suggests that the Stoics went beyond Stilpo and the Cynics and indeed must have returned to the more specific formulations of the *Phaedrus* passage itself. In one of the two legs of Socrates' dilemma in passage [iii] above, that is 'a more cultivated and simpler living being', both 'cultivated' and 'simple' can be traced back in our Stoic sources. Both terms are relatively infrequent, and thus make it probable that the Stoics took it from the *Phaedrus* passage. 'Simple' reoccurs as a characterisation of the sage and can be found in Stobaeus 2.108.11 (*SVF* 3.630).[94] The term is easily explained within the framework of Stoic theory: the simplicity (or non-complexity) of the sage is that the sage has got a rational nature, free from alien elements.[95] 'Cultivated' is also used with regard to the sage, that is to say it can be derived *e contrario* from Stobaeus 2.104.3–4 (*SVF* 3.677), where the inferior person is described as 'uncultivated'.

91 τῦφον τὰ πάντα, ὅπερ οἴησίς ἐστι τῶν οὐκ ὄντων ὡς ὄντων.

92 τὸ γὰρ ὑποληφθὲν τῦφον εἶναι πᾶν.

93 ῥῆμά τι / ἐφθέγξατ' οὐδὲν ἐμφερές, μὰ τὸν Δία, / τῷ γνῶθι σαυτόν.

94 τὸν δὲ σπουδαῖον . . . ἁπλοῦν.

95 Cf. Diogenes Laertius 7.98 (*SVF* 3.102), where knowledge is described as a simple good. In physical terms the soul (or rather its leading part) of the sage differs from the soul of the inferior person in that the latter consists of fire and air, whereas the former has freed itself from the air and consists of (a special kind of) fire only – see Section 2.2.3c.

However, there is more in this passage in Stobaeus, at 2.103.24–4.5, which really ought to make us think of the beginning of the *Phaedrus*. It is therefore worthwhile to quote the whole passage in full:

> They also say that every inferior person is rustic. For rusticity is inexperience of the practices and laws in a city: of which every inferior person is guilty. He is also wild, being hostile to that lifestyle which is in accord with the law, bestial and a harmful human being. And he is uncultivated and tyrannical, inclined to do despotic acts, and even to cruel, violent, and lawless acts when he is given the opportunities.[96]

'Uncultivated' is preceded by 'bestial' at 2.104.3 and followed by 'violent' at 2.104.5, which should remind us of 'the beast more complex and more violent than Typhon'.[97] 'Rustic' at the beginning of the section, and explained by Stobaeus as 'not having the experience of the customs and laws of the city' can be contrasted with 'urban' (*asteios*) as a characterisation of the city, discussed in the preceding section at 2.103.12–17 (*SVF* 1.587, 3.328, LS 67I), one of the most elaborate passages on the Stoic city we still possess.[98] This pair of opposites should again remind us of the beginning of the *Phaedrus*.[99]

It may be argued that in these passages the Stoics' usage of 'simple' and 'cultivated' is rather different from the use Socrates made of the adjectives in passage [iii]: whereas the Stoics applied them to the sage, Socrates applied these – in the comparative – to a human being. From a Stoic point of view this objection can be fully rebutted, precisely because of the

96 φασὶ δὲ καὶ ἄγροικον εἶναι πάντα φαῦλον· τὴν γὰρ ἀγροικίαν ἀπειρίαν εἶναι τῶν κατὰ πόλιν ἐθῶν καὶ νόμων· ᾗ πάντα φαῦλον ἔνοχον ὑπάρχειν. εἶναι δὲ καὶ ἄγριον, ἐναντιωτικὸν ὄντα τῇ κατὰ νόμον διεξαγωγῇ καὶ θηριώδη καὶ βλαπτικὸν ἄνθρωπον. τὸν δ' αὐτὸν τοῦτον καὶ ἀνήμερον ὑπάρχειν καὶ τυραννικόν, οὕτως διακείμενον ὥστε δεσποτικὰ ποιεῖν, ἔτι δὲ ὠμὰ καὶ βίαια καὶ παράνομα καιρῶν ἐπιλαβόμενον.

97 'Tyrannical' can also be brought into connection with Typhon: see Dio Chrysostomus (second half of the first century CE), *Orations* 1.67, on which Dudley (1983) 57.

98 See Schofield (1999) 131–5. For the Stoic usage of ἀστεῖος predominantly attested in relation to the law pervading the world see Schofield (1999) 136–41. On the opposition between ἄγροικος and ἀστεῖος with regard to the Stoics see further Ribbeck (1888) 46–7.

99 Cicero, who might be following the early Stoics here, uses this opposition in the beginning of his (Stoicised) *On the Laws* 1, too, with explicit reference (at 3) to the beginning of the *Phaedrus*. See e.g. Dyck (2004) 20–2.

usage of the comparative. The Stoics, especially in this kind of context – that is, the contrast between the sage and the non-sage or inferior person – reinterpret Socrates' use of the comparative in a special, 'paradoxical', way. Rejecting the commonsense reading of a comparative expressing 'more of the same' as in 'among all sweet objects one sweet object can be sweeter than the others', they offer their non-commonsense or 'paradoxical' reading of the comparative as an expression of approximation that in the end has nothing to do with the basic quality from which the comparative is derived.[100] The most prominent Socratic example can be found in Plato's *Apology* 21A–3B, in which – as we have seen above in Section 4.3 – Socrates finds himself declared wiser than all other human beings, but not at all truly wise;[101] the best-known Stoic example is surely with regard to someone who makes progress towards the good: someone who makes progress, becomes a better person, but is in no way a truly good or virtuous person.[102] In the same manner, 'more cultivated' and 'simpler' can be taken as approximations of cultivated and simple only, which as such can only be said of the sage. So for the Stoics Socrates' ignorance about whether he is either a beast or a human being, at the same time offers a hint as to what self-knowledge should amount to. Socrates' confession of ignorance thus interpreted contains both an analysis of his present condition as an inferior person as well as a hint at how this condition might be overcome or, perhaps better still, what this would entail: i.e. being simple and cultivated.

[100] Perhaps this reading is not so paradoxical after all: a person who is ill can start feeling better, but may still be far off from a good, healthy condition.

[101] Another example is Xenophon's version of the oracle story in his *Apology*, at 14 (cf. n. 13): 'In the presence of many people Apollo answered that no human being was more free than I, or more just, or more moderate.' The 'many people' do not only function as witnesses of what the Pythia said, it may also be with them that Socrates needs to be compared here. Also, in *Memorabilia* 4.8.11, where Xenophon describes Socrates as the most excellent and happiest *among men*, it is left open whether Socrates is here truly excellent or happy, and hence a sage after all, as e.g. Beckman (1979) 223 and Sellars (2009) 62 maintain, since he can be wiser than all other human beings, but still not at all truly wise in comparison with the god.

[102] See above, Section 2.2.3a.

The apposite 'divine and *atuphos* portion' can also be understood on these two levels of imperfection and perfection, as imperfect reason possessed by all full-grown human beings, on the one hand, and as perfect reason acquired by the sage, on the other. 'Portion' (*moira*) was used by the Stoics, notably by Chrysippus, as we know from the Diogenianus passage, discussed in Section 3.2.4e. According to Diogenianus *ap.* Eusebius of Caesarea, *Preparation for the Gospel* 6.8.9 (*SVF* 2.914), Chrysippus holds the view that the different names given to fate, such as *Moirai*, support the doctrine that everything is fated: 'The *Moirai* have been so called as they have been assigned and distributed to each of us',[103] thus relating *moira* to the verb *meiromai*, 'to receive as one's portion'. As everything is determined by fate and we all have a share in it, *moira* is thus one's personal fate that is a portion of the fate of the whole.[104] As, according to the Stoics, the fate of the whole is just another expression for the reason pervading the cosmos,[105] *moira* as individual fate must be just another expression for one's personal portion of the reason of the cosmos. 'Sharing' (*metechon*) and 'by nature' (*phusei*) fit in well, too. 'Sharing' might be read as sharing alongside other *moirai* which together constitute divine cosmic reason,[106] and nature in 'by nature' might be read as human nature, in which our portion of divine reason can be developed by our rational capacity.

[103] ἀλλὰ καὶ τὰς Μοίρας ὠνομάσθαι ἀπὸ τοῦ μεμερίσθαι καὶ κατανενεμῆσθαί τινα ἡμῶν ἑκάστῳ. Chrysippus continues with the individual goddesses of fate: '*Lachesis* is so called from 'casting lots' (λαγχάνειν) for each man's destiny; *Atropos* from the 'unchanging' (ἄτρεπτος) and unalterable character of distribution; and *Clotho* from all things being 'twisted together' (συγκεκλῶσθαι) and woven, and from their having only one appointed solution.' The same etymologies are ascribed to Chrysippus in Stobaeus 1.79.12–20 (*SVF* 2.913, LS 55M): Μοίρας δὲ καλεῖσθαι ἀπὸ τοῦ κατ' αὐτὰς διαμερισμοῦ etc.

[104] Like μοῖρα, 'fate' (εἱμαρμένη) is presumably also related to μείρομαι (see e.g. LSJ s.v. μείρομαι, Gundel (1912) 2623–4, Greene (1944) 402). The Stoics also relate fate to εἴρω, 'to connect', as in Diogenes Laertius 7.149 (*SVF* 2.915): ἔστι δ' εἱμαρμένη αἰτία τῶν ὄντων [or ὅλων] εἰρομένη.

[105] See e.g. Chrysippus in *On Definitions* [or *On Seasons*?, the text is uncertain] 2 and in the books *On Fate* and elsewhere according to Stobaeus 1.79.5–6 (*SVF* 2.913, LS 55M): εἱμαρμένη ἐστὶν ὁ τοῦ κόσμου λόγος, Stobaeus 1.133.3–5 (Arius Didymus fr. 20 Diels, *SVF* 1.87): διὰ ταύτης [sc. matter] δὲ διαθεῖν τὸν τοῦ παντὸς λόγον, ὃν ἔνιοι εἱμαρμένην καλοῦσιν, Diogenes Laertius 7.149 (*SVF* 2.915).

[106] On sharing cf. Section 1.2.2c.

The problem raised earlier (see pp. 152–3), whether *theia moira* should be interpreted transcendentally as divine grace or immanently as a (divine) portion in us, would thus have been decided by the Stoics in favour of the immanent reading.

What is more, Socrates even offers a method as to how to achieve this good state, that is by applying the reductive method from [i]. As is well known, the Stoics were interested in the method of 'reducing' mythological accounts, that is – in standard Stoic terminology – of reading myths allegorically.[107] In contrast to all these other strange creatures inhabiting the countryside mentioned at *Phaedrus* 229D–E and for which he has no leisure, Socrates *does* have time to mention Typhon in his inquiry of himself, which suggests that it *does* make sense 'to reduce' this monster. If we leave aside the interpretation of Typhon as a source of wind (see n. 59), there are various other and more meaningful ways to allegorise upon Typhon. As the Stoics identified Zeus with cosmic reason,[108] his battle with Typhon may well be understood as a metaphor for reason prevailing over unreason,[109] and hence of (the possibility of) overcoming ignorance. Another possible manner in which the mythological acccount of Typhon can be 'reduced', is in connection with Python, the monster that had to be beaten by Apollo before he was able to set up his sanctuary at Delphi, so that even 'before the fifth century some Greeks, if not all, called Apollo's opponent Typhon' and that 'the names Typhon and Python are in fact variants of a single name'.[110]

107 On allegorical interpretation in early Stoicism see e.g. Steinmetz (1986) 18–30, Boys-Stones (2001) 31–43, Goulet (2005), Ramelli (2007) 1–107 (a collection of the passages in *SVF* on allegory, with brief commentary).

108 See e.g. Chrysippus, *On Gods* 1 according to Philodemus *On Piety* col. 4.12–18 Henrichs (*SVF* 2.1076): ἀλ[λὰ μὴν] καὶ (i.e. the Stoics earlier than Chrysippus, cf. Obbink (2002) 200 n. 40) Χρύσιπ[πος τὸ π]ᾶν ἐπὶ Δι' ἀ[νάγων ἐ]ν τῷ πρώ[τῳ Περὶ θεῶ]ν Δία φη[σὶν εἶναι τὸ]ν ἅπαντ[α διοικοῦ]ντα λόγον, Diogenes Laertius 7.88 (*SVF* 3.4, LS 63C): ὁ ὀρθὸς λόγος, διὰ πάντων ἐρχόμενος, ὁ αὐτὸς ὢν τῷ Διί, καθηγεμόνι τούτῳ τῆς τῶν ὄντων διοικήσεως ὄντι.

109 Typhon has been characterised as '*acosmia* incarnate' by Clay (2003) 26 and as 'un anti-Zeus parfait', 'une menace pour l'organisation du cosmos' by Blaise (1992) 362, 363.

110 The identification was argued for by Fontenrose (1959) 77–93, 95, 252, the parallel noted by e.g. Weniger (1870) 28, Gruppe (1906) 102, 812 (followed by Höfer (1902–9) 3398) and West (2007) 257–8.

Interpreting Socrates' inquiry into himself 'in accordance with the Delphic inscription' (or as in Plato, *Apology* 23C 'in the service to the god') as a search for self-knowledge, the Stoics may have thought that Socrates allegorically brought up the suggestion that to find self-knowledge is to repeat what Apollo did.[111] Like Apollo beating Typhon, we should beat Typhon or ignorance or badness. This reductive interpretation of Typhon/Python has an interesting implication concerning our relation to the gods: whereas in the search for self-knowledge one is a servant to Apollo, by finding self-knowledge or developing one's divine portion in the world one becomes equal to the god, or even divine oneself. This victory could thus have been the true *apotheōsis* (or better *entheōsis*), as we discover the divine in ourselves.[112]

It is time to conclude this long discussion of how the Stoics used the *Phaedrus* portrait of Socrates. As with the *Apology* they must have picked up the fundamental themes of Socrates presenting himself both searching for (self-)knowledge and claiming that he does not possess it. But, as we can see now, the Stoics must have studied and used the *Phaedrus* passage in a careful and detailed manner, too. Apart from *tuphos*, which can well be regarded as a common theme among the Cynics also, not only the string of adjectives 'rustic', 'urban', 'bestial', 'violent', 'urban', 'simple' and '(un-)cultivated', but also the use of the reductive method, make clear that the Stoics used this depiction of Socrates in relation both to the diagnosis of the human condition, and as a way to overcome this condition, up to the point that they read their ideal of wisdom in it.

4.5 A sage after all?

In order to round off this discussion of the Stoic interpretation of Socrates' philosophical stance, I will deal in this section with the possibility that the Stoics, despite Socrates' denial in

[111] On Stoic wisdom as self-knowledge see Section 1.2.2c.
[112] For the Stoic sage as a divine being see Section 2.2.2c.

Plato's *Apology* and *Phaedrus*, may have considered Socrates a sage after all.

We may first recall the evidence discussed in Section 3.2.2, where we found that the Stoics were at the very least reluctant to refer to others as sages. At best the sage is 'rarely found' (Sextus Empiricus, *Against the Professors* 2.43), or there have been just 'one or two' (Alexander of Aphrodisias, *On Fate* 199.16–17 and Chrysippus *ap.* Diogenianus *ap.* Eusebius of Caesarea, *Preparation for the Gospel* 6.8.14), or the sage 'like the Ethiopians' phoenix springs into being once in five hundred years' (Alexander of Aphrodisias, *On Fate* 199.18, Seneca, *Letter* 42.1). The most likely candidates for sagehood are Heracles and Odysseus, in line with the references to the sage that he or she is 'dreamed up' (Sextus Empiricus, *Outlines of Pyrrhonism* 1.91) or 'related about fabulously' (Alexander of Aphrodisias, *On Fate* 199.17). We may secondly recall that despite this reluctance there is one passage in which Socrates is presented as an early Stoic sage. (We can neglect Seneca's Cato here, whose sagehood can of course for chronological reasons be left aside for the early Stoic view.) In this one passage, Tatian, *Address to the Greeks* 3.2, makes it unambiguously clear that Zeno did refer to Socrates as a sage, alongside 'Heracles and a few more others'.

This identification of Socrates as a sage obviously contradicts the portraits of Socrates discussed thus far in this chapter, as someone searching for wisdom, and denying that he has found it yet. However, if we accept this single piece of evidence,[113] the apparent contradiction between Tatian and the portraits can be resolved in two ways.

If we take the portraits, and especially Socrates' speeches in Plato's *Apology* at face value, the contradiction can be removed by interpreting Socrates as a sage after all, notably in the final days of his life in prison, as depicted by Plato in the *Crito* and the *Phaedo*. Cleanthes may have hinted at Socrates' sagehood in his final days when he describes in very general

[113] As von Arnim apparently does not (see my discussion of Tatian in Section 3.2.2c), but Sedley (2007) 233 n. 67 surely does.

terms how, if a human being were to acquire virtue, this possibility occurs only 'late and at the sunset of life',[114] where a verbal allusion may be intended to the final scene in Plato's *Phaedo*, in which Socrates' life lasts until the setting of the sun.[115] Perhaps Chrysippus, too, hinted at Socrates having acquired his wisdom late, when he used the example 'Socrates will die on that day', as an illustration of his doctrine that some things are 'simply' fated, preserved at Cicero, *On Fate* 30 (*SVF* 2.956, LS 55S).[116] If something is simply fated, one can either accept it or go against it. If one were to choose the latter, though, this would not make any difference, as it will happen anyway. The example can well refer back to the prison scene as depicted in Plato's *Crito*, and be interpreted, as Sedley does, to mean that Socrates 'in view of his wisdom and justice' understands and willingly accepts his death as a part of the divine course of things.[117] In either scene, in the *Phaedo* and in the *Crito*, it is indeed remarkable that Socrates has insight into the course of things. However, this insight would still not make him a sage, as all inferior human beings can have cognitions, too. His calm acceptance of what is incumbent on him, though, the constancy with which he accepts his fate and is able to console the distressed Crito, as well as his confident reliance on divine signs, are indeed remarkable, and could perhaps be tokens of his sagehood.

Another way to resolve this apparent contradiction is that the Stoics understood Socrates as a sage unaware of his wisdom, as discussed in Section 2.3 – that is, a sage who at first is not yet

114 Sextus Empiricus, *Against the Professors* 9.90 (*SVF* 1.529), which we already encountered on p. 127 n. 111.

115 See 116B: καὶ ἦν ἤδη ἐγγὺς ἡλίου δυσμῶν, and at 116E: καὶ ὁ Κρίτων· ἀλλ' οἶμαι, ἔφη, ἔγωγε, ὦ Σώκρατες, ἔτι ἥλιον εἶναι ἐπὶ τοῖς ὄρεσιν καὶ οὔπω δεδυκέναι. The expression may well be a commonplace, however: it occurs in passing in the *Laws*, at 770A, and Aristotle, *Poetics* 1457a24, presents it as one of the examples of the metaphor for 'old age'. (Aristotle mentions Empedocles, too, here: if it is indeed this particular example, which should be attributed to Empedocles (but see the doubts expressed by Diels and Kranz *ad* fr. 152), the expression becomes even more a commonplace.)

116 I owe the example and the context of the *Crito* to Sedley (2007) 233. Cf. Sedley (1993) 316–17.

117 See Sedley (2007) 233.

aware of the fact that he has become one. Again this understanding could apply to Socrates in prison, where the same pieces of Cleanthean and Chrysippean evidence could be used to support it. It could perhaps already be applied earlier, that is, for example, to the Socrates who defended himself against the accusations of Anytus and Meletus. Whereas during his trial Socrates still does not claim sagehood for himself, he had in fact already become a sage, but was not aware of that. For the Stoics the moment of awareness can presumably not be pushed back much earlier: if we carefully apply to Socrates the Stoic characteristic of the unnoticed change, the fact that the new sage is at first not yet aware in particular implies that he will have to become aware of his wisdom after a while.

This identification of Socrates as a sage who is unaware of his wisdom would thus give a further reason as to why the Stoics developed this doctrine that someone could be a sage without noticing it. It would also give a further reason why the Stoics defended a conception of wisdom as a way in the world, against Plato's transcendental interpretation of wisdom as a vision (see Section 2.4). If Socrates is a sage who has not yet noticed his wisdom, Plato, while even using Socrates as his mouthpiece, must have been surely wrong in depicting the moment of becoming wise as a moment of great exaltation, as in the *Phaedrus* 250B–C or in the *Republic* 532C, where unawareness is obviously not an option. Finally, it would also give us some explanation as to why the Stoics may have been reluctant to present Socrates as a sage. The doctrine is a subtle one, and Socrates' unawareness could easily be interpreted negatively as a sign of his dishonesty (see Section 4.6).

Of course, without any further evidence we can only speculate. But whether the Stoics considered Socrates a sage or not, this much has become clear: that for the Stoics, Socrates was a major source of inspiration, if not outright veneration.

4.6 The portraits debated

The Stoics' almost hagiographical interpretation of Socrates must have infuriated Epicurus. In any case it stands in stark contrast with the interpretation the Epicureans developed of the portraits of Socrates, especially the one in the *Phaedrus*. Here I will reconstruct the traces of what presumably must have become a fierce debate.[118] This controversy confirms the role of Socrates as a key figure in the development of the new Hellenistic systems of thought, either as someone to be despised, as by the Epicureans, or as someone to be inspired by, as for the Stoics.

With regard to the Epicureans, a first important piece of evidence stems – indirectly – from the Epicurean Colotes, a contemporary of Zeno and Cleanthes, in his book fully entitled *On the Point that it is Impossible Even to Live According to the Doctrines of the Other Philosophers*.[119] Colotes' treatise is lost, but from Plutarch's reply, entitled *Against Colotes*, we can reconstruct that it contained several attacks against Socrates. At *Against Colotes* 1118F–9C Colotes argues that the quest for self-knowledge leads to the 'collapse of life',[120] saying: 'It is these enormities in the *Phaedrus* that bring our affairs into disorder',[121] after which the latter part of [iii] is quoted. Plutarch replies that he cannot see how asking questions like 'what am I?' can lead to the collapse of life, and continues with a counter-attack upon Colotes' 'master' Epicurus (fr. 558 Usener), in which he explicitly refers to Typhon, playing on its different connotations: 'He [Socrates] cleared life from madness and confusion, and from burdensome and excessive illusions about oneself and arrogance. For this is what Typhon signifies.'[122] A little earlier on in the treatise, at 1118C, Plutarch had already presented Colotes' argument against Socrates' quest for self-knowledge and the accompanying claim (made 'with youthful insolence' (*neanieuomenos*), as Colotes

118 For a discussion of the evidence on the first exchanges between Epicureans and Stoics, with focus on the *Lysis* rather than the *Phaedrus*, see Kechagia (2010).

119 The title Περὶ τοῦ ὅτι κατὰ τὰ τῶν ἄλλων φιλοσόφων δόγματα οὐδὲ ζῆν ἔστιν is in Plutarch, *Against Colotes* 1107E.

120 1119A: τοῦ βίου σύγχυσις.

121 1119B: ἐκεῖνα δ' ἦν τὰ ἐν Φαίδρῳ δεινὰ καὶ ταρακτικὰ τῶν πραγμάτων.

122 τὴν δ' ἐμβροντησίαν ἐκ τοῦ βίου καὶ τὸν τῦφον ἐξήλαυνε καὶ τὰς ἐπαχθεῖς καὶ ὑπερόγκους κατοιήσεις καὶ μεγαλαυχίας. ταῦτα γὰρ ὁ Τυφών ἐστιν.

characterised it) that he knew nothing himself. (As both the quest and the claim occur in *Phaedrus* 230A, Colotes may yet again have been referring to the *Phaedrus* passage here.[123]) This argument, more than the earlier one, reveals why Epicureans like Colotes rejected the *Phaedrus* passage and the (self-)portrait of Socrates in it. For Colotes, quoted by Plutarch at 1117D, Socrates' words or arguments were simply 'dishonest' (*alazōn*): 'What you said to people in your conversations was one thing, but what you actually did was something else.'[124] As reported in other sources, for Epicureans Socrates' dishonesty consisted in claiming not to know anything, whereas in fact he did know a few things, and hence – even more importantly from the Epicurean perspective – not sharing this hidden 'wisdom' with people he should have treated as his friends, thereby making life impossible, that is: making the Epicurean ideal of living together with friends impossible.[125] Yet again we find the *Phaedrus* passage subjected to another Hellenistic interpretation or, more precisely, rejected as a sincere characterisation of Socrates. Thus, not only the Stoics seem to have engaged themselves with the *Phaedrus* passage, Epicureans like Colotes did so, too.

It may be objected that if this were true, Colotes would have had every reason to attack the Stoics as well, but that no trace of this appears to have survived in Plutarch's treatise.[126] A simple rebuttal is that with regard to Socrates, Platonists and Stoics were rivals. A Platonist, like Plutarch, might hence have wanted to present himself as the true defender of Socrates. By rebutting the Epicurean Colotes without referring to the Stoics, Plutarch could not only give the Epicureans a

[123] Cf. Einarson and de Lacy (1967) *ad loc.*

[124] καὶ ἕτερα μὲν διελέγου τοῖς ἐντυγχάνουσιν, ἕτερα δ' ἔπραττες.

[125] See Philodemus *On Freedom of Speech* fr. 41.1–2 Olivieri and Cicero, *Brutus* 292, cf. Riley (1980) 65–6. The things he thus did know would, of course, not have appealed to the Epicureans, either, whether interpreted in a Stoic way, as I have done above, or in a Platonic way, as discussed in Warren (2002) 351–4.

[126] Cf. Einarson and de Lacy (1967) 156: 'Colotes did not mention . . . the Stoics', Kechagia (2011) 93, 98–9, who calls it 'puzzling'.

beating, but also convey the impression that Socrates' legacy simply belonged to the Platonists.[127]

Epicurus even went a step further in his critique of Socrates. Far from wanting to be a 'hypocrite' like Socrates, Epicurus broke the taboo on proclaiming oneself a sage. He did call himself a sage, and as a consequence referred to the epistemic status of his doctrines as wisdom. If we look at the evidence, it is already surprising that Sextus Empiricus, *Against the Professors* 1.57 and 11.21 (both fr. 255 Usener), refers to Epicurus as a sage without further ado, but in these cases the context leaves it unclear whether Epicurus himself would have endorsed it. Three other pieces of evidence are of a more compelling nature.[128] In *Against Colotes* 1108E–F (Metrodorus fr. 33 Körte), Plutarch tells us that Metrodorus (*c.* 331–278), one of Epicurus' pupils, 'states outright in his work *On Philosophy* that if Democritus had not shown the way Epicurus would not have attained wisdom'.[129] Of course, 'wisdom' could be used here in a loose, non-technical sense.[130] This becomes doubtful, however, once we consider Plutarch's report in his treatise *That It is Impossible* 1100A (Epicurus fr. 146 Usener): 'He [Epicurus] said that except for himself and his pupils no one had ever been a sage.'[131] Conclusive confirmation that Epicurus did consider himself a sage can be found in Cicero, *On Ends* 2.7 (Epicurus fr. 146 Usener). Cicero's spokesman tells us that Epicurus' pupil Metrodorus was prepared to call himself a sage, at the instigation of Epicurus. For as Cicero says, one does not call oneself a sage, only others can do so, just as with regard to the Seven Sages:

[127] The silence about Pyrrho among Platonists may already go back to Arcesilaus, 'to keep skepticism within the Academic family', as suggested by Sedley (1983) 16. For the debate about Socrates between Pyrrhonists and Arcesilaus' Academy see Decleva Caizzi (1986) 173–6.

[128] Cf. Hirzel (1882) 279, Isnardi Parente (1993) 7: 'Gli epicurei proclamavano sapienti i loro *kathegemónes*.'

[129] ὁ δὲ Μητρόδωρος ἄντικρυς <ἐν τῷ> Περὶ φιλοσοφίας εἴρηκεν ὡς, εἰ μὴ προκαθηγήσατο Δημόκριτος, οὐκ ἂν προῆλθεν Ἐπίκουρος ἐπὶ τὴν σοφίαν. Remarkably enough, in his fr. 33, Körte (1890) 556 decided to leave out ἐπὶ τὴν σοφίαν without even mentioning it.

[130] Perhaps this is why Körte left ἐπὶ τὴν σοφίαν out. Einarson and De Lacy's translation in their Loeb edition seems to imply as much, where they translate 'his wisdom'.

[131] σοφὸν δὲ μηδένα φάναι πλὴν αὑτοῦ γεγονέναι καὶ τῶν μαθητῶν.

But I do not doubt, I said, that you can do this easily [to explain what Epicurus meant by his words] nor that it is shameful to agree with the sage [Epicurus], who is the only one, as far as I know, who has dared to present himself as a sage. Because I do not think that Metrodorus dared to call himself a sage, but when he was called such by Epicurus, he did not want to refuse such a favour; for the Seven Sages were named not by their own vote but by that of all the people.[132]

Important for our discussion is the information that Epicurus was the only one who dared to profess himself a sage. From this passage it is not clear whether Cicero means that Epicurus was the only one among the *Epicureans* who dared to call himself a sage, or that he was the only one among the *Athenian thinkers* who dared to do so. But that it is likely the latter is meant follows from Cicero, *On Old Age* 43 (fr. 146 Usener, in the apparatus), who reports that Gaius Fabricius Luscinus, himself reportedly a paradigm of virtue and integrity (for this see Plutarch, *Life of Pyrrhus* 20), 'used to marvel at the story . . . that there was a man at Athens who professed himself a sage, and said that everything we do should be judged by the standard of pleasure'.[133] Thus these passages do not only offer evidence for the fact that whether or not to consider yourself a sage was a topic in those days, but also that among the philosophers in general, Epicurus, exceptionally, did declare himself a sage.[134]

The Epicurean position appears to have been directed above all against the Stoics. In the debate with his main professional

132 *ego vero non dubito, inquam, quin facile possis, nec est quod te pudeat sapienti adsentiri, qui se unus, quod sciam, sapientem profiteri sit ausus. nam Metrodorum non puto ipsum professum, sed, cum appellaretur ab Epicuro, repudiare tantum beneficium noluisse; septem autem illi non suo, sed populorum suffragio omnium nominati sunt.*

133 *saepe audivi e maioribus natu, qui se porro pueros e senibus audisse dicebant, mirari solitum C. Fabricium quod, cum apud regem Pyrrhum legatus esset, audisset e Thessalo Cinea esse quendam Athenis qui se sapientem profiteretur, eumque dicere omnia quae faceremus, ad voluptatem esse referenda.*

134 This restriction may also shed more light on Aristo's alleged sagehood in the anecdote in Diogenes Laertius 7.162 (discussed in Section 3.2.4b). If Sphaerus had indeed refuted Aristo, Epicurus (according to Plutarch, *That it is Impossible* 1100A) could thus rightly have considered himself as the only real sage that had ever lived (on his own terms, of course), and Cicero (*On Ends* 2.7), if at all aware of Aristo's claim (see *quod sciam*), could thus have left it aside.

rivals, Epicurus seems to have responded to the Stoic reverence of Socrates by explicitly positioning himself as anti-Socratic, in both his claim to be a sage as well as in referring to his own doctrines as wisdom. Perhaps, if the Stoics indeed considered Socrates as a sage who is unaware of his wisdom, as I suggested in Section 4.5, the debate between Epicureans and Stoics resolved around this issue, too. What the Stoics interpreted as unawareness might have been taken by Epicurus and his followers as (further) evidence for Socrates' insincerity: how can someone who has become a sage not be aware of it?[135]

The positions in the controversy between, on the one hand, Epicurus, claiming to be in the possession of wisdom, and on the other, the Stoics, searching in a Socratic manner for wisdom, are at any rate satirised by the New Comedy poet Damoxenus (dated third century BCE, and thus a contemporary of Zeno and Epicurus), in a passage from his *Foster Brothers (Suntrophoi)*, preserved by Athenaeus, at 3.103B (fr. 2 ll. 61–7 Kassel and Austin).[136] The passage is part of a speech by a cook, who presents himself as a disciple of the 'sage' Epicurus.[137] This cook praises Epicurus for his wisdom and criticises the Stoics for searching for wisdom, not knowing yet what it is:

Into †wisdom† Epicurus intensified pleasure.[138] He kneaded[139] it with care. The only one who knows the nature of the good, is he: those in the Stoa are

[135] Schofield (1999) 152–6 presents a different sequence. Following Hirzel's developmental approach discussed in Chapter 3, he argues that if 'in the time of Zeno the Stoics began to acknowledge that they could not identify a sage', they did this as an anti-Epicurean move, since it would have been Epicurus, who 'made the running on the general issue'. Only after Epicurus had proclaimed himself a sage would the Stoics have taken Socrates' position into account, and declared themselves not to be sages.

[136] The passage (for which I owe the reference to Decleva Caizzi (1993) 322) is elaborately discussed by Dohm (1964) esp. 187–9 (see also 181 n. 2), Gallo (1981) 127–30.

[137] Athenaeus 3.102A (fr. 2 ll. 1–2 Kassel and Austin): Ἐπικούρου δέ με / ὁρᾷς μαθητὴν ὄντα τοῦ σοφοῦ.

[138] The sentence is corrupt: †σοφὸν† Ἐπίκουρος οὕτω κατεπύκνου τὴν ἡδονήν. For κατεπύκνου see Epicurus, *Principal Doctrines* 9 (Diogenes Laertius 10.142): εἰ κατεπυκνοῦτο πᾶσα ἡδονή, . . . οὐκ ἄν ποτε διέφερον ἀλλήλων αἱ ἡδοναί.

[139] The manuscripts have ἐμασᾶτ', 'he chewed', but if we were to read ἐμάξατ', as an aorist middle of μάσσω, 'he kneaded', the sentence makes even more sense, with a cook saying that Epicurus carefully kneaded pleasure into something wise, who would thus be able to offer it to others, too.

always seeking for it, as they do not know what it is. Therefore what they have not got and do not know, they cannot give to others.[140]

4.7 A Socratic definition

If Socrates is indeed the main source behind the Stoics' interest in and search for wisdom, as well as of their denial of their own sagehood, the question can also be posed whether the Stoic definitions of wisdom, with which I began this reconstruction, can be regarded as Socratic in inspiration. I will claim that the definition of wisdom as knowledge of human and divine matters can indeed be understood in this manner. Here, too, Stoics appropriated Socratic thought, by making his conception of wisdom explicit.

For this definition of wisdom two passages are of particular importance. The first passage is in Plato's *Apology*, the other is in Xenophon's *Memorabilia*. I can be brief on the passage in the *Apology*, already considered in Section 4.3, but I will elaborate on the lesser-known passage in the *Memorabilia*.

In the *Apology*, at 22C–E, of the three groups Socrates investigated in order to refute the saying of the oracle, Socrates has the most positive things to say about the craftsmen. They indeed have knowledge, and knowledge of many fine things, too. However, their knowledge does not extend to 'the most important matters'. The inference is simple. The wisdom Socrates is striving for must contain both the element 'knowledge' and the element 'the most important matters'. Of course, the definition of wisdom as 'knowledge of the most important matters' is only an approximation of the Stoic definition of wisdom of 'knowledge of human and divine matters'.

For 'human and divine matters' we can best turn to the passage in Xenophon's *Memorabilia*. At 4.6.1, Xenophon describes Socrates' dialectical 'research method',[141] that is 'investigating with his companions, what any given thing

140 †σοφὸν† / Ἐπίκουρος οὕτω κατεπύκνου τὴν ἡδονήν· / ἐμαξᾶτ᾽ ἐπιμελῶς. οἶδε τἀγαθὸν μόνος / ἐκεῖνος οἷόν ἐστιν· οἱ δ᾽ ἐν τῇ Στοᾷ / ζητοῦσι συνεχῶς, οἷόν ἐστ᾽ οὐκ εἰδότες. / οὐκοῦν ὅ γ᾽ οὐκ ἔχουσιν, ἀγνοοῦσι δέ, / οὐδ᾽ ἂν ἑτέρῳ δοίησαν.

141 τὸν τρόπον τῆς ἐπισκέψεως.

is'.[142] At 4.6.2, Socrates and Euthydemus apply this method. After having done so, and having formulated definitions of piety and justice, they make wisdom the explicit topic of a somewhat longer conversation, worth quoting here in full, at 7:

> With regard to wisdom, what can we say about it? Tell me, does it seem to you that the wise are wise about what they know or are some wise about what they do not know? – It is clear that it is about what they know, he [Euthydemus] said. For how can a man be wise about the things he does not know? – Thus the wise are wise by knowledge? – How else, he said, can a man be wise if not by knowledge? – Do you think that wisdom is something else than that by which sages are sages? – I do not think so. – Wisdom is therefore knowledge? – I think so. – Now then do you think that it is possible that a man knows all things? – No, by Zeus, not even a fraction of these. – Thus it is not possible for a man to be wise with respect to everything? – By Zeus, no! he said. – Thus everyone is wise about what he knows. – I think so.[143]

For my purposes two points can be noted. First, wisdom is identified with knowledge (and sages are said to be sages because of this knowledge). Second, Socrates and Euthydemus agree that wisdom cannot be omniscience, as man can only know a very small amount of all the things that can be known. It can already be noticed that the Xenophontic Socrates thus goes against the characteristic of universality in Plato's *Republic* 598D–E or *Laws* 631B–C (see Section 1.2.1) and is in line with the Stoic rejection of wisdom as omniscience (see Section 1.2.2c).

If wisdom is knowledge, and if knowledge is not encompassing, what does it relate to? Here the preceding discussions in the *Memorabilia* on the definitions of piety and justice offer an answer. As with regard to wisdom, Socrates and

142 σκοπῶν σὺν τοῖς συνοῦσι, τί ἕκαστον εἴη τῶν ὄντων. On this method see further Döring (1892) 189, Breitenbach (1967) 1833, Gourinat (2008) 154, Dorion (2011) 187–8.

143 σοφίαν δὲ τί ἂν φήσαιμεν εἶναι; εἰπέ μοι, πότερά σοι δοκοῦσιν οἱ σοφοί, ἃ ἐπίστανται, ταῦτα σοφοὶ εἶναι, ἢ εἰσί τινες ἃ μὴ ἐπίστανται σοφοί; – ἃ ἐπίστανται δῆλον ὅτι, ἔφη· πῶς γὰρ ἄν τις, ἅ γε μὴ ἐπίσταιτο, ταῦτα σοφὸς εἴη; – ἆρ᾽ οὖν οἱ σοφοὶ ἐπιστήμῃ σοφοί εἰσι; – τίνι γὰρ ἄν, ἔφη, ἄλλῳ τις εἴη σοφός, εἴ γε μὴ ἐπιστήμῃ; – ἄλλο δέ τι σοφίαν οἴει εἶναι ἢ ᾧ σοφοί εἰσιν; – οὐκ ἔγωγε. – ἐπιστήμη ἄρα σοφία ἐστίν; – ἔμοιγε δοκεῖ. – ἆρ᾽ οὖν δοκεῖ σοι ἀνθρώπῳ δυνατὸν εἶναι τὰ ὄντα πάντα ἐπίστασθαι; – οὐδὲ μὰ Δί᾽ ἔμοιγε πολλοστὸν μέρος αὐτῶν. – πάντα μὲν ἄρα σοφὸν οὐχ οἷόν τε ἄνθρωπον εἶναι; – μὰ Δί᾽ οὐ δῆτα, ἔφη. – ὃ ἄρα ἐπίσταται ἕκαστος, τοῦτο καὶ σοφός ἐστιν; – ἔμοιγε δοκεῖ.

Euthydemus formulate the definitions of piety and justice in terms of knowledge. With which objects of knowledge are piety and justice brought into connection? In 4.6.2–4 Socrates and Euthydemus arrive at the conclusion that piety is knowledge of 'what is lawful concerning the gods';[144] in 4.6.5–7 they define justice in almost exactly the same wording as 'the knowledge of what is lawful', where this time the knowledge is 'concerning men'.[145] Thus, if the two preceding passages on piety and justice are read in combination with the passage on wisdom, they offer us a definition of wisdom as knowledge of what is lawful concerning divine and human matters, which obviously closely resembles the Stoic definition. However, in contrast to the Stoic definition, in both Xenophontic definitions the term 'lawful' is used. How should this expression be understood? Does 'lawful' refer to the positive laws in a city, or to a rudimentary understanding of natural law? In principle both meanings are possible: the Greek word used here, *nomima*, can refer not only to the norms and customs of a city in a conventionalist, positivist way, but also to norms and customs in a general, natural law-type fashion. As Socrates and Euthydemus use *nomimos* in relation to justice as well as piety, *nomimos* has to be understood here as going beyond a mere conventionalist sense.[146] It is likely that the Stoics would have followed this interpretation. For them, law is one of the many names for the one active, divine principle that orders the universe, and in which human beings can actively participate.[147] Even more so than in Plato's *Apology*, with

144 4.6.4: ὁ ἄρα τὰ περὶ τοὺς θεοὺς νόμιμα εἰδὼς ὀρθῶς ἂν ἡμῖν εὐσεβὴς ὡρισμένος εἴη;

145 4.6.6: ὀρθῶς ἂν ποτε ἄρα ὁριζοίμεθα δικαίους εἶναι τοὺς εἰδότας τὰ περὶ ἀνθρώπους νόμιμια;

146 See Johnson (2003) 273–4, who attributes to the Xenophontic Socrates 'the rudiments of a natural law theory' (256).

147 On the Stoic doctrine of law as reason evidence is extant for Zeno, Cleanthes and Chrysippus. For Zeno see Cicero, *On the Nature of the Gods* 1.36 (*SVF* 1.162): *Zeno naturalem legem divinam esse censet eamque vim obtinere recta imperantem prohibentemque contraria* ('Zeno thinks that the law of nature is divine and that it has the power to order the right things and to forbid the opposite things'), for Cleanthes see his *Hymn to Zeus* l. 2 (*SVF* 1.537, LS 54I): Ζεῦ, . . . νόμου μετὰ πάντα κυβερνῶν ('Zeus, . . . steering everything with his law'), for Chrysippus see his *On Ends* 1 *ap*. Diogenes Laertius 7.88 (*SVF* 3.4, LS 63C): ὁ νόμος ὁ κοινός, ὅσπερ ἐστὶν ὁ

its implicit definition of wisdom as 'knowledge of the most important matters', the passage in the *Memorabilia* could thus have served as the cradle of the Stoic definition of wisdom as 'knowledge of human and divine matters'. Of course, as in Plato's *Apology*, in Xenophon's extended discussion of the elements of the Stoic definition of wisdom the exact formulation of the definition remains implicit. In line with their philosophical position as 'followers of Socrates', the spelling out of this hidden definition is precisely what the Stoics may have considered their 'Socratic' mission.

There is even evidence that suggests that the Stoics may have had the Xenophontic passage in mind, when formulating their definition of wisdom. In *On the Nature of the Gods* 2.153 (not in *SVF*) Cicero brings his Stoic exposition of the superiority of the perfect human being to a close. The sage, differing from the gods only with respect to immortality, is praised as having knowledge of the gods, from which piety arises, and with which justice and the other virtues are connected:

> Such matters [i.e. observation of the heavens] allow the mind to attain knowledge of the gods, and this gives rise to piety, with which justice and the other virtues are closely linked. These virtues are the basis of the good life, which is similar and equivalent to that enjoyed by the gods; it yields to them only in their immortality, which has no relevance to living well.[148]

Here Cicero offers us an explicit connection between knowledge, on the one hand, and the virtues of piety and justice, on the other. The parallelism of this Stoic text with the passage in Xenophon's *Memorabilia* is obvious: the sage's knowledge is connected here with notably the virtues of piety and justice or, in the words of the Socratic definitions in Xenophon's *Memorabilia*, with 'divine and human matters'.

ὀρθὸς λόγος, διὰ πάντων ἐρχόμενος ('The common law, which is right reason, pervading all things'). On participation in law see e.g. Cleanthes' admonition to all non-sages in his *Hymn* ll. 25: ᾧ [sc. κοινός νόμος] κεν πειθόμενοι σὺν νῷ βίον ἐσθλὸν ἔχοιεν ('Obeying the common law would lead to a good life in partnership with intelligence'). See further Brouwer (2011a).

148 The text is already quoted in Chapter 2, n. 35.

4.8 Conclusion

'Follow that man.' If this chapter has made anything clear, it should be that Zeno put into practice these words spoken by the bookseller in the anecdote that marked the start of his philosophical career. We have seen that Zeno indeed followed the footsteps of Socrates, by becoming the pupil of Socratically inspired teachers like Crates the Cynic and Stilpo, and by studying with Diodorus Cronus, while even sneaking in through the back door of Polemo's Academy. He and his students followed Socrates' footsteps, too, by carefully studying texts about him, using among others Plato's *Apology*, as well as the self-characterisation of Socrates in Plato's *Phaedrus*. They thus consciously fashioned themselves as followers of Socrates, striving for wisdom, without claiming to be sages themselves. Even their definition of wisdom as knowledge of human and divine matters can be regarded as a conscious attempt to make Socratic thought explicit. This brings me back to the statement with which I started out in my Introduction (p. 6), but which can now be read as a conclusion, that the Stoics tried to give their best possible answer to the question of what Socrates had been looking for, and what he perhaps even – without himself noticing? – had found.

CONCLUSION

In this monograph I have offered a reconstruction of the Stoic views on wisdom, dealing with the question of what the Stoics understood by it, but also how this wisdom can be achieved, how difficult it is to become a sage and how this difficulty can be explained.

In Chapter 1, I presented the Stoic view on wisdom by starting out from the two extant definitions: 'knowledge of human and divine matters', and 'fitting expertise'.

I began by showing that the first and best-known definition of wisdom, as knowledge of human and divine matters is indeed Stoic, arguing against the widely accepted view that the definition is simply a commonplace, or that its origins go back to Plato's *Republic* or *Laws*. Thereafter I reconstructed the meaning of this definition, arguing that the three elements in it (knowledge, human matters and divine matters) can be taken to correspond with the three parts of philosophical discourse distinguished by the Stoics (dialectic, ethics and physics, respectively). Just as these parts constitute an organic unity, so do the elements of wisdom. We have seen that this unity does not imply that the Stoics interpreted wisdom as being omniscience or as having an all-encompassing set of doctrines. Rather, according to the Stoics, wisdom consists in the perfectly rational stable disposition, which makes one participate in the active principle that as a force or breath pervades and orders the world.

With regard to the second and more neglected Stoic definition of wisdom as 'fitting expertise', I argued that the Stoics understood wisdom as an expert-like disposition, which is 'fitting' precisely because it enables the sage to understand and act in accordance with the expert-like structure of the world. In this manner, the second definition provides a perfect parallel to the first, in terms of both the integration of dialectic, ethics and physics and with regard to the sage's perfectly rational disposition.

In Chapter 2, the central question was how to become a sage, with particular emphasis on the last, pivotal step in this process of becoming. I argued that the Stoics presented this step in physiological terms, as a qualitative change in the disposition of the human soul. As we saw, this physiological nature of the change to wisdom can help to explain the ethical and logical paradoxes for which the Stoics were famous. Whereas the change to wisdom is exceptional, it is 'ordinary', too, in the sense that the sage will continue to operate in the same manner as the inferior person he was just a moment before. However, different from the inferior person, the sage in his particular physiological disposition will no longer make any of the mistakes of the inferior person. Comparably to the experience of someone who has mastered a craft, becoming a sage thus goes with an initial unawareness. This unawareness stands in a stark contrast with Plato's exalted versions of seeing the truth.

In Chapter 3, I dealt with the question of whether the Stoics believed that someone ever achieved this state of perfection, and in particular whether they took themselves to be sages. Against the developmental view, according to which the earliest of the Stoics did consider themselves wise, we found that the Stoics stressed the extreme rarity of the sage, and that from the beginning onwards they either did not put forward the claim that they were sages, or even explicitly disavowed sagehood.

In the final Chapter 4, I explained the sage's rarity by looking at the intellectual settings against which the Stoics developed their system. They consciously fashioned themselves as followers of Socrates, who did not claim wisdom for himself, but nevertheless devoted his life to striving for it, perhaps even – without him being aware thereof – achieving this goal. Even the Stoic understanding of wisdom can be regarded as a conscious attempt to make Socratic thought explicit. Epicurus, in the debate with his professional rivals, responded to this

Stoic reverence for Socrates by explicitly positioning himself as anti-Socratic as well as a self-declared sage, thereby implicitly confirming the origin of the Stoic interpretation of wisdom.

Even if Stoicism became one of the dominant intellectual outlooks among the Roman elite,[1] in the end, after five centuries of promoting its regulative ideal of the sage, which was so difficult to achieve, it had to make way for ideologies according to which wisdom or happiness was to be found elsewhere, in another life, more real than this one, in another world, more real than this one, and with a conception of a god that is not part of this world.[2]

[1] The explanation in Stoic terms of Rome's expansion to an empire by Polybius, as set out in Brouwer (2011b), may well have contributed to the success of Stoicism among the Roman elite.

[2] See Frede (1999) 796–7.

SELECT BIBLIOGRAPHY

Sigla

ANRW: H. Temporini and W. Haase (eds.) (1972–) *Aufstieg und Niedergang der römischen Welt*, Berlin

CAG: *Commentaria in Aristotelem graeca* (1882–1909), Berlin

DK: H. Diels and W. Kranz (eds.) (1952) *Die Fragmente der Vorsokratiker*, 6th edn., Berlin

DNP: H. Cancik and H. Schneider (eds.) (1996–2011) *Der neue Pauly*, Stuttgart

FDS: K. Hülser (ed.) (1987–8) *Fragmente der Dialektik der Stoiker*, Stuttgart

LS: A.A. Long and D.N. Sedley (1987) *The Hellenistic Philosophers*, Cambridge

LSJ: H.G. Liddell, R. Scott and H.S. Jones (1996) *A Greek-English Lexicon. With a Revised Supplement*, Oxford

RE: G. Wissowa, W. Kroll and K. Mittelhaus (eds.) (1894–1974) *Paulys Realencyclopädie der classischen Altertumswissenschaft*, Stuttgart

SVF: H. von Arnim (ed.) (1903–5) *Stoicorum veterum fragmenta 1–3*, Leipzig

Primary literature

4 Maccabees, in A. Rahlfs (ed.) (1979) *Septuaginta* 1, Stuttgart 1157–84

Aeschylus, *Prometheus Unbound*: in D.L. Page (ed.) (1972) *Aeschyli septem quam supersunt tragoediae*, Oxford 287–329

'Aëtius': G. Lachenaud (ed.) (2003) *Plutarque. Oeuvres morales* 12.2: *Opinions des philosophes*, Paris, but I also give (Diels's) chapter and verse as in: J. Mau (ed.) (1971) *Plutarchi moralia* 5.2.1, Berlin 50–153 A new edition is in preparation; for book 2 see already: in J. Mansfeld and D.T. Runia (eds.) (2009) *Aëtiana* 2, Leiden 664–714

Alcinous, *Handbook of Platonism*: J. Whittaker (ed.) (1990) *Alcinoos. Enseignement des doctrines de Platon*, Paris

Alexander of Aphrodisias, *Commentary on Aristotle's Topics*: M. Wallies (ed.) (1891) *Alexandri Aphrodisiensis in Aristotelis topicorum libros octo commentaria (CAG 2.2)*, Berlin

Ethical Questions: in I. Bruns (ed.) (1892) *Alexandri Aphrodisiensis praeter commentaria scripta minora: Quaestiones, De fato, De mixtione (CAG. Supplementum aristotelicum 2.2)*, Berlin 118–63

On Fate: R.W. Sharples (ed.) (1893) *Alexander of Aphrodisias. On Fate*, London

On Mixture: R.B. Todd (ed.) (1976) *Alexander of Aphrodisias on Stoic Physics*, Leiden

Supplement to On the Soul: in I. Bruns (ed.) (1887) *Alexandri Aphrodisiensis praeter commentaria scripta minora. De anima liber cum mantissa (CAG. Supplementum aristotelicum 2.1)*, Berlin

Alexinus, *Fragments*: in K. Döring (ed.) (1972) *Die Megariker*, Amsterdam 21–7

Ammonius, *Commentary on Aristotle's Prior Analytics*: M. Wallies (ed.) (1899) *Ammonius in Aristotelis Analyticorum priorum librum I commentarium (CAG 4.6)*, Berlin

ps.-Andronicus, *On Emotions*: A. Glibert-Thirry (ed.) (1977) *Pseudo-Andronicus.* Περὶ παθῶν *(Corpus latinum commentariorum in Aristotelem Graecorum.* Suppl. 2*)*, Leiden

Anecdota Graeca Parisiensa: J.A. Cramer (ed.) (1839–51) *Anecdota Graeca e codd. manuscriptis bibliothecae regiae Parisiensis*, Oxford

Antiochus of Ascalon, *Fragments*: in H.J. Mette (1986) 'Philon von Larissa und Antiochos von Askalon', *Lustrum* 28 25–63

Antigonus of Carystus: T. Dorandi (ed.) (1999) *Antigone de Caryste*, Paris

Antisthenes, *Fragments*: see Giannantoni (1990) vol. 2, 137–225

Apollonius of Rhodes, *Argonautica*: H. Fränkel (ed.) (1970) *Apollonii Rhodii Argonautica*, 2nd edn., Oxford

Apuleius, *On Plato and His Doctrines*: in J. Beaujeu (ed.) (1973) *Apulée. Opuscules philosophiques (Du dieu de Socrate, Platon et sa doctrine, Du monde) et fragments*, Paris 47–107

Arcesilaus, *Fragments*: H.J. Mette (1984) 'Zwei Akademiker heute: Krantor von Soloi und Arkesilaus von Pitane', *Lustrum* 26: 7–94

Aristocles of Messene, *Fragments*: H. Heiland (ed.) (1925) *Aristoclis Messenii reliquiae*, Giessen, and M.L. Chiesara (ed.) (2001) *Aristocles of Messene. Testimonia and Fragments*, Oxford

Aristotle, *Metaphysics*: W.D. Ross (ed.) (1924) *Aristotle's Metaphysics. A Revised Text with Introduction and Commentary*, Oxford

Nicomachean Ethics: L. Bywater (ed.) (1894) *Aristotelis Ethica Nicomacheia*, Oxford

Poetics: S. Halliwell (ed.) (1995) *Aristotle. Poetics*, Cambridge, Mass.

Sophistical Refutations: W.D. Ross (ed.) (1958) *Aristotelis Sophistici elenchi*, Oxford

Topics: J. Brunschwig (ed.) (1967–2007) *Aristote. Topiques*, Paris

Fragments: W.D. Ross (ed.) (1955) *Aristotelis fragmenta selecta*, Oxford

Arius Didymus, *Fragments*: in H. Diels (1879) *Doxographi Graeci, Berlin* 445–72

Aspasius, *Commentary on Aristotle's Nicomachean Ethics*: G. Heylbut (ed.) (1889) *Aspasii in Ethica Nicomacheia quae supersunt commentaria (CAG* 19.1*)*, Berlin

Athenaeus: S.D. Olson (ed.) (2006–12) *Athenaeus. The Learned Banqueters*, Cambridge, Mass.

Augustine, *Against the Academics*: P. Knöll (ed.) (1922) *Sancti Aureli Augustini Contra academicos libri tres, De beata vita liber unus, De ordine liber duo (Corpus scriptorum ecclesiasticorum Latinorum* 83*)*, Vienna

On the Trinity: W.J. Mountain and F. Glorie (eds.) (1968) *Sancti Aurelii Augustini. De trinitate libri XV. Libri XIII–XV*, Turnhout

Cicero, *In Defence of Murena*: in A.C. Clark (ed.) (1905) *M. Tulli Ciceronis orationes* 1, Oxford 243–91

On Divination: A.S. Pease (ed.) (1955) *M. Tulli Ciceronis De divinatione* [1920–3], 2nd edn., Darmstadt

On Ends: T. Schiche (ed.) (1915) *M. Tulli Ciceronis De finibus bonorum et malorum*, Leipzig

On Fate: in R. Giomini (ed.) (1975) *M. Tulli Ciceronis scripta quae manserunt omnia* 46*: De divinatione, De fato, Timaeus*, Leipzig 149–76

On Friendship: in J.G.F. Powell (ed.) (2006) *M. Tulli Ciceronis De re publica, De legibus, Cato maior de senectute, Laelius de amicitia*, Oxford 317–65

On the Laws: in J.G.F. Powell (ed.) (2006) *M. Tulli Ciceronis De re publica, De legibus, Cato maior de senectute, Laelius de amicitia*, Oxford 155–266

Lucullus: C. Schäublin et al. (eds.) (1995) *Cicero. Akademische Abhandlungen. Lucullus*, Hamburg

On the Nature of the Gods: A.S. Pease (ed.) (1955–8) *M. Tulli Ciceronis De natura deorum*, Cambridge, Mass.

On Old Age: in J.G.F. Powell (ed.) (2006) *M. Tulli Ciceronis De re publica, De legibus, Cato maior de senectute, Laelius de amicitia*, Oxford 267–315

On the Orator: A.S. Wilkins (ed.) (1902) *M. Tullius Cicero. De Oratore*, Oxford

On the Paradoxes of the Stoics: M.V. Ronnick (ed.) (1991) *Cicero's 'Paradoxa Stoicorum'*, Frankfurt am Main

On Proper Functions: M. Winterbottom (ed.) (1994) *M. Tulli Ciceronis de officiis*, Oxford

Tusculan Disputations: M. Pohlenz (ed.) (1918) *M. Tulli Ciceronis scripta quae manserunt omnia* 44*. Tusculanae disputationes*, Leipzig

Varro: in O. Plasberg (ed.) (1922) *Cicero. Academicorum reliquiae cum Lucullo*, Leipzig 1–25

Cleanthes, *Hymn to Zeus*: J.C. Thom (ed.) (2005) *Cleanthes' Hymn to Zeus*, Tübingen

Clement of Alexandria, *Miscellanies 1–6*: O. Stählin and L. Früchtel (eds.) (1960) *Clemens Alexandrinus* 2*: Stromata Buch 1–6*, 3rd edn., Berlin

Miscellanies 7–8: in O. Stählin and L. Früchtel (eds.) (1970) *Clemens Alexandrinus* 3*: Stromata Buch 7 und 8, Excerpta ex Theodoto, Eclogae propheticae, Quis dives salvetur, Fragmente*, 2nd edn., Berlin 1–102

Protrepticus: in O. Stählin and U. Treu (eds.) (1972) *Clemens Alexandrinus 1: Protrepticus und Paedagogus*, 3rd edn., Berlin 1–88
Selections from the Prophets: in O. Stählin and L. Früchtel (eds.) (1970) *Clemens Alexandrinus 3: Stromata Buch 7 und 8. Excerpta ex Theodoto, Eclogae propheticae, Quis dives salvetur, Fragmente*, 2nd edn., Berlin 136–55
The Teacher: in O. Stählin and U. Treu (eds.) (1972) *Clemens Alexandrinus 1: Protrepticus und Paedagogus*, 3rd edn., Berlin 89–292
Cornutus, *Compendium of Greek Theology*: C. Lang (ed.) (1881) *Cornuti theologiae Graecae compendium*, Leipzig
Crates, *Fragments*: see Giannantoni (1990), vol. 2, 523–75
Damoxenus, *Fragments*: in R. Kassel and C. Austin (eds.) (1986) *Poetae comici Graeci 5. Damoxenus-Magnes*, Berlin 1–7
David, *Introduction*: in A. Busse (ed.) (1904) *Davidis prolegomena philosophiae et in Porphyrii isagogen commentarium (CAG 18.2)*, Berlin 1–79
Demetrius of Magnesia, *Fragments*: J. Mejer (1981) 'Demetrius of Magnesia: on Poets and Authors of the Same Name', *Hermes* 109 447–72
Digest: in T. Mommsen (ed.) (1911) *Corpus iuris civilis* 1, 12th edn., Berlin
Dio Chrysostomus, *Orations*: H. von Arnim (1893–6) *Quae exstant omnia Dionis prusaensis*, Berlin
Diodorus Cronus, *Fragments*: in K. Döring (ed.) (1972) *Die Megariker* (Amsterdam) 28–44, and Giannantoni (1990) vol. 1 413–31
Diogenes of Sinope, *Fragments*: in Giannantoni (1990) vol. 2 227–509
Diogenes Laertius: Dorandi, T. (ed.) (2013) *Diogenes Laertius. Lives of Eminent Philosophers*, Cambridge
Diogenianus, *Fragments*: A. Gercke (ed.) (1885) *Jahrbücher für classische Philologie*. Suppl. 14 748–55
[Dionysius Thrax] *Scholia on Dionysius Thrax*: A. Hilgard (ed.) (1901) *Scholia in Dionysii Thracis artem grammaticam (Grammatici graeci 1.3)*, Leipzig
Empedocles, *Fragments*: in DK 1 276–375
Epictetus, *Dissertations*: H. Schenkl (ed.) (1916) *Epicteti dissertationes ab Arriano digestae. Editio maior*, Leipzig
Epicurus, *Fragments*: H. Usener (ed.) (1887) *Epicurea*, Leipzig
Epiphanius, *On Faith*: in K. Holl and J. Dummer (eds.) (1985) *Epiphanius 3. Panarion haer. 65–80, De fide*, 2nd edn., Berlin 496–526
Eusebius of Casarea, *Preparation for the Gospel*: K. Mras (ed.) (1954) *Eusebius Werke 8. Die Praeparatio evangelica*, Berlin
Galen, *On the Different Pulses*: in C.G. Kühn (ed.) (1824) C. *Galeni opera omnia* 8, Leipzig 493–961
On the Doctrines of Hippocrates and Plato: P.H. de Lacy (ed.) (1978–84) *Galeni de placitis Hippocratis et Platonis (Corpus medicorum Graecorum 5.4.1.2)*, Berlin

On the Natural Faculties: in C.G. Kühn (ed.) (1821) C. *Galeni opera omnia* 2, Leipzig 1–204

The Soul's Dependence on the Body (= Quod animi mores): in I. Müller (ed.), *Claudii Galeni Pergameni scripta minora* 2, Leipzig 32–79

ps.-Galen, *On the History of Philosophy*: in H. Diels (ed.) (1879) *Doxographi Graeci*, Berlin 595–648

Medical Definitions: in C.G. Kühn (ed.) (1830) C. *Galeni opera omnia* 19, Leipzig 346–462

Great Etymological Dictionary: T. Gaisford (ed.) (1848) *Etymologicon magnum*, Oxford

Gregory of Nazianzus, *Letters*: P. Gallay (ed.) (1964–7) *Saint Grégoire de Nazianze. Lettres*, Paris

Hecato, *Fragments*: H. Gomoll (1933) *Der stoische Philosoph Hekaton. Seine Begriffswelt und Nachwirkung unter Beigaben seiner Fragmente*, Borsdorf

Heraclitus, *Fragments*: in DK 1 139–90

Heraclitus, *Homeric Problems*: F. Buffière (ed.) (1962) *Héraclite. Allégories d'Homère*, Paris

Hermias of Alexandria, *Commentary on Plato's Phaedrus*: P. Couvreur (ed.) (1901) *Hermiae Alexandrini in Platonis Phaedrum scholia*, Paris

Hermias, *Derision of the Heathen Philosophers*: R.P.C. Hanson (ed.) (1993) *Hermias. Satire des philosophes païens*, Paris

Hermippus, *Fragments*: J. Bollansée (ed.) (1999) *Hermippus of Smyrna (Die Fragmente der griechischen Historiker IVA3, 1026)*, Leiden

Herodotus: Ph.-E. Legrand (ed.) (1930–54), *Herodote. Histoires*, Paris

Hesiod, *Theogony*: M.L. West (ed.) (1966) *Hesiod. Theogony*, Oxford

Hierocles, *Elements of Ethics*: G. Bastianini and A.A. Long (eds.) (1992) 'Hierocles. 1. *Elementa moralia*' in *Corpus dei papiri filosofici greci e latini (CPF). Parte* I: *Autore noti:* 1**, Florence 268–451

Hippobotus, *Fragments*: M. Gigante (1983) 'Frammenti di Ippoboto' in A. Mastrocinque (ed.) *Omaggio a P. Treves*, Padua 151–93

Homer, *Iliad*: T.W. Allen (ed.) (1931) *Homeri Ilias*, Oxford

Odyssee: P. von der Mühll (ed.) (1962) *Homeri Odyssea*, Stuttgart

Isidorus of Pelusion, *Letters*: J.P. Migne (ed.) (1864) *Isidori Pelusiotae epistularum libri quinque (Patrologia Graeca 78)*, Paris

Jerome, *Commentary on the Letter to the Ephesians*: in J.P. Migne (ed.) (1845) *Hieronymii opera omina 7 (Patrologia Latina* 26), Paris 439–554

Julian, *Orations 6*: in G. Rochefort (ed.) (1963) *L'empereur Julien. Oeuvres complètes* 2.1, Paris 133–73

Lactantius, *Institutions*: S. Brandt (ed.) (1890) *L. Caeli Firmiani Lactanti opera omnia* 1 *(CSEL* 19*)*, Vienna

[Lucanus] *Scholia on Lucanus' Civil War*: H. Usener (ed.) (1889) *Scholia in Lucani Bellum civile* 1. *Commenta Bernensia*, Leipzig

Lucian, *Philosophers for Sale*: in A.D. Harmon (ed.) (1915) *Lucian* 2, Cambridge, Mass. 449–511

Macrobius, *Commentary on the Dream of Scipio*: I. Willis (ed.) (1963) *Ambrosii Theodosii Macrobii Commentarii in somnium Scipionis*, Leipzig

Marcus Aurelius, *Meditations*: J. Dalfen (ed.) (1987) *Marci Aurelii Antonini ad se ipsum libri xii*, 2nd edn., Leipzig

Menander, *Fragments*: R. Kassel and C. Austin (eds.) (1983) *Menander (PCG* 6.2*)*, Berlin

Metrodorus, *Fragments*: A. Körte (ed.) (1890) 'metrodori epicurei fragmenta', *Jahrbücher für classische Philologie*. Suppl. 17 529–97

Monimus of Syracuse, *Fragments*: see Giannantoni (1990) vol. 2 519–21

Nemesius, *On the Nature of Man*: M. Morani (ed.) (1987) *Nemesii Emeseni de natura hominis*, Leipzig

Numenius, *Fragments*: E. Des Places (ed.) (1973) *Numénius. Fragments*, Paris

Olympiodorus, *Commentary on the Gorgias*: L.G. Westerink (ed.) (1970) *Olympiodori in Platonis Gorgiam commentaria*, Berlin

Commentary on Plato's First Alcibiades: L.G. Westerink (ed.) (1982) *Olympiodorus. Commentary on the first Alcibiades of Plato*, 2nd edn., Amsterdam

Origen, *Against Celsus*: M. Borret (ed.) (1967–76) *Origène. Contre Celse*, Paris

Homily on Jeremiah: in E. Klostermann (ed.) (1901) *Origenes. Werke* 3, Leipzig 1–195

On Prayer: P. Koetschau (ed.) (1899) *Origenes. Werke* 2, Leipzig

On Principles: H. Crouzel and M. Simonetti (eds.) (1979–80) *Origène. Traité des principes*, Paris

Panaetius, *Fragments*: F. Alesse (ed.) (1997) *Panezio di Rodi. Testimonianze*, Naples, and M. van Straaten (ed.) (1962) *Panaetii Rhodii fragmenta*, 3rd edn., Leiden

Pausanias, *Description of Greece*: F. Spiro (ed.) (1903) *Pausaniae Graeciae descriptio*, Leipzig

PHerc. 1020: See FDS, 88

Philo of Alexandria, *Allegorical Interpretation*: in L. Cohn and P. Wendland (eds.) (1896) *Philonis Alexandrini opera quae supersunt* 1, Berlin 61–169

On Agriculture: in L. Cohn and P. Wendland (eds.) (1897) *Philonis Alexandrini opera quae supersunt* 2, Berlin 1–60

On the Change of Names: in L. Cohn and P. Wendland (eds.) (1898) *Philonis Alexandrini opera quae supersunt* 3, Berlin 156–203

On the Creation: in L. Cohn and P. Wendland (eds.) (1896) *Philonis Alexandrini opera quae supersunt* 1, Berlin 1–60

On Dreams: in L. Cohn and P. Wendland (eds.) (1898) *Philonis Alexandrini opera quae supersunt* 3, Berlin 204–58

On the Eternity of the World: in L. Cohn and P. Wendland (eds.) (1915) *Philonis Alexandrini opera quae supersunt* 6, Berlin 72–119

On God: F. Siegert (ed.) (1988) *Philon von Alexandrien. Über die Gottesbezeichnung 'wohltätig verzehrendes Feuer' (De deo). Rückübersetzung des Fragments aus dem Armenischen, deutsche Übersetzung und Kommentar*, Tübingen

On the Migration of Abraham: in L. Cohn and P. Wendland (eds.) (1897) *Philonis Alexandrini opera quae supersunt* 2, Berlin 268–314

On Noah's Work as a Planter: in L. Cohn and P. Wendland (eds.) (1897) *Philonis Alexandrini opera quae supersunt* 2, Berlin 133–69

On the Preliminary Studies: in L. Cohn and P. Wendland (eds.) (1898) *Philonis Alexandrini opera quae supersunt* 3, Berlin 72–109

Questions and Answers on Genesis: C. Mercier (ed.) (1979–84) *Quaestiones et solutiones in Genesim I–VI e versione armenica (Les œuvres de Philon d'Alexandrie* 34a-b*)*, Paris

On Sobriety: in L. Cohn and P. Wendland (eds.), *Philonis Alexandrini opera quae supersunt* 2, Berlin 170–214

Philodemus, *On Freedom of Speech*: A. Olivieri (ed.) (1914) *Philodemi* Περὶ παρρησίας, Leipzig

Index of the Stoics: T. Dorandi (ed.) (1994) *Philodemus. Storia dei filosofi. La Stoa da Zenone a Panezio (PHerc.* 1018*)*, Leiden

On Music: D. Delattre (ed.) (2007) *Philodème de Gadara. Sur la musique* 4, Paris

On Piety: A. Henrichs (1974) 'Die Kritik der stoischen Theologie im PHerc. 1428', *Cronache ercolanesi* 4: 5–32 and D. Obbink (ed.) (1996) *Philodemus. On Piety* 1, Oxford

On the Stoics: T. Dorandi (ed.) (1982) 'Filodemo. *Gli Stoici* (*PHerc.* 155 e 339)', *Cronache ercolanesi* 12 92–133

Philoponus, *Commentary on Nichomachus' Introduction to Arithmetic*: G.R. Giardina (ed.) (1999) *Giovanni Filopono matematico tra neopitagorismo e neoplatonismo (Symbolon* 20*)*, Catania

Pindar: H. Maehler (ed.) (1989) *Pindari carmina cum fragmentis* 2*. Fragmenta. Indices*, Leipzig

Plato: Plato's dialogues are quoted from the *Oxford Classical Texts* editions

[Plato] *Old Scholia on the Alcibiades*: in W.C. Greene (ed.) (1938) *Scholia Platonica (Philological monographs* 8*)*, Haverford 89–107

Plutarch, *Against Colotes*: in B. Einarson and P.H. de Lacy (eds.) (1967) *Plutarch. Moralia* 14*: 1086C–1147A*, Cambridge, Mass. 190–315

On Common Notions: in H. Cherniss (ed.) (1976) *Plutarch. Moralia* 13.2*: 1033A–1086B*, Cambridge, Mass. 660–873

On the Face of the Moon: M. Pohlenz (ed.) (1955) *Plutarchi moralia* 5.3 Leipzig 31–89

On the Fortune or Virtue of Alexander: in W. Nachstädt, W. Sieveking and J. Titchener (eds.) (1935) *Plutarchi moralia* 2.2, Leipzig 75–120

Isis and Osiris: W. Sieveking and W. Nachstädt (eds.) (1935) *Plutarchi moralia* 2.3, Leipzig

Life of Aratus: in C. Lindskog and K. Ziegler (eds.) (1971) *Plutarchi vitae parallelae* 3.1, 2nd edn., Leipzig

Life of Cato the Younger: in C. Lindskog and K. Ziegler (eds.) (1964) *Plutarchi vitae parallelae* 2.1, 2nd edn., Leipzig

Life of Pyrrhus: in C. Lindskog and K. Ziegler (ed.) (1971) *Plutarchi vitae parallelae* 3.1, 2nd edn., Leipzig

On Moral Virtue: in W.R. Paton, M. Pohlenz and W. Sieveking (eds.) (1972) *Plutarchi moralia* 3, Berlin 127–56

Progress = *How a Man May Become Aware of his Progress in Virtue*: in W.R. Paton, I. Wegehaupt, M. Pohlenz and H. Gärtner (eds.) (1993) *Plutarchi moralia* 1, 3rd edn., Stuttgart 149–71

On Stoic Contradictions: in H. Cherniss (ed.) (1976) *Plutarch. Moralia* 13.2: *1033A–1086B*, Cambridge, Mass. 412–603

Synopsis = *Synopsis of the Treatise 'The Stoics talk More Paradoxically than the Poets'* in H. Cherniss (ed.) (1976) *Plutarch. Moralia* 13.2: *1033A–1086B*, Cambridge, Mass. 610–19

That It is Impossible: in B. Einarson and P.H. de Lacy (eds.) (1967) *Plutarch. Moralia* 14: *1086C–1147A*, Cambridge, Mass. 14–149

On the Tranquillity of Mind: in W.R. Paton, M. Pohlenz and W. Sieveking (eds.) (1972) *Plutarchi moralia* 3, Berlin 187–220

ps.-Plutarch, *On Homer*: J.F. Kindstrand (ed.) (1990) *[Plutarchi] De Homero*, Leipzig

PMilVogliano 1241: F. Decleva Caizzi and M.S. Funghi (1988) 'Un testo sul concetto stoico di progresso morale (PMil Vogliano inv. 1241)' in *Aristoxenica, Menandrea. Fragmenta philosophica (Studi e testi per il corpus dei papiri filosofici greci e latini* 3), Florence 85–124

Posidonius, *Fragments*: L. Edelstein and I.G. Kidd (eds.) (1972) *Posidonius* I. *The Fragments*, Cambridge

Proclus, *Commentary on Plato's Alcibiades*: L.G. Westerink (ed.) (1954) *Proclus diadochus. Commentary on the First Alcibiades of Plato*, Amsterdam

Commentary on Plato's Republic: G. Kroll (ed.) (1899–1901) *Procli diadochi in Platonis Rem publicam commentarii*, Leipzig

Commentary on Plato's Timaeus: E. Diehl (ed.) (1903–5) *Procli diadochi in Platonis Timaeum commentaria*, Leipzig

Pyrrho, *Fragments*: F. Decleva Caizzi (ed.) (1981) *Pirrone. Testimonianze*, Naples

Quintilian, *Institutions*: J. Cousin (ed.) (1975–80) *Quintilien. Institution oratoire*, Paris

Seneca, *On Constancy*: in L.D. Reynolds (ed.) (1977) *L. Annaei Senecae dialogorum libri duodecim*, Oxford 18–38

To Helvia: in L.D. Reynolds (ed.) (1977) *L. Annaei Senecae dialogorum libri duodecim*, Oxford 291–317

Letter(s): L.D. Reynolds (ed.) (1965) *L. Annaei Senecae ad Luculium epistulae morales*, Oxford

To Marcia: in L.D. Reynolds (ed.) (1977) *L. Annaei Senecae dialogorum libri duodecim*, Oxford 129–66

Natural Questions: H.M. Hine (ed.) (1996) *L. Annaei Senecae naturalium quaestionum libri*, Stuttgart

On Tranquillity: in L.D. Reynolds (ed.) (1977) *L. Annaei Senecae dialogorum libri duodecim*, Oxford 207–38

Sextus Empiricus, *Against the Professors 1–6*: H. Mutschmann and I. Mau (eds.), *Sexti Empirici opera* 3. *Adversus mathematicos libri 1–6*, 2nd edn., Berlin

Against the Professors 7–11: H. Mutschmann (ed.) (1914) *Sexti Empirici opera* 2. *Adversus dogmaticos libri quinque (Adv. Mathem. 7–11)*, Berlin

Outlines of Pyrrhonism: H. Mutschmann and I. Mau (eds.) (1958) *Sexti Empirici opera* 1: ΠΥΡΡΩΝΕΙΩΝ ΥΠΟΤΥΠΩΣΕΩΝ, 2nd edn., Berlin

Simplicius, *Commentary on Aristotle's Categories*: C. Kalbfleisch (ed.) (1907) *Simplicius. Commentarium in Aristotelis categorias (CAG 8)*, Berlin

Stilpo, *Fragments*: in K. Döring (ed.) (1972) *Die Megariker*, Amsterdam 46–61, and Giannantoni (1990), vol. 2 449–68

Stobaeus: C. Wachsmuth and O. Hense (eds.) (1884–1923) *Ioannis Stobaei anthologium*, Berlin

Strabo: S. Radt (ed.) (2002–11) *Strabons Geographika*, Göttingen

Tatian, *Address to the Greeks*: M. Whittaker (ed.) (1982) *Tatian. Oratio ad Graecos and fragments*, Oxford

Tertullian, *Apology*: in T.R. Glover (ed.) (1931) *Tertullian. Apology, De spectaculis*, Cambridge, Mass. 1–227

Themistius, *Commentary on the Soul*: R. Heinze (ed.) (1899) *Themistii in libros Aristotelis de anima paraphrasis (CAG 5.3)*, Berlin

Orations: H. Schenkl *et al.* (eds.) (1965–74) *Themistii orationes quae supersunt*, Leipzig

Timon, *Fragments*: M. di Marco (ed.) (1989) *Timone di Fluente. Silli*, Rome, and in H. Lloyd-Jones and P. Parsons (eds.) (1983) *Supplementum Hellenisticum*, Berlin 369–95

Xenocrates, *Fragments*: R. Heinze (ed.) (1892) *Xenokrates. Darstellung der Lehre und Sammlung der Fragmente*, Leipzig, and M. Isnardi Parente and T. Dorandi (eds.) (2012) *Senocrate e Ermodoro. Testimonianze e frammenti*, Pisa

Xenophon, *Apology*: in E.C. Marchant and O.J. Todd (eds.) (1923) Xenophon, *Memorabilia. Oeconomicus. Symposium. Apology*, Cambridge, Mass. 637–63

Memorabilia: M. Bandini and L.-A. Dorion (eds.) (2000–11) *Xénophon. Mémorables*, Paris

Bibliography

Secondary literature

Aall, A. (1896) *Geschichte der Logosidee in der griechischen Philosophie*, Leipzig

Ackermann, E. (1907) *De Senecae Hercule Oetaeo, Philologus. Suppl.* 10 323–428

(1912) 'Der leidende Hercules des Seneca', *Rheinisches Museum* 67 425–71

Adam, J. (1911) *The Vitality of Platonism and Other Essays*, Cambridge

Albert, K. (1989) *Über Platons Begriff der Philosophie*, Sankt Augustin

Alesse, F. (1997) 'Il tema stoico del διαλεληθὼς σοφός e il διαλανθάνων λόγος dell'eristica megarica', *Elenchos* 18 57–75

(2000) *La Stoa e la tradizione socratica*, Naples

Alexander, W.H. (1946) 'Cato of Utica in the Work of Seneca philosophus', *Transactions of the Royal Society of Canada. Section II: Literature, History, Archeology, Sociology, Political Economy and Allied Subjects, in English 3*.40 59–74

Alpers, I. (1912) 'Hercules in bivio', diss. Göttingen

Althoff, J. and D. Zeller (eds.) (2006) *Die Worte der sieben Weisen*, Darmstadt

Amand, D. (1945) *Fatalisme et liberté dans l'antiquité grecque*, Louvain.

Annas, J. (1993) *The Morality of Happiness*, New York

(1995) 'Reply to Cooper', *Philosophy and Phenomenological Research* 55 599–610

(2007) 'Ethics in Stoic Philosophy', *Phronesis* 52 58–87

(2008) 'The Sage in Ancient Philosophy' in F. Alesse *et al.* (eds.) *Anthropine sophia*, Naples 11–27

Annas, J. and J. Barnes (2000) *Sextus Empiricus. Outlines of Scepticism*, 2nd edn., Cambridge 777–8

Appel, B. (1914) *Das Bildungs- und Erziehungsideal Quintilians nach der Institutio oratoria*, Donauwörth

Arnim, H. von (1903) 'Diogenianos 3', *RE* 5.1 777–8

(1921) 'Kleanthes 2', *RE* 11 558–74

Assmann, A. (1991) 'Was ist Weisheit? Wegmarken in einem weiten Feld' in A. Assmann (ed.) *Weisheit, Archäologie der literarischen Kommunikation 3*, Munich 15–44

Barker, A. (1984) *Greek Musical Writings* 1: *The Musician and His Art*, Cambridge

Barnes, J. (1999) 'Logic and Language: Introduction' in K. Algra, J. Barnes, J. Mansfeld and M. Schofield (eds.) *The Cambridge History of Hellenistic Philosophy*, Cambridge 65–76

Battaly, H. (2008) 'Virtue Epistemology', *Philosophy Compass* 3/4 639–63

Baumstark, A. (1922) *Geschichte der syrischen Literatur mit Ausschluß der christlich-palästinensischen Texte*, Bonn

Beaujeu, J. (ed.) (1973) *Apulée. Opuscules philosophiques (Du dieu de Socrate, Platon et sa doctrine, Du monde) et fragments*, Paris

Beckman, J. (1979) *The Religious Dimension of Socrates' Thought*, Waterloo
Bees, R. (2010) '"Natur" in der Telosformel Zenons von Kition', *Antike Naturwissenschaft und ihre Rezeption* 20 45–64
(2011) *Zenons Politeia*, Leiden
Bekker, I. (ed.) (1842) *Sextus Empiricus*, Berlin
Bénatouïl, T. (2002) 'Logos et scala naturae dans le stoïcisme de Zenon et Cleanthe', *Elenchos* 23 297–331
(2005) 'Force, fermeté et froid: la dimension physique de la vertu stoïcienne', *Philosophie antique* 5 5–30
Bernard, H. (1997) *Hermeias von Alexandrien. Kommentar zu Platons 'Phaidros'*, Tübingen
Berry, E.G. (1940) *The History and Development of the Concept* of θεία μοῖρα *and* θεία τύχη *Down To and Including Plato*, Chicago
Betegh, G. (2003) 'Cosmological Ethics in the *Timaeus* and Early Stoicism', *Oxford Studies in Ancient Philosophy* 24 273–302
Bett, R. (1997) *Sextus Empiricus. Against the Ethicists (Adversus mathematicos XI)*, Oxford
(2005) *Sextus Empiricus. Against the Logicians*, Cambridge
(2009) 'Stoic Ethics' in M.L. Gill and P. Pellegrin (eds.) *A Companion to Ancient Philosophy*, Chichester
(2011) 'Socratic Ignorance' in D.R. Morrison (ed.) *The Cambridge Companion to Socrates*, Cambridge 215–36
(2012) *Sextus Empiricus. Against the Physicists*, Cambridge
Bickel, E. (1957) 'μετασχηματίζεσθαι. Ein übersehener Grundbegriff des Poseidonios', *Rheinisches Museum* 100 98–9
Billerbeck, M. (1987) 'Faule Fische. Zu Timon von Phleius und seiner Philosophensatire', *Museum Helveticum* 44 127–33
Blaise, F. (1992) 'L'épisode de Typhée dans la *Théogonie* d'Hésiode (v. 820–885). La stabilisation du monde', *Revue des études grecques* 90 349–70
Bloos, L. (1973) *Probleme der stoischen Physik*, Hamburg
Bluck, R.S. (ed.) (1961) *Plato's Meno*, Cambridge
Bobzien, S. (1998) *Determinism and Freedom in Stoic Philosophy*, Oxford
Boeri, M.D. (2009) 'Does Cosmic Nature Matter? Some Remarks on the Cosmological Aspects of Stoic Ethics' in R. Salles (ed.) *God and Cosmos in Stoicism*, Oxford 173–200
Bonazzi, M. (2011) *Platone. Fedro*, Turin
(2012) 'Antiochus and Platonism' in D. Sedley (ed.) *The Philosophy of Antiochus*, Cambridge 307–33
Bonhöffer, A. (1890) *Epictet und die Stoa*, Stuttgart
(1894) *Die Ethik des Stoikers Epictet*, Stuttgart
Boyancé, P. (1963) 'Cicéron et le Premier Alcibiade', *Revue des études latines* 41 210–29
(1975) 'L'éloge de la philosophie dans le *De legibus* 1, 58–62', *Ciceroniana* NS 2 21–42

Boys-Stones, G.R. (2001) *Post-Hellenistic Philosophy*, Oxford
Breitenbach, H.B. (1967) 'Xenophon', *RE* 9A 1567–2052
Brennan, T. (1996) 'Reasonable Impressions in Stoicism', *Phronesis* 41 318–34
Bridoux, A. (1966) *Le stoicisme et son influence*, Paris
Brisson, L. (ed.) (1989) *Platon. Phèdre*, Paris
(ed.) (2008) *Platon. Œuvres complètes*, Paris
Brouwer, R. (2002) 'Stoic Sagehood', *Oxford Studies in Ancient Philosophy* 23 181–224
(2006) *'Zeno's Political Thought: the City of Sages'*, http://www.archelogos.com/zeno/phessay.htm, consulted 5 September 2013
(2007) 'The Early Stoic Doctrine of the Change to Wisdom', *Oxford Studies in Ancient Philosophy* 33 285–315
(2008) 'Hellenistic Philosophers on *Phaedrus* 229B–230A', *Proceedings of the Cambridge Philological Society* 235/*Cambridge Classical Journal* N.S. 55 30–48
(2011a) 'On Law and Equity: the Stoic View', *Zeitschrift der Savigny-Stiftung für Rechtsgeschichte. Romanistische Abteilung* 128 17–38.
(2011b) 'Polybius on Stoic *tyche*', *Greek, Roman, and Byzantine Studies* 51 111–32
(forthcoming) 'Stoic Sympathy' in E. Schliesser (ed.) *Sympathy. Key Concepts in Philosophy*, New York
Brunschwig, J. (1988) 'Sextus Empiricus on the kritērion' in J.M. Dillon and A.A. Long (eds.) *The Question of 'Eclecticism'. Studies in Later Greek Philosophy*, Berkeley, Calif. 145–175, repr. in J. Brunschwig (1995) *Études sur les philosophies hellénistiques*, Paris 289–319
(1991) 'On a Book-Title by Chrysippus: "On the Fact that the Ancients Admitted Dialectic Along with Demonstrations"', *Oxford Studies in Ancient Philosophy*. Suppl. 81–95, in French as (1995) 'Sur un titre d'ouvrage de Chrysippe: "Que les Anciens ont admis la dialectique aux côtés de démonstration"' in J. Brunschwig, *Études sur les philosophies hellénistiques*, Paris 233–50
(1994) 'Did Diogenes of Babylon Invent the Ontological Argument?' in J. Brunschwig, *Papers in Hellenistic Philosophy*, Cambridge 170–89
(2002) 'Zeno between Kition and Athens' in T. Scaltsas and A. Mason (eds.) *The Philosophy of Zeno*, Larnaca 11–27
Brunschwig, J. and P. Pellegrin (2001) *Long et Sedley. Les philosophes hellénistiques*, Paris
Buffière, F. (1956) *Les mythes d'Homère et la pensée grecque*, Paris
Burkert, W. (1960) 'Platon oder Pythagoras. Zum Ursprung des Wortes "Philosophie"', *Hermes* 88 159–77
(1987) *Ancient Mystery Cults*, Cambridge, Mass.
(1995) 'Der geheime Reiz des Verborgenen: Antike Mysterienkulte' in H.G. Kippenberg and G.G. Stroumsa (eds.), *Secrecy and Concealment*, Leiden 79–100

Bury, R.G. (1933–49) *Sextus Empiricus in Four Volumes*, Cambridge, Mass.
Busine, A. (2002) *Les sept sages de la Grèce antique*, Paris
Canto, M. (1993) *Platon. Gorgias*, Paris
Casevitz, M. (ed.) (2002) *Plutarque. Oeuvres morales* 15.2: *Traité 72: Sur les notions communes, contre les Stoïciens,* traduit et commenté par D. Babut, Paris
(2004) *Plutarque. Oeuvres morales* 15.1*: Traité 70: Sur les contradictions stoïciennes; Traité 71: Synopsis du traité 'Que les stoïciens tiennent des propos plus paradoxaux que les poètes',* traduit et commenté par D. Babut, Paris
Castagnoli, L. (2010) 'How Dialectical was Stoic Dialectic?' in A. Nightingale and D. Sedley (eds.), *Ancient Models of Mind*, Cambridge 153–79
Chadwick, H. (1980) *Origen. Contra Celsum* [1953] 3rd edn., Cambridge
Chantraine, P. (1999) *Dictionnaire étymologique de la langue grecque* [1968] 2nd edn., Paris
Charlton, W.W. (1985) 'Greek Philosophy and the Concept of an Academic Discipline', *History of Political Thought* 6 47–61
Cherniss, H. (1959) '[Review of] H.D. Saffrey (1955) *Le* περὶ φιλοσοφίας *d'Aristote et la théorie platonicienne des idées et des nombres*, Leiden', *Gnomon* 31 36–51
(ed.) (1976) *Plutarch's Moralia* 13.2: *1033A–1086B*, Cambridge, Mass.
Chiesara, M.L. (ed.) (2001) *Aristocles of Messene. Testimonia and Fragments*, Oxford.
Christensen, J. (1962) *An Essay on the Unity of Stoic Philosophy*, Munksgaard
Clay, J.S. (2003) *Hesiod's Cosmos*, Cambridge
Clayman, D.L. (2009) *Timon of Phlius. Pyrrhonism into Poetry*, Berlin
Colson, F.H. (ed.) (1924) *M. Fabii Quintiliani Institutionis oratoriae liber I*, Cambridge
Cooper, J.M. (1995) 'Eudaimonism and the Appeal to Nature in the Morality of Happiness. Comments on Julia Annas, *The Morality of Happiness*', *Philosophy and Phenomenological Research* 55 587–98
(2012) *Pursuits of Wisdom*, Princeton
Costa, C.D.N. (ed.) (1994) *Seneca. Four dialogues: De vita beata, De tranquilitate animi, De constantia sapientiae, Ad Helviam matrem de consolatione*, Warminster
Courcelle, P. (1974–5) *Connais-toi toi-même de Socrate à Saint Bernard*, Paris
Craig, E. (1987) *The Mind of God and the Works of Man*, Oxford
Crisp, R. (2010) 'Virtue Ethics and Virtue Epistemology', *Metaphilosophy* 41 22–40
Daiber, H. (1980) *Aetius arabus. Die Vorsokratiker in arabischer Überlieferung (Akademie der Wissenschaften und der Literatur. Veröffentlichungen der orientalischen Kommission 33)*, Wiesbaden

Daraki, M. (1989) *Une religiosité sans Dieu. Essai sur les stoïciens d'Athènes et Saint Augustin*, Paris

Decleva Caizzi, F. (1980) 'Τῦφος: contributo alla storia di un concetto', *Sandalion* 3 53–66, repr. in M. Billerbeck (ed.) (1991), *Die Kyniker in der modernen Forschung*, Amsterdam 273–85

(1986) 'Pirroniani ed accademici nel III secolo AC' in H. Flashar and O. Gigon (eds.), *Aspects de la philosophie hellenistique*, Vandoevres 147–83

(1993) 'The Porch and the Garden: Early Hellenistic Images of the Philosophical Life' in A. Bulloch, E.S. Gruen, A.A. Long and A. Stewart (eds.) *Images and Ideologies. Self-Definition in the Hellenistic World*, Berkeley 303–29

Decleva Caizzi, F. and M.S. Funghi (1988) 'Un testo sul concetto stoico di progresso morale (PMil Vogliano inv. 1241)' in *Aristoxenica, Menandrea. Fragmenta philosophica (Studi e testi per il corpus dei papiri filosofici greci e latini 3)*, Florence 85–124

(1991) 'Dossografia stoica. Riposta a Marcello Gigante' in F. Decleva Caizzi *et al.* (eds.), *Varia papyrologica*, Florence 127–34

Deichgräber, K. (1937) 'Persaios', *RE* 19 926–31

Denyer, N. (2001) *Plato. Alcibiades*, Cambridge

Diels, H. (1879) *Doxographi Graeci*, Berlin

(1901) *Poetarum philosophorum fragmenta*, Berlin

(1917) *Philodemus. Über die Götter. Drittes Buch. 2. Erläuterung des Textes (Abhandlungen der Königlich Preußischen Akademie der Wissenschaften. Jahrgang 1916. Philosopisch-historische Klasse. Nr. 6)*, Berlin

Deißner, K. (1930) *Das Idealbild des stoischen Weisen*, Greifswald

Descartes, R. [1644] *Principia philosophiae*, reprinted in C. Adam and P. Tannery (eds.) (1905) *Oeuvres de Descartes* 8.1, Paris

Di Marco, M. (ed.) (1989) *Timone di Fluente. Silli. Introduzione, edizione critica, traduzione e commento*, Rome

Dobbin, R.F. (1998) *Epictetus. Discourses. Book 1*, Oxford

Doege, H. (1896) *Quae ratio intercedat inter Panaetium et Antiochum Ascolintam in morali philosophia*, Halle

Döring, A. (1892) 'Der Begriff der Dialektik in den Memorabilien', *Archiv für Geschichte der Philosophie* 5 185–97

Döring, K. (ed.) (1972) *Die Megariker*, Amsterdam

Dörrie, H. (1987) *Der Platonismus in der Antike 1: Die geschichtlichen Wurzeln des Platonismus. Bausteine 1–35: Text, Übersetzung, Kommentar*, Stuttgart

Dörrie, H. and M. Baltes (1996) *Der Platonismus in der Antike 4: Die philosophische Lehre des Platonismus. Einige grundlegende Axiome: Platonische Physik (im antiken Verständnis) I Bausteine 101–124: Text, Übersetzung, Kommentar*, Stuttgart

Dohm, H. (1964) *Mageiros. Die Rolle des Kochs in der griechisch-römischen Komödie*, Munich

Dorandi, T. (1994) 'Diogénianos' in R. Goulet (ed.) *Dictionnaire des philosophes antiques* 2, Paris 833–4

(ed.) (1994) *Philodemus. Storia dei filosofi. La Stoa da Zenone a Panezio (PHerc. 1018)*, Leiden

Dorion, L.-A. (2011) 'The Rise and Fall of the Socratic Problem' in D.R. Morrison (ed.) *The Cambridge Companion to Socrates*, Cambridge 1–23

Dougan, T.W. (ed.) (1904) *M. Tulli Ciceronis Tusculanarum disputationum libri quinque* 1, Cambridge

Dougan, T.W. and R.M. Henry (eds) (1934) *M. Tulli Ciceronis Tusculanarum disputationum libri quinque* 2, Cambridge

Ernesti, J.A. (1739) *Clavis Ciceroniana*, Leipzig

Du Toit, D.S. (1997) *Theios anthropos*, Tübingen

Dudley, D. (1983) *A History of Cynicism* [1937], 2nd edn., Bristol

Dufour, R. (2004) *Chrysippe. Oeuvre philosophique*, Paris

Duhot, J.-J. (1989) *La conception stoïcienne de la causalité*, Paris

Dyck, A.R. (2004) *A Commentary on Cicero, De legibus*, Ann Arbor

Edelstein, L. (1966) *The Meaning of Stoicism*, Cambridge, Mass.

Edert, O. (1909) *Über Senecas Herakles und den Herakles auf dem Oeta*, Kiel

Einarson, B. and P.H. de Lacy (eds.) (1967) *Plutarch's Moralia 14: 1086A–1147A*, Cambridge, Mass.

Engberg-Pedersen, T. (1986) 'Discovering the Good: *oikeiōsis* and *kathēkonta* in Stoic Ethics' in M. Schofield and G. Striker (eds.) *The Norms of Nature*, Cambridge 145–83

Engels, J. (2010) *Die sieben Weisen*, Munich

Fabricius, J.A. (ed.) (1718) *Sexti Empirici opera Graece et Latine*, Leipzig

Ferrari, G.R.F. (1987) *Listening to the Cicadas. A Study of Plato's Phaedrus*, Cambridge

Festa, N. (1932–5) *I frammenti degli Stoici antichi*, Bari

Festugière, A.-J. (1932) *L'idéal religieux des Grecs et l'Évangile*, Paris

Fiodora, A. and D. Werner (eds.) (2007) *Dominicus Gundissalinus. De divisione philosophiae*, Freiburg im Breisgau

Fladerer, L. (1996) *Antiochos von Askalon. Hellenist und Humanist*, Graz

Fontenrose, J. (1959) *Python. A Study of Delphic Myth and its Origins*, Berkeley

Forschner, M. (1995) 'Theoria und stoische Tugend. Zenons Erbe in Cicero, Tusculanae disputationes v', *Zeitschrift für philosophische Forschung* 53 163–87

Fowler, H.N. (ed.) (1914) *Plato. Euthyphro, Apology, Crito, Phaedo, Phaedrus*, Cambridge, Mass.

Frede, M. (1994) 'The Stoic Conception of Reason' in K. Boudouris (ed.) *Hellenistic Philosophy* 2, Athens 50–63

(1996) 'Introduction' in M. Frede and G. Striker (eds.) *Rationality in Greek Thought*, Oxford 1–28

(1999) 'Epilogue' in K. Algra, J. Barnes, J. Mansfeld and M. Schofield (eds.) *The Cambridge History of Hellenistic Philosophy*, Cambridge 770–97

(2004) 'Aristotle's Account of the Origins of Philosophy', *Rhizai* 1 9–44

Frisk, H. (1960–72) *Griechisches etymologisches Wörterbuch*, Heidelberg

Fritz, K. von (1931) 'Megariker', *RE* Suppl. 5 707–24

Früchtel, U. (1968) *Die kosmologischen Vorstellungen bei Philo von Alexandrien*, Leiden

Furlani, G. (1926) *Il libro delle definizione e divisioni di Michele l'interprete (Atti della reale accademia nazionale dei Lincei. Memorie della classe di scienze morali, storiche e filolologiche 6.2)*, Rome

Gallo, I. (1981) *Teatro ellenistico minore*, Rome

Gannon, J.F. (1987) 'An Interpretation of Timon of Phlius Fr. 38 D', *American Journal of Philology* 108 603–11

Ganss, W. (1952) *Das Bild des Weisen bei Seneca*, Schaan

Gauss, H. (1937) *Plato's Conception of Philosophy*, London

Gawlick, G. and W. Görler (1994) 'Cicero' in H. Flashar (ed.) *Die hellenistische philosophie*, Basel 995–1083

Gercke, A. (ed.) (1885a) *Chrysippea. Particulam priorem*, Leipzig

(1885b) 'Chrysippea cont.', *Jahrbücher für classische Philologie*. Suppl. 14 691–781

Gerson, L.P. (1990) *God and Greek Philosophy*, London

Giannantoni, G. (1990) *Socratis et Socraticorum reliquiae*, 2nd edn., Naples

Gigante, M. (1998) *Diogene Laerzio. Vite dei filosofi*, 3rd edn., Rome

Gigon, O. (1946) 'Antike Erzählungen über die Berufung zur Philosophie', *Museum Helveticum* 3 1–21

Gladigow, B. (1965) *Sophia und Kosmos*, Hildesheim

Glucker, J. (1978) *Antiochus and the Late Academy*, Göttingen

(1988) 'Πρὸς τὸν εἰπόντα. Sources and Credibility of *De Stoicorum repugnantiis* 8', *Illinois Classical Studies* 13 473–89

Görler, W. (1990) 'Antiochos von Askalon über die Alten und über die Stoa. Beobachtungen zu Cicero, Academici posteriores 1, 24–43' in P. Steinmetz (ed.) *Beiträge zur hellenistischen Literatur und ihrer Rezeption in Rom*, Stuttgart 123–39

Goldschmidt, V. (1979) *Le système stoïcien et l'idée de temps* [1953], 4th edn., Paris

Gomperz, T. (ed.) (1866) *Philodem. Über Frömmigkeit. Erste Abteilung. Der Text*, Leipzig

Gorman, R. (2001) 'οἱ περὶ in Strabo', *Zeitschrift für Papyrologie und Epigraphik* 136 201–13

Gottschalk, H.B. (1987) 'Aristotelian Philosophy in the Roman World', *ANRW* 2.36.4 1079–174

Goulet, R. (2005) 'La méthode allégorique des stoïciens' in J.-B. Gourinat (ed.) *Les stoïciens*, Paris 93–119

Goulet-Cazé, M.-O. (1982) 'Un syllogisme stoïcien sur la loi dans la doxographie de Diogène le Cynique. À propos de Diogène Laërce VI 72', *Rheinisches Museum* 125 214–40

(1986) *L'ascèse cynique. Un commentaire de Diogène Laërce 6.70–1*, Paris

(ed.) (1999) *Diogène Laërce. Vies et doctrines des philosophes illustres*, Paris

Gourinat, J.-B. (2008) 'La dialectique de Socrate selon les Mémorables de Xénophon' in M. Narcy and A. Tordesillas (eds.) *Xénophon et Socrate*, Paris 129–59

(2011) 'Aëtius et Arius Didyme sources de Stobée' in G. Reydams-Schils (ed.) *Thinking Through Excerpts: Studies on Stobaeus*, Turnhout 143–201

Graver, M. (2007) *Stoicism and Emotion*, Chicago

Green, P. (1990) *Alexander to Actium*, Berkeley

Greene, W.C. (1944) *Moira. Fate, Good, and Evil in Greek Thought*, Cambridge, Mass.

Grimal, P. (1994) *Sénèque*, 2nd edn., Paris

Griswold jr., C.L. (1986) *Self-knowledge in Plato's Phaedrus*, New Haven

Gruppe, O. (1906) *Griechische Mythologie und Religionsgeschichte*, Munich

Gundel, H. (1912) 'Heimarmene', *RE* 7 2622–45

Haase, W. (1965) 'Ein vermeintliches Aristoteles-Fragment bei Johannes Philoponus' in H. Flashar and K. Gaiser (eds.) *Synusia. Festgabe für Wolfgang Schadewaldt zum 15. März 1965*, Pfullingen 323–54

Hackforth, R. (1952) *Plato's Phaedrus*, Cambridge

Hadot, P. (1979) 'Les divisions des parties de la philosophie dans l'Antiquité', *Museum Helveticum* 36: 201–23, repr. in P. Hadot (1998) *Études de philosophie ancienne*, Paris 125–58

(1989) 'Philosophie I Antike: E. Hellenismus F. Die Einteilung der Philosophie in der Antike' in J. Ritter and K. Gründer (eds.) *Historisches Wörterbuch der Philosophie* 7, Basel 592–607

(1991) 'La figure du sage dans l'Antiquité gréco-latine' in G. Gadoffre (ed.) *Les sagesses du monde*, Paris 9–24, repr. in P. Hadot (1998) *Études de philosophie ancienne*, Paris 233–57

(1995) *Qu'est-ce que la philosophie antique?*, Paris

(2002) *Exercises spirituels et philosophie antique*, 4th edn., Paris

Hahm, D. (1977) *The Origins of Stoic Cosmology*, Columbus

(1992) 'Diogenes Laertius 7: On the Stoics', *ANRW* 2.36.6 4076–182

Harbach, A. (2010) *Die Wahl des Lebens in der antiken Literatur*, Stuttgart

Hatzimichali, M. (2011) *Potamo of Alexandria and the Emergence of Eclecticism in Late Hellenistic Philosophy*, Cambridge

Hays, R.S. (1983) 'Lucius Annaeus Cornutus' Epidrome', diss. Austin, Tex.

Heine, O. (1869) 'Kritische Beiträge zum siebenten Buche des Laertios Diogenes', *Jahrbücher für classische Philologie* 15 611–28

Heitmann, P.A. (1940) *Imitatio dei. Die ethische Nachahmung Gottes nach der Väterlehre der zwei ersten Jahrhunderte*, Rome

Heitsch, E. (1993) *Platon. Phaidros*, Göttingen

Hengelbrock, M. (2000) *Das Problem des ethischen Fortschritts in Senecas Briefen*, Hildesheim

Henrichs, A. (1974) 'Die Kritik der stoischen Theologie im *PHerc*. 1428', *Cronache ercolanesi* 4 5–32

Hermann, K.F. (1839) *Geschichte und System der platonischen Philosophie*, Heidelberg

Hicks, R.D. (ed.) (1925) *Diogenes Laertius. Lives of Eminent Philosophers*, Cambridge, Mass.

Hillgruber, M. (1994–9) *Die pseudoplutarchische Schrift De Homero*, Stuttgart

Hirzel, R. (1877–83) *Untersuchungen zu Cicero's philosophischen Schriften*, Leipzig, esp.

(1882) *Untersuchungen zu Cicero's philosophischen Schriften* 2.1. *Die Entwicklung der stoischen Philosophie*, Leipzig

Höfer, O. (1902–9) 'Pythios' in W.H. Roscher (ed.) *Ausführliches Lexikon der griechischen und römischen Mythologie* 3.2, Leipzig

Höistad, R. (1948) *Cynic Hero and Cynic King*, Uppsala

Holl, K., and J. Dümmer (eds.) (1985) *Epiphanius* 3*: Panarion haer. 65–80. De fide*, 2nd edn., Berlin

Horn, C. (2002) *Antike Lebenskunst*, Munich

(2006) 'Was weiß der stoische Weise? Zur Epistemologie der stoischen Ethik' in C. Rapp and T. Wagner (eds.) *Wissen und Bildung in der antiken Philosophie*, Stuttgart 341–57

Hoyer, R. (1883) 'De Antiocho ascalonita', diss. Bonn

Hunter, R. (2012) *Plato and the Traditions of Ancient Literature*, Cambridge

Ierodiakonou, K. (1993) 'The Stoic Division of Philosophy', *Phronesis* 38 57–74

Inwood, B. (1984) 'Hierocles: Theory and Argument in the Second Century AD', *Oxford Studies in Ancient Philosophy* 2 151–83

(1985) *Ethics and Human Action in Early Stoicism*, Oxford

(1993) 'Seneca and Psychological Dualism' in J. Brunschwig and M.C. Nussbaum (eds.) *Passions and Perceptions*, Cambridge 150–83, repr. in Inwood (2005) 23–64

(1995) '[Review of] J. Annas (1993) *The Morality of Happiness*, New York', *Ancient Philosophy* 15 647–65

(2005) *Reading Seneca*, Oxford

Inwood, B. and L.P. Gerson (1997) *Hellenistic Philosophy*, 2nd edn., Indianapolis

(2008) *The Stoics Reader*, Indianapolis

Ioppolo, A.M. (1977) 'Aristone di Chio' in G. Giannantoni (ed.) *Scuole socratiche minori e filosofia ellenistica*, Bologna 115–40

(1980) *Aristone di Chio e lo stoicismo antico*, Naples

(1986) *Opinione e scienza. Il dibattito tra Stoici e Accademici nel III e nel II secolo AC*, Naples

Irwin, T.H. (1986) 'Stoic and Aristotelian Conceptions of Happiness' in M. Schofield and G. Striker (eds.) *The Norms of Nature*, Cambridge 205–44

(1998) 'Socratic Paradox and Stoic Theory' in S. Everson (ed.) *Ethics, (Companions to Ancient Thought 4)*, Cambridge 151–92

Isnardi Parente, M. (1994) *Gli Stoici. Opere e testimonianze*, Milan

(1966) *Techne. Momenti del pensiero greco da Platone ad Epicuro*, Florence

(1993) *Lo stoicismo ellenistico*, Rome

(1990) 'Diogeniano, gli epicurei e la τύχη', *ANRW* 2.36.4 2424–45

Jaeger, W. (1934) *Aristotle. Fundamentals of the History of his Development.* Translated with the Author's Corrections and Additions by R. Robinson, Oxford

Johnson, D.M. (2003) 'Xenophon's Socrates on Law and Justice', *Ancient Philosophy* 23 255–81

Kahn, C.H. (1996) *Plato and the Socratic Dialogue: The Philosophical Use of a Literary Form*, Cambridge

Karamanolis, G.E. (2006) *Plato and Aristotle in Agreement?*, Oxford

(2011) 'The Place of Ethics in Aristotle's Philosophy', *Oxford Studies in Ancient Philosophy* 40 133–56

Kechagia, E. (2010) 'Rethinking a Professional Rivalry: Early Epicureans Against the Stoa', *Classical Quarterly* 60 132–55

(2011) *Plutarch against Colotes*, Oxford

Kerferd, G.B. (1976) 'The Wise Man in Greece Before Plato' in C. Laga *et al.* (eds.), *Images of Man in Ancient and Medieval Thought*, Leuven 17–28

(1978) 'What Does the Wise Man Know?' in J.M. Rist (ed.) *The Stoics*, Berkeley 125–36

Kidd, I.G. (1978) 'Philosophy and Science in Posidonius', *Antike und Abendland* 24 7–15

(1988) *Posidonius II. The Commentary*, Cambridge

(1999) *Posidonius III. The Translation of the Fragments*, Cambridge

Kleingeld, P. (2012) *Kant and Cosmopolitanism*, New York

Kleingeld, P. and E. Brown (2006) 'Cosmopolitanism', *Stanford Encyclopedia of Philosophy* (online)

Körte, A. (ed.) (1890) 'metrodori epicurei fragmenta', *Jahrbücher für classische Philologie*. Suppl. 17 529–97

Korhonen, T. (1997) 'Self-Concept and Public Image of Philosophers and Philosophical Schools at the Beginning of the Hellenistic Period' in

J. Frösén (ed.) *Early Hellenistic Image. Symptoms of a Change*, Helsinki 33–102

Kühn, W. (2009) *Quel savoir après le scepticisme? Plotin et ses predecesseurs sur la connaissance de soi*, Paris

Kühner, R. and B. Gerth (1898) *Ausführliche Grammatik der griechischen Sprache 2: Satzlehre* 1, 3rd edn., Hanover

(1904) *Ausführliche Grammatik der griechischen Sprache 2: Satzlehre* 2, 3rd edn., Hanover

Lachenaud, G. (ed.) (2003) *Plutarque. Oeuvres morales 12.2: Opinions des philosophes*, Paris

Laks, A. (1994) '[Review of] M. Schofield (1991) *The Stoic Idea of the City*, Cambridge', *Ancient Philosophy* 14 452–60

Lapidge, M. (1973) 'ἀρχαί and στοιχεῖα. A Problem in Stoic Cosmology', *Phronesis* 18 240–78

Lavecchia, S. (2006) *Una via che conduce al divino. La 'homoiosis theo* [sic]*' nella filosofia di Platone*, Milan

Leibniz, G.W. (1676) 'On the Happy Life' in H. Schepers, W. Schneiders and W. Kabitz (eds.) (1980) *Gottfried Wilhelm Leibniz. Sämtliche Schriften und Briefe* 6*: Philosophische Schriften* 3, Berlin 636–44

Leisegang, H. (1927) 'Sophia', *RE* 3A.1 1019–39

Lévy, C. (2010) 'Note sur un aspect de Quintilien lecteur de Cicéron. Sceptiques et stoïciens dans l'Institution oratoire' in P. Galand, F. Hallyn, C. Lévy and W. Verbaal (eds.) *Quintilien: ancien et moderne*, Turnhout 109–24

Lipsius, J. (1604) *Manuductionis ad Stoicam philosophiam libri tres, L. Annaeo Senecae, aliisque scriptoribus illustrandis*, Antwerp, repr. in M.N. Bouillet (ed.) (1827) *L. Annaei Senecae pars prima sive opera philosophica quae recognovit tum suis illustravit notis* 4, Paris li–ccxliii

Liu, I. (2009) 'Nature and Knowledge in Stoicism. On the Ordinariness of the Stoic Sage', *Apeiron* 41 247–75

Lloyd-Jones and Parsons (1983) *Supplementum Hellenisticum*, Berlin

Lobeck, C.A. (1829) *Aglaophamus sive de theologiae mysticae Graecorum causis*, Königsberg

Long, A.A. (1967) 'Carneades and the Stoic telos', *Phronesis* 12 59–90.

(1970–1) 'The Logical Basis of Stoic Ethics' *Proceedings of the Aristotelian Society* 71 85–104, repr. in A.A. Long (1996) *Stoic Studies*, Cambridge 179–201

(1978a) 'Sextus Empiricus on the Criterion of Truth', *Bulletin of the Institute for Classical Studies* 25 35–49

(1978b) 'Timon of Phlius: Pyrrhonist and Satirist', *Proceedings of the Cambridge Philological Society* 204/N.S. 24 68–91, repr. in A.A. Long (2006) *From Epicurus to Epictetus*, Oxford 70–96

(1982) 'Soul and Body in Stoicism', *Phronesis* 27 34–57, repr. in A.A. Long (1996) *Stoic Studies*, Cambridge 224–49

(1988) 'Socrates in Hellenistic Philosophy', *Classical Quarterly* 38 150–71, repr. in A.A. Long (1996) *Stoic Studies*, Cambridge 1–34

(1989) 'Stoic Eudaimonism' in J.J. Cleary and D.C. Shartin (eds.) *Proceedings of the Boston Area Colloquium in Ancient Philosophy* 4 77–112, repr. in A.A. Long (1996) *Stoic Studies*, Cambridge 179–201

(2002) *Epictetus. A Stoic and Socratic Mentor*, Oxford

(2011) 'Socrates in Later Greek Philosophy' in D.R. Morrison (ed.) *The Cambridge Companion to Socrates*, Cambridge 355–79

Lukoschus, J. (1999) *Gesetz und Glück: Untersuchungen zum Naturalismus der stoischen Ethik*, Frankfurt am Main

Luschnat, O. (1958) 'Das Problem des ethischen Fortschritts in der alten Stoa', *Philologus* 102 178–214

Mackenzie, M.M. (1988) 'The Virtues of Socratic Ignorance', *Classical Quarterly* N.S. 38 331–50

Madvig, J.N. (1871) *Adversaria critica ad scriptores Graecos et Latinos 1*, Copenhagen

Männlein-Robert, I. (2002) '"Wissen um die göttlichen und die menschlichen Dinge". Eine Philosophiedefinition Platons und ihre Folgen', *Würzburger Jahrbücher für die Altertumswissenschaft* N.F. 26 13–38

Maier, F. (1970) 'Der σοφός–Begriff. Zur Bedeutung, Wertung und Rolle des Begriffes von Homer bis Euripides', diss. Munich

Malingrey, A.-M. (1961) *'Philosophia'. Étude d'un groupe de mots dans la littérature grecque, des Présocratiques au ive siècle après J-C*, Paris

Mansfeld, J. (1979) 'Providence and the Destruction of the Universe in Early Stoic Thought. With Some Remarks on the "Mysteries of Philosophy"' in M.J. Vermaseren (ed.) *Studies in Hellenistic Religions*, Leiden 129–88

(1983) '*Techne*: a New Fragment of Chrysippus', *Greek, Roman and Byzantine Studies* 24 57–65

(1986) 'Diogenes Laertius on Stoic Philosophy', *Elenchos* 7 295–382

(1990) 'Doxography and Dialectic: the *Sitz im Leben* of the "Placita"', *ANRW* 2.36.4 3056–229

(1992) 'περὶ κοσμοῦ. A Note on the History of a Title', *Vigiliae christianae* 46 391–411

Mansfeld, J. and D.T. Runia (1997) *Aëtiana 1*, Leiden

(2009) *Aëtiana 2*, Leiden

Marcovich, M. (ed.) (1999) *Diogenis Laertii Vitae philosophorum 1. Libri 1–10*, Stuttgart

Marquard, O. (1989) 'Philosophie IV E' in H. Ritter and K. Gründer (eds.) *Historisches Wörterbuch der Philosophie* 7, Basel 714–32

Mayet, K. (2010) *Chrysipps Logik in Ciceros philosophischen Schriften*, Tübingen

Mayor, J.E.B. (ed.) (1880) *Thirteen Satires of Juvenal 1*, London

McPherran, M.L. (1996) *The Religion of Socrates*, University Park, Pa.

Meinwald, C. (2005) 'Ignorance and Opinion in Stoic Epistemology', *Phronesis* 55 215–31
Mejer, J. (1978) *Diogenes Laertius and his Hellenistic Background*, Wiesbaden
Menn, S. (1995) 'Physics as a Virtue' in J.J. Clearly and W.C. Wians (eds.) *Proceedings of the Boston Area Colloquium in Ancient Philosophy* 11 1–33
Mignucci, M. (1999) 'Logic 3: The Stoics 8: Paradoxes' in K. Algra, J. Barnes, J. Mansfeld and M. Schofield (eds.) *The Cambridge History of Hellenistic Philosophy*, Cambridge 157–76
Moraux, P. (1984) *Der Aristotelismus bei den Griechen. Von Andronikos bis Alexander von Aphrodisias 2: Der Aristotelismus im I. und II. JH. n. Chr.*, Berlin
Moreschini, C. (ed.) (1985) *Platon, Phèdre, notice de Léon Robin, traduit par P. Vicaire*, Paris
(1998) *Platon, Phèdre, traduit par P. Vicaire, préface de J. Brunschwig, introduction et notes par G. Samama*, Paris
Morgan, K. (2000) *Myth and Philosophy From the Presocratics to Plato*, Cambridge
Most, G.W. (2006) *Hesiod, Theogony. Works and Days. Testimonia*, Cambridge, Mass.
Muller, R. (1989) 'Alexinos d'Élis' in R. Goulet (ed.) *Dictionnaire des philosophes antiques* 1, Paris 150–1.
(1994) 'Diodorus, dit Cronos' in R. Goulet (ed.) *Dictionnaire des philosophes antiques* 2, Paris 779–81
Mutschmann, H. (ed.) (1914) *Sexti Empirici opera 2: Adversus dogmaticos libros quinque (Adv. Mathem. 7–11)*, Berlin
Mutschmann, H. and I. Mau (eds.) (1961) *Sexti Empirici opera 3: Adversus mathematicos libros 1–6* [1954], 2nd edn., Berlin
Nadler, S. (2007) *Spinoza's Ethics*, Cambridge
Natali, C. (ed.) (1999) *Etica stoica. Ario Didimo, trad. e note di C. Viano. Diogene Laerzio, trad. e note di M. Gigante. Introduzione di J. Annas*, Rome
Nehamas, A. and P. Woodruff (1997) 'Plato. Phaedrus' in J. Cooper (ed.) *Plato. Complete Works*, Princeton 506–56
Norden, E. (1892) 'In Varronis saturas menippeas observationes selectae', *Jahrbücher für classische Philologie*. Suppl. 18 265–352
Nussbaum, M.C. (1994) *The Therapy of Desire*, Princeton
(1995) 'Commentary on Menn' in J.J. Clearly and W.C. Wians (eds.) *Proceedings of the Boston Area Colloquium in Ancient Philosophy* 11 34–45
O'Meara, J.J. (1951) *St. Augustine. Against the Academics*, Westminster, Md.
Obbink, D. (1999) 'The Stoic Sage in the Cosmic City' in K. Ierodiakonou (ed.) *Topics in Stoic Philosophy*, Oxford 178–95
(2002) '"All Gods are True" in Epicurus' in D. Frede and A. Laks (eds.) *Traditions of Theology*, Leiden 183–221

Parker, R. (2011) *On Greek Religion*, Ithaca
Pearson, A.C. (1891) *The Fragments of Zeno and Cleanthes with Introduction and Explanatory Notes*, London
Passmore, J. (2000) *The Perfectibility of Man*, 3rd edn., Indianapolis
Pease, A.S. (ed.) (1955) *M. Tulli Ciceronis. De divinatione* [1920–3], 2nd edn., Darmstadt
(ed.) (1955–8) *M. Tulli Ciceronis. De natura deorum*, Cambridge, Mass.
Pembroke, E.G. (1971) 'Oikeiōsis' in A.A. Long (ed.) *Problems in Stoicism*, London 114–49
Penella, R.J. (2000) *The Private Orations of Themistius*, Berkeley
Pérez Ruiz, F. (1959) *El concepto de filosofia en los escritos de Platon*, Comillas
Pfister, F. (1937) 'Herakles und Christus', *Archiv für Religionswissenschaft* 34 42–60
Pianko, G. (1948–9) 'De Timonis Phlasii *Sillorum* dispositione', *Eos* 43 120–6
Places, É. des (1949) *Pindare et Platon*, Paris
Pohlenz, M. (1904) '[Review of] SVF 3', *Berliner philologische Wochenschrift* 24 932–8
(1926) 'Stoa und Semitismus', *Neue Jahrbücher für Wissenschaft und Jugendbildung* 2 257–69
(1939) 'Plutarchs Schriften gegen die Stoiker', *Hermes* 74 1–33
(1992) *Die Stoa. Geschichte einer geistigen Bewegung* 1 [1949], 7th edn., Göttingen
(1990) *Die Stoa. Geschichte einer geistigen Bewegung 2. Erläuterungen* [1949], 6th edn., Göttingen
Pohlenz, M. and R. Westman (eds.) (1959) *Plutarchi Moralia* 6.2, 2nd edn., Leipzig
Polito, R. (2012) 'Antiochus and the Academy' in D. Sedley (ed.) *The Philosophy of Antiochus*, Cambridge 31–54
Pomeroy, A.J. (1999) *Arius Didymus. Epitome of Stoic Ethics*, Atlanta
Pourkier, A. (1992) *L'hérésiologie chez Épiphane de Salamine*, Paris
Powell, J.G.F. (1990) *Cicero. On Friendship and the Dream of Scipio*, Warminster
Powers, N. (2009) 'The Natural Theology of Xenophon's Socrates', *Ancient Philosophy* 29 249–66
Prantl, C. (1855) *Geschichte der Logik im Abendlande 1*, Leipzig
Prost, F. (2004) *Les théories hellénistiques de la douleur*, Leuven
Rabbow, P. (1914) *Antike Schriften über Seelenheilung und Seelenleitung auf ihre Quellen untersucht 1*, Leipzig
Radermacher, L. (1915) in S. Sudhaus (ed.) *Philodemi volumina rhetorica*. Suppl., Leipzig ix–xxvi
Radt, S.L. (1980) 'Noch einmal Aischylos, Niobe fr. 162 N.[2] (278 M.)', *Zeitschrift für Papyrologie und Epigraphik* 38 47–58
Ramelli, I. (2007) *Allegoristi dell'età classica. Opera e frammenti*, Milan

Raubenheimer, H. (1911) 'Quintilianus quae debere videatur Stoicis popularibusque, qui dicuntur, philosophis', diss. Würzburg

Ravaisson, F. (1877) 'Mémoire sur le Stoïcisme', *Mémoires de l'institut impérial de France. Académie des inscriptions et belles-lettres* 21 1–94

Reale, G. (1998) *Platone. Fedro*, Milan

Reeve, C.D.C. (1989) *Socrates in the Apology*, Indianapolis

Reid, J.S. (ed.) (1879) *M. Tulli Ciceronis Laelius de amicitia edited for schools and colleges*, Cambridge

(1885) *M. Tulli Ciceronis Academica*, London

Reinhardt, K. (1921) *Poseidonios*, Munich

(1954) 'Poseidonios von Apameia, der Rhodier genannt', *RE* 22 558–826

Renehan, R. (1972) 'The Greek Philosophic Background of Fourth Maccabees', *Rheinisches Museum* 115 223–38

Repici, L. (1993) 'The Stoics and the elenchos' in K. Döring and T. Ebert (eds.) *Dialektiker und Stoiker*, Stuttgart 253–69

Reynolds, L.D. (ed.) (1977) *L. Annaei Senecae dialogorum libri duodecim*, Oxford

Ribbeck, O. (1888) 'Agroikos. Eine ethologische Studie', *Abhandlungen der philologisch-historischen Classe der Königlich-Sächsischen Gesellschaft der Wissenschaften* 10 1–68

Rice, E.F. (1958) *The Renaissance Idea of Wisdom*, Cambridge, Mass.

Richardson, N.J. (1975) 'Homeric Professors in the Age of the Sophists', *Proceedings of the Cambridge Philological Society* 201/N.S. 21 65–81

Riedweg, C. (1987) *Mysterienterminologie bei Platon, Philon und Klemens von Alexandrien*, Berlin

Riley, M.T. (1980) 'The Epicurean Criticism of Socrates', *Phoenix* 34 55–68

Rist, J.M. (1969) *Stoic Philosophy*, Cambridge

(1977) 'Zeno and Stoic Consistency', *Phronesis* 22 161–74

(1989) 'Seneca and Stoic Orthodoxy', *ANRW* 2.36.3 1993–2012

Ritter, H., L. Preller and E. Wellmann (eds.) (1914) *Historia philosophiae Graecae*, 9th edn., Gotha

Ritter, C. (1922) *Platons Dialog Phaidros*, 2nd edn., Leipzig

Rolke, K.-H. (1975) *Die bildhaften Vergleiche in den Fragmenten der Stoiker von Zenon bis Panaitios*, Hildesheim

Roskam, G. (2005) *On the Path to Virtue*, Leuven

Rowe, C.J. (1988) *Plato. Phaedrus*, Warminster

(2007) *Plato and the Art of Philosophical Writing*, Cambridge

(2011) 'Self-examination' in D.R. Morrison (ed.) *The Cambridge Companion to Socrates*, Cambridge 201–14

Runia, D.T. (1996) 'Aetius', *DNP* s.v.

(2001) *Philo of Alexandria, On the Creation of the Cosmos According to Moses*, Leiden

Sandbach, F.H. (1989) *The Stoics* [1975], 2nd edn., London
Schäfer, C. (2007) 'Philosophie (philosophia)' in C. Schäfer (ed.) *Platon-Lexikon*, Darmstadt 220–3
Schenkl, H. (ed.) (1916) *Epicteti dissertationes ab Arriano digestae. Editio maior*, Leipzig
Schleiermacher, F. (1996) *Über die Philosophie Platons [1804–28], herausgegeben und eingeleitet von P.M. Steiner*, Hamburg
Schmekel, A. (1892) *Die Philosophie der mittleren Stoa in ihrem geschichtlichen Zusammenhange*, Berlin
Schmidt, E.G. (1960) 'Eine Frühform der Lehre vom Umschlag Quantität-Qualität bei Seneca', *Forschungen und Fortschritte* 34 112–5, repr. as 'Der Umschlag von Quantität und Qualität bei Seneca und Hegel' in E.G. Schmidt (1988) *Erworbenes Erbe*, Berlin 392–404
Schofield, M. (1982) 'The Earliest Ontological Argument for the Existence of God' (unpublished typescript)
(1983) 'The Syllogisms of Zeno of Citium', *Phronesis* 28 31–58
(1999) *The Stoic Idea of the City* [1991] 2nd edn., Chicago
(2012) 'The Neutralizing Argument: Carneades, Antiochus, Cicero' in D. Sedley (ed.), *The Philosophy of Antiochus*, Cambridge 237–49
(2013) 'Cardinal Virtues: A Contested Socratic Inheritance' in A. Long (ed.) *Plato and the Stoics*, Cambridge
Schröder, H.O. (1969) 'Fatum (Heimarmene)' in T. Klauser (ed.) *Reallexikon für Antike und Christentum* 7 524–636
Schwabe, L. von (1909) '137) M. Fabius Quintilianus', *RE* 6 1845–65
Sedley, D. (1977) 'Diodorus Cronus and Hellenistic Philosophy', *Proceedings of the Cambridge Philological Society* 203/N.S. 23 74–120
(1983) 'The Motivation of Greek Skepticism' in M. Burnyeat (ed.) *The Skeptical Tradition*, Berkeley 9–29
(1993) 'Chrysippus on Psychophysical Causality' in J. Brunschwig and M.C. Nussbaum (eds.) *Passions and Perceptions*, Cambridge 313–31
(1997) '"Becoming Like God" in the Timaeus and Aristotle' in T. Calvo and L. Brisson (eds.) *Interpreting the Timaeus – Critias*, Sankt Augustin 327–39
(1999a) 'Hellenistic Physics and Metaphysics' in K. Algra, J. Barnes, J. Mansfeld and M. Schofield (eds.) *The Cambridge History of Hellenistic Philosophy*, Cambridge 355–411
(1999b) 'The Ideal of Godlikeness' in G. Fine (ed.) *Plato 2: Ethics, Politics, Religion and the Soul*, Oxford 309–28
(1999c) 'The Stoic–Platonist Debate on *kathêkonta*' in K. Ierodiakonou (ed.) *Topics in Stoic Philosophy*, Oxford 128–52
(2007) *Creationism and its Critics in Antiquity*, Berkeley
(2012a) 'Introduction' in D. Sedley (ed.), *The Philosophy of Antiochus*, Cambridge 1–8

(2012b) 'A Guide to the Testimonies for Antiochus' in D. Sedley (ed.) *The Philosophy of Antiochus*, Cambridge 334–46

Sellars, J. (2009) *The Art of Living. The Stoics on the Nature and Function of Philosophy* [2003], 2nd edn., London

Seyffert, M. and C.F.W. Müller (eds.) (1876) *Cicero. Laelius de amicitia dialogus*, 2nd edn., Leipzig

Sharples, R.W. (ed.) (1983) *Alexander of Aphrodisias. On Fate*, London

(1984) 'On Fire in Heraclitus and in Zeno of Citium', *Classical Quarterly* N.S. 34 231–3

Siegert, F. (1980–92) *Drei hellenistisch-jüdische Predigten. Ps.-Philon, 'Über Jona', 'Über Simson', 'Über die Gottesbezeichnung "wohltätig verzehrendes Feuer"'*, Tübingen

Shorey, P. (1933) *What Plato Said*, Chicago

Smeal, J.G. (1989) 'Themistios: The Twenty-Third Oration', diss. Vanderbilt

Smith, N.D. and P.B. Woodruff (eds.) (2000) *Reason and Religion in Socratic Philosophy*, New York

Snell, B. (1971) *Leben und Meinungen der Sieben Weisen*, 4th edn., Munich

Solmsen, F. (1961) *Cleanthes or Posidonius. The Basis of Stoic Physics*, Amsterdam

Souilhé, J. (1930) 'La θεία μοῖρα chez Platon' in F.-J. von Rintelen (ed.) *Philosophia perennis. Abhandlungen zu ihrer Vergangenheit und Gegenwart* 1, Regensburg 13–25

Spalding, G.L. (ed.) (1798–1829) *M. Fabius Quintilianus. De institutione oratoria*, Leipzig

Sparshott, F.E. (1978) 'Zeno on Art: Anatomy of a Definition' in J.M. Rist (ed.) *The Stoics*, Berkeley 273–90

Spinoza, B. de (1677) *Ethica ordine geometrico demonstrata* in C. Gebhardt (ed.) (1925) *Spinoza. Opera* 2, Heidelberg 41–308

Stählin, O. and U. Treu (eds.) (1972) *Clemens Alexandrinus* 1*: Protrepticus und Paedagogus*, 3rd edn., Berlin

Stanford, W.B. (1963) *The Ulysses Theme*, 2nd edn., Oxford

Steinmetz, F.-A. (1967) *Die Freundschaftslehre des Panaitios nach einer Analyse von Cicero's 'Laelius de amicitia'*, Wiesbaden

Steinmetz, P. (1986) 'Allegorische Deutung und allegorische Dichtung in der alten Stoa', *Rheinisches Museum* 129 18–30

Stellwag, H.W.F. (1933) *Epictetus. Het eerste boek der Diatriben*, Amsterdam

Striker, G. (1991) 'Following Nature. A Study in Stoic Ethics', *Oxford Studies in Ancient Philosophy* 9 1–73, repr. in her (1996) *Essays on Hellenistic Epistemology and Ethics*, Cambridge 221–80

(1997) 'Academics Fighting Academics' in B. Inwood and J. Mansfeld (eds.) *Assent and Argument*, Leiden 257–76

Strycker, E. de and S.R. Slings (1994) *Plato's Apology of Socrates*, Leiden

Tarán, L. (1966) '[Review of] M. Untersteiner (1963) *Aristotele. Della filosofia*, Rome', *American Journal of Philology* 87 464–72

(1969) *Asclepius of Tralles. Commentary to Nicomachus' Introduction to Arithmetic (Transactions of the American Philosophical Society. N.S. 59.4)*, Philadelphia

Tarn, W.W. (1913) *Antigonos Gonatas*, Oxford

Theiler, W. (1982) *Poseidonios. Die Fragmente II. Erläuterungen*, Berlin

Thom, J.C. (2005) *Cleanthes' Hymn to Zeus*, Tübingen

Thompson, W.H. (1868) *The Phaedrus of Plato with English Notes and Dissertations*, London

Tiberius, V. and J. Swartwood (eds.) (2011) 'Wisdom Revisited: a Case Study in Normative Theorizing', *Philosophical Explorations* 14 277–95

Tieleman, T. (1996) *Galen and Chrysippus on the Soul*, Leiden.

Togni, P. (2010) *Conoscenza e virtù nella dialettica stoica*, Naples

Trapp, M.B. (1991) '[Review of] Di Marco (1989)', *Classical Review* N.S. 41 469–70

Tsekourakis, D. (1974) *Studies in the Terminology of Early Stoic Ethics*, Wiesbaden

Tsouna, V. (2001) 'Socrate et la connaissance de soi' in M. Nancy (ed.) *Figures de Socrate*, Villeneuve d'Asq 37–64

Türk, G. (1884–1937) 'Phoinix' in W.H. Roscher (ed.) *Ausführliches Lexikon der griechischen und römischen Mythologie* 3, Leipzig 3450–72

Überweg, F. and K. Praechter (1926) *Grundriß der Geschichte der Philosophie* 1*: Die Philosophie des Altertums*, 12th edn., Berlin

Vegetti, M. (1998) *L'etica degli antichi*, 5th edn., Rome

Verdenius, W.J. (1955) 'Notes on Plato's *Phaedrus*', *Mnemosyne* 4.8 265–89

Veyne, P. (2005) 'Passion, perfection et âme matérielle dans l'utopie stoïcienne et chez saint Augustin' in P. Veyne, *L'empire gréco-romain*, Paris 683–712

Viano, C. (1999) *Etica stoica*, Rome

(2005) 'L'Epitomê de l'éthique stoïcienne d'Arius Didyme (Stobée, Eclog. II, 5, 7, 57, 13–116, 18)' in J.-B. Gourinat (ed.), *Les stoïciens*, Paris 335–55

Vimercati, E. (2011) 'Stobeo sul saggio stoico' in G. Reydams-Schils (ed.), *Thinking Through Excerpts: Studies on Stobaeus*, Turnhout 577–614

Vlastos, G. (1991) *Socrates. Ironist and Moral Philosopher*, Cambridge

Vogt, K. (2008) *Law, Reason, and the Cosmic City*, New York

(2012) *Belief and Truth*, New York

Vries, G.J. de (1969) *A Commentary on the Phaedrus of Plato*, Amsterdam

Wachsmuth, C. (1885) *Sillographorum Graecorum reliquiae*, Lipsiae

Walbank, F.W. (1984) 'Macedonia and Greece' in F.W. Walbank *et al.* (eds) *The Cambridge Ancient History* 7.1, Cambridge 221–56

Walsh, P.G. (1997) *Cicero. The Nature of the Gods*, Oxford

Warren, J. (2002) *Epicurus and Democritean Ethics*, Cambridge

Watanabe, A.T. (1988) '*Cleanthes*, Fragments: Text and Commentary', diss. Illinois

Weniger, L. (1870) *Die religiöse Seite der großen Pythien*, Breslau
West, M.L. (ed.) (1966) *Hesiod. Theogony*, Oxford
(2007) *Indo-European Poetry and Myth*, Oxford
White, M.J. (2003) 'Stoic Natural Philosophy' in B. Inwood (ed.) *The Cambridge Companion to the Stoics*, Cambridge 124–52
White, N.P. (1979) 'The Basis of Stoic Ethics', *Harvard Studies in Classical Philology* 83 143–78
Whittaker, J. (ed.) (1990) *Alcinoos. Enseignement des doctrines de Platon*, Paris
Wilamowitz-Moellendorff, U. von (1881) *Antigonos von Karystos*, Berlin
Wilckens, U. (1959) *Weisheit und Torheit. Eine exegetisch-religionsgeschichtliche Untersuchung zu 1. Kor. 1 und 2*, Tübingen
Wilkins, E.G. (1917) *'Know thyself' in Greek and Latin literature*, Chicago
Williams, G.D. (2012) *The Cosmic Viewpoint. A Study of Seneca's Natural Questions*, Oxford
Wilpert, P. (1957) 'Die Stellung der Schrift 'Über die Philosophie' in der Gedankenentwicklung des Aristoteles', *Journal of Hellenic Studies* 77 155–62
Winterbottom, M. (1964) 'Quintilian and the *vir bonus*', *Journal of Roman Studies* 54 90–7
Wlosok, A. (1960) *Laktanz und die philosophische gnosis*, Heidelberg
Wohlfart, G. (1991) 'Das Weise. Bemerkungen zur anfänglichen Bedeutung des Begriffs der Philosophie im Anschluss an Heraklits Fragment B108', *Philosophisches Jahrbuch* 98 18–33
Wolfson, H.A. (1934) *The Philosophy of Spinoza*, Cambridge, Mass.
Wundt, M. (1911) *Geschichte der griechischen Ethik* 2, Leipzig
Wyttenbach, D. (ed.) (1810) *Plutarchi Chaeronensis moralia* 6.1, Oxford
Yunis, H. (2011) *Plato. Phaedrus*, Cambridge
Zeller, E. and M. Wellmann (1923) *Die Philosophie der Griechen in ihrer geschichtlichen Entwicklung* 3.1*: Die nacharistotelische Philosophie, erste Hälfte*, 5th edn., Leipzig
Ziegler, K. (1951) 'Plutarch von Chaironeia', *RE* 22.1 636–962

GENERAL INDEX

The index has been compiled predominantly from the main text, with a particular emphasis on the systematic nature of the subjects discussed. *Italicised* terms are Greek except where Latin (Lat.) is indicated. Dates of historical persons can be found where they are first mentioned in the text according to this index.

INDEX LOCORUM

This index contains all passages quoted or referred to. References in **bold** indicate passages translated into English.

Index locorum

Made in the USA
Columbia, SC
24 October 2020